CURRICULUM FOR EXCELLENCE BENCHMARKS

PRIMARY EDITION – EARLY TO SECOND LEVEL

All the primary school Benchmarks, redesigned to be easier to use and grouped by individual organisers to help you enable progress to the next level

See Hear Teach .scot

The original content of *Curriculum for Excellence* is © Crown copyright, 2009-2018. It is reproduced under the terms of the Open Government Licence. To view this licence, visit http://www.nationalarchives.gov.uk/doc/open-government-licence. The original content is available for free on the Education Scotland website at education.gov.scot*.

This edition of the Benchmarks and related materials as *Curriculum for Excellence: Benchmarks (Primary Edition) – Early to Second Level* is © Harold Raitt (t/a SeeHearTeach), 2019.

SeeHearTeach is a trademark of Harold Raitt.

ISBN 978 1 9164836 2 0

All efforts have been made by the publisher of this edition to ensure its accuracy; several corrections have been made to errors found in the original material, which are indicated with footnotes where necessary. Please report any errors you find to mail@seehearteach.scot, and we will correct them in future editions. [A]

* At the time of going to press, the material in this document was available as follows: **Benchmarks, HMCIe Statement and Achievement of a Level poster:** https://education.gov.scot/improvement/learning-resources/Curriculum%20for%20Excellence%20Benchmarks. **Experiences & Outcomes materials:** https://education.gov.scot/scottish-education-system/policy-for-scottish-education/policy-drivers/cfe-(building-from-the-statement-appendix-incl-btc1-5)/Experiences%20and%20outcomes.

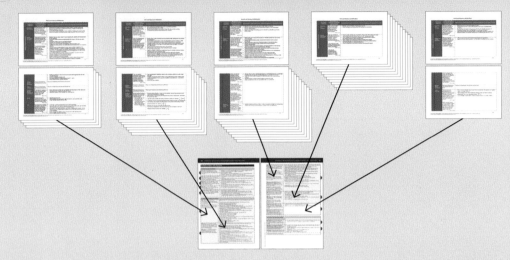

According to the introduction to the Benchmarks (March 2017, page 2 of this book) "their purpose is to make clear what learners need to know and be able to do to progress through the levels." Meanwhile, the 'Statement for Practitioners from HMCIe' (August 2016, page 4 of this book) states "there is currently too much support material and guidance for practitioners … we are taking action to significantly streamline all our support and guidance materials for the curriculum."

At present, this laudable aim of streamlining documentation and guidance materials for the curriculum has failed to tackle the immensely poor design of Scottish education's two most fundamental documents, the *Experiences & Outcomes* ('Es & Os') and the *Benchmarks*. Following the popularity of my redesigned version of the Experiences & Outcomes (*Curriculum for Excellence: Streamlined*, SeeHearTeach, 2018), I have now decided to see what I can do to improve the design of the Benchmarks, with *Benchmarks – The Next Steps* and *Benchmarks: Primary Edition*.

The approach taken in this volume can be easily seen in the diagram above. Suppose a teacher wants to be "clear what learners need to know and be able to do to progress through the levels", and wants to compare the Benchmarks for 'Number and number processes' from Early to Fourth Level. To start off with, the Es & Os and Benchmarks at most levels are spread over two pages each, making it overly difficult just to read the Benchmarks at one level, let alone five. Then, because the Benchmarks PDFs provide us with every benchmark for each level before moving on to the next level, you have to leaf through 37 other pages to find the other relevant sections.

If facilitating learners' progress is indeed the key aim of the Benchmarks, wouldn't it make it easier for teachers to have all the Es & Os and Benchmarks for 'Number and number processes' together on one double-page spread? That's precisely what you'll find – for Early to Second Level – on pages 80-81 of this book. You'll even find the Es & Os and Benchmarks for 'Estimation and Rounding', 'Multiples, Factors and Primes', 'Fractions, Decimals and Percentages' and 'Money' on those pages, too.

I've achieved this through several means similar to those used in my earlier edition of the Experiences & Outcomes: a small but highly-legible font, optimised margin widths and cell padding on tables, and the elimination of unnecessarily repetitive labelling (although please see the editorial notes on page 3 for an important point about column headings).

Following this approach throughout this book, 441 pages of Benchmarks material (from Early to Fourth Level) have been reduced to just 73 (from Early to Second Level). **Please note: it is highly recommended that teachers of later years in primary schools, particularly P6 and P7, use our full *Benchmarks – The Next Steps* edition, so that they can plan learning for pupils who are capable of working beyond Second Level.**

The inclusion of other crucial documentation not included in the Benchmarks PDFs has brought the full page count up to 129:

▸ All Experiences & Outcomes, even those with no Benchmarks (this volume can therefore be used as a complete guide to *Curriculum for Excellence*, without needing to refer to a separate copy of the Es & Os)
▸ Principles & Practice papers and relevant footnotes and appendices from the Experiences & Outcomes documents
▸ The introductions to both the Benchmarks and Experiences & Outcomes, plus August 2016's 'Statement for Practitioners from HMCIe' and March 2018's answers to Frequently Asked Questions about the Benchmarks.

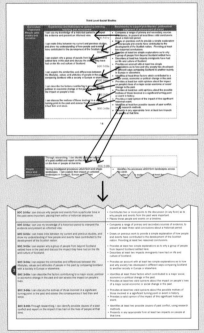

I have silently corrected a number of mistakes from the original documents, or noted them with footnotes where necessary. This is especially true of a number of inconsistencies between the Es & Os and the Benchmarks.

I have also taken care to try and align all Benchmarks with their relevant Experience(s) & Outcome(s). For example, in the original version of the Social Studies Benchmarks shown on the left, the Benchmarks are presented in a single block, and it is not at all obvious that they are connected to specific Es & Os. The version which you will find on page 117 of this document uses tabulation and small line breaks to make these relationships clear.

I am a firm believer that *Curriculum for Excellence* still has a lot to offer both learners and practitioners in Scotland, and I hope these documents will make it much easier for colleagues to plan great learning and progression. They will also prove a timely contribution to the developing discussions about 'Curriculum for Excellence 2.0' …

Harold Raitt, mail@seehearteach.scot
Kelso, June/August 2019

INTRODUCTION TO THE BENCHMARKS (MARCH 2017)

GUIDANCE ON USING BENCHMARKS FOR ASSESSMENT

Education Scotland's *Curriculum for Excellence (CfE) Statement for Practitioners* (August 2016, [see pages 4-7]) stated that the two key resources which support practitioners to plan learning, teaching and assessment are:

▸ **Experiences and Outcomes**

▸ **Benchmarks**

Benchmarks have been developed to provide clarity on the national standards expected within each curriculum area at each level. They set out clear lines of progression in literacy and English and numeracy and mathematics, and across all other curriculum areas from Early to Fourth Levels (First to Fourth Levels in Modern Languages). Their purpose is to make clear what learners need to know and be able to do to progress through the levels, and to support consistency in teachers' and other practitioners' professional judgements.

Skills development is integrated into the Benchmarks to support greater shared understanding. An understanding of skills and how well they are developing will enable learners to make links between their current learning and their future career options and employment.

Benchmarks draw together and streamline a wide range of previous assessment guidance (including significant aspects of learning, progression frameworks and annotated exemplars) into one key resource to support teachers' and other practitioners' professional judgement of children's and young people's progress across all curriculum areas.

Benchmarks have been designed to support professional dialogue as part of the moderation process to assess where children and young people are in their learning. They will help to support holistic assessment approaches across learning. They should not be ticked off individually for assessment purposes.

Benchmarks for literacy and numeracy should be used to support teachers' professional judgement of achievement of a level. In other curriculum areas, Benchmarks support teachers and other practitioners to understand standards and identify children's and young people's next steps in learning. Evidence of progress and achievement will come from a variety of sources including:

▸ observing day-to-day learning within the classroom, playroom or working area

▸ observation and feedback from learning activities that takes place in other environments, for example, outdoors, on work placements

▸ coursework, including tests

▸ learning conversations
and

▸ planned periodic holistic assessment.

BENCHMARKS IN CURRICULUM AREAS

Benchmarks in each curriculum area are designed to be concise and accessible, with sufficient detail to communicate clearly the standards expected for each curriculum level.

Teachers and other practitioners can draw upon the Benchmarks to assess the knowledge, understanding, and skills for learning, life and work which children are developing in each curriculum area.

In secondary schools, Benchmarks can support subject specialist teachers in making robust assessments of learners' progress and the standards they achieve. They will help teachers ensure that learners make appropriate choices and are presented at an appropriate level for National Qualifications in the senior phase. This can help avoid excessive workload for teachers and unnecessary assessments for learners. For example, learners should have achieved relevant Fourth level Experiences and Outcomes before embarking on the National 5 qualifications. Schools should take careful account of this when options for S4 are being agreed. Benchmarks should be used to help with these important considerations.

LITERACY AND NUMERACY

In literacy and numeracy, Benchmarks support teachers' professional judgement of achievement of a level. Teachers' professional judgements will be collected and published at national, local and school levels. It is important that these judgements are robust and reliable. This can only be achieved through effective moderation of planning learning, teaching and assessment.

Achievement of a level is based on teacher professional judgement, well informed by a wide range of evidence. Benchmarks should be used to review the range of evidence gathered to determine if the expected standard has been achieved and the learner has:

▸ achieved a **breadth** of learning across the knowledge, understanding and skills as set out in the experiences and outcomes for the level;

▸ responded consistently well to the level of **challenge** set out in the Experiences and Outcomes for the level and has moved forward to learning at the next level in some aspects; and

▸ demonstrated **application** of what they have learned in new and unfamiliar situations.

It is not necessary for learners to demonstrate mastery of every individual aspect of learning within Benchmarks at a particular level and before moving on to the next level. However, it is important that there are no major gaps in children's and young people's learning when looking across the major organisers in each curriculum area.

PLANNING LEARNING, TEACHING AND ASSESSMENT USING THE BENCHMARKS

In addition to the *Curriculum for Excellence (CfE) Statement for Practitioners* from HM Chief Inspector of Education, August 2016 [see pages 4-7] on the purpose and use of Benchmarks, teachers and other practitioners should note the following advice.

KEY MESSAGES – WHAT TO DO	KEY MESSAGES – WHAT NOT TO DO
✓ Use literacy and numeracy Benchmarks to help monitor progress towards achievement of a level, and to support overall professional judgement of when a learner has achieved a level.	✗ Avoid undue focus on individual Benchmarks which may result in over-assessing or recording of learners' progress.
✓ Become familiar with other curriculum area Benchmarks over time.	✗ Avoid the requirement to spend time collating excessive evidence to assess learners' achievement.
✓ Use Benchmarks to help assess whether learners are making suitable progress towards the national standards expected and use the evidence to plan their next, challenging steps in learning.	✗ There is no need to provide curriculum level judgements in all curriculum areas – stick to literacy and numeracy.
	✗ Do not create excessive or elaborate approaches to monitoring and tracking.
✓ Discuss Benchmarks within and across schools to achieve a shared understanding of the national standards expected across curriculum areas.	✗ Do not assess Benchmarks individually. Plan periodic, holistic assessment of children's and young people's learning.
	✗ Do not tick off individual Benchmarks.

EDITORIAL NOTE ON COLUMN HEADINGS

The basic principle of this edition is to present a complete edition of the Benchmarks, grouped by individual curriculum organisers, alongside all the material from the Experiences & Outcomes documents.

Although the compilation of the Principles & Practice statements has involved de-duplication of a substantial amount of text (for, example, the overlapping material for 'Literacy: Responsibility of All', 'Literacy & English' and 'Literacy and Gàidhlig' is presented once only), nothing has been removed.

The sole exception to this are the column headings which appear at the start of the Benchmark tables at each level:

▶ Above the Experiences & Outcomes:
   "Experiences and Outcomes for planning learning, teaching and assessment"

▶ Above the Benchmarks:
   "Benchmarks to support practitioners' professional judgement"

The latter of these, read in the light of the introduction on these two pages, and the 'Statement for Practitioners' on pages 4-7 is obviously particularly important; the intention is to support practitioners, not to overrule or overburden them.

In addition, the section headings in Principles & Practice documents have mostly been rephrased from being questions to shorter headings which facilitate scanning and skim-reading. So, for example, "How will we build on children and young people's prior learning in the expressive arts?" becomes, in the Expressive Arts section, just "Building on prior learning".

EDITORIAL NOTE ON USE OF SQUARE BRACKETS AND ITALICS

All material included in square brackets is editorial. The main use for this is in footnotes, to distinguish text which appears as footnotes in the original *Benchmarks* or *Es & Os* from editorial comments.

Some titles of curriculum organisers have additional text, as with Health & Wellbeing's "Diet, rest and sleep", which has been changed to "[Activity,] diet, rest and sleep" to better reflect the actual content of the Experiences & Outcomes and Benchmarks.

Where Benchmarks themselves appear in square brackets, this is to denote inter-disciplinary material which has been copied from another curriculum area, and helps to reduce the need to turn pages back and forth unnecessarily.

Italics are used to differentiate documents from their content. For example, *Benchmarks* refers to the various PDFs on the Education Scotland website, while 'Benchmarks' refers to their content.

STATEMENT

RE-FOCUSING CURRICULUM FOR EXCELLENCE

This definitive statement is for teachers and practitioners, including those in early learning and childcare, youth work, colleges and local authorities. It will be important for teachers, practitioners, leaders and local authority staff to consider how it applies in the context of their own stage, phase, sector and local authority.

Curriculum for Excellence (CfE) is transforming learning experiences for children and young people across Scotland. The range of learning opportunities and the breadth of children's and young people's achievements is greater than ever before. In recent years there has been a great deal of very positive improvement work in early learning and childcare, schools and colleges on which we can continue to build. Moving forward, the two key priorities for CfE are:

▶ ensuring the best possible progression in literacy, numeracy and health and wellbeing for every child and young person

and

▶ closing the attainment gap.

To deliver this focus, a number of challenges remain. There is currently too much support material and guidance for practitioners. This is contributing to the growth of over-bureaucratic approaches to planning and assessment in many schools and classrooms across the country. Despite the recognition of these issues in the Tackling Bureaucracy report, progress has been far too slow. As a result we are taking action to significantly streamline all our support and guidance materials for the curriculum. This statement and the benchmarks to be published this session are key to this streamlined approach.

This statement is intended to provide clear, practical advice for teachers and practitioners on planning learning, teaching and assessment. It provides key messages about what teachers and practitioners are expected to do to effectively plan learning, teaching and assessment for all learners, and also suggests what should be avoided. Teachers should be empowered to use the flexibility that CfE provides to organise learning for children and young people in ways that best meets learners' needs. Schools should be working in a collegiate way to make key decisions.

The appendix to this statement summarises the key components of the curriculum framework within which teachers and practitioners are now expected to teach. Moving forward, the two key resources which teachers should use to plan learning, teaching and assessment are:

▶ **Experiences and Outcomes**

▶ **Benchmarks**

PLANNING LEARNING, TEACHING AND ASSESSMENT USING THE EXPERIENCES AND OUTCOMES

WHAT TO DO	WHAT NOT TO DO
✓ Use long-term plans to outline the structure of the year and the ways in which learning is organised throughout the whole year.	✗ Avoid writing overly-detailed plans for the year ahead which limit your flexibility to respond to children's and young people's needs, interests and progression.
✓ Keep medium-term planning short and focused on the main learning activities developed from the Experiences and Outcomes (Es & Os). Group Es & Os together in ways which best suit learners.	✗ Do not plan for individual Es & Os or spend excessive time writing detailed descriptions of learning activities.
✓ Short-term planning on a daily or weekly basis should be flexible and be regarded as working notes to help organise learning.	✗ Do not 'tick off' all of the Es & Os separately.
✓ Take a collegiate approach to moderation of planning learning, teaching and assessment.	✗ Do not spend excessive time completing detailed daily or weekly planning templates or writing detailed evaluations of plans.
✓ Work together with colleagues to review and reduce any unnecessary bureaucracy. Plan and organise learning in a way which avoids each week at school feeling too cluttered to provide space and time for depth of learning.	✗ Avoid unnecessary bureaucracy creeping back in over time.
✓ Planning should include consideration of how best the needs of individual and groups of children and young people will be met.	✗ Stop doing too many things at the same time. For example, in a primary school, covering all eight curriculum areas every week.
✓ Prioritise literacy, numeracy and health and wellbeing across the curriculum to ensure that all learners make the best possible progress.	✗ Do not lose a clear focus on helping all children and young people to progress at an appropriate pace and achieve the highest standards in literacy, numeracy and health and wellbeing.
✓ Plan interdisciplinary learning (IDL) to make natural links across learning. Be aware of what is happening in other subjects and make connections.	✗ Do not spend time on IDL which does not provide opportunities to apply and deepen learning or is contrived.
✓ All planning must focus directly on enhancing the learner journey. When asked to complete paperwork which does not directly relate to improving the learner journey, challenge this with your colleagues.	

PLANNING LEARNING, TEACHING AND ASSESSMENT USING THE BENCHMARKS

The purpose of the Benchmarks is to set out very clear statements about what children and young people need to learn to achieve each level of the curriculum. Benchmarks streamline and embed a wide range of existing assessment guidance (significant aspects of learning, progression frameworks and annotated exemplification) into one key resource to support teachers' professional judgement.

KEY MESSAGES – WHAT TO DO	KEY MESSAGES – WHAT NOT TO DO
✓ Periodically (from time to time) use assessments to sample and pull together learning in a joined-up way.	✗ Avoid spending time on assessment activities which do not help to identify children's and young people's next steps in learning.
✓ Plan an appropriate balance between on-going and periodic assessment – this will vary from stage to stage.	✗ Do not over-assess learners or assess the same content repeatedly in different ways. Do not create large portfolios of evidence.
✓ Moderate assessment judgements by taking account of a sample of evidence from different sources to discuss standards and the progress of learners.	✗ Avoid duplication and keeping evidence of every detail within the Benchmark.
✓ As a school, develop simple and effective approaches to monitoring and tracking learners' progress particularly in literacy and numeracy. Tracking needs to be as easy to use as possible.	✗ Avoid waiting until learners have demonstrated evidence of every aspect of learning within the Benchmarks before moving on to the next level.
✓ Regularly discuss tracking information with colleagues to plan additional support and interventions to help improve learners' progress.	✗ Avoid undue pressure on learners with too many assessments in different subjects at once.
✓ Evaluate learners' progress on an on-going basis and keep short concise notes to help planning for next steps in learning. This will include identifying where additional support and challenge may be needed.	✗ Avoid spending too much time collecting a wide range of evidence for moderation purposes.
✓ Use the benchmarks to help monitor progress and support overall professional judgement of when a learner has achieved a curriculum level.	✗ Do not track and record progress against individual Es & Os.
✓ Involve children and young people in leading their own learning and involve them in profiling their achievements.	✗ Do not track progress and achievement using the terms 'developing, consolidating, secure'.
✓ Reporting to parents should highlight latest progress, identify next steps in learning and build on profiling. Discussions should highlight ways in which parents can support their child's progress.	✗ Do not spend time writing long reports for parents which describe lots of classwork or use professional jargon.

ACHIEVEMENT OF A LEVEL (reproduced from 'Achievements of a Level Poster' PDF on Benchmarks webpage)

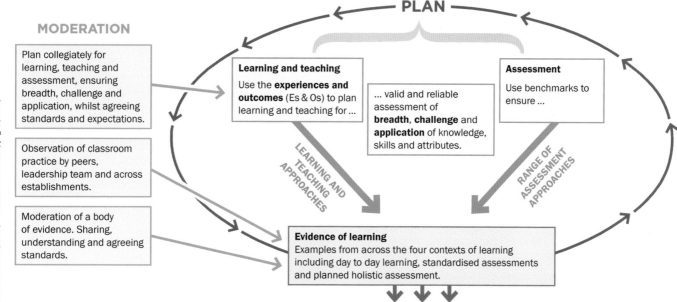

Design: © Harold Raitt / SeeHearTeach.scot (2019)   Content: © Crown copyright (2017)

APPENDIX:
SUMMARY OF THE CURRICULUM FRAMEWORK IN SCOTLAND – AUGUST 2016

This summary is for teachers and practitioners, including those in early learning and childcare, youth work and colleges. It provides clarity of the main messages.

▼ CORE INFORMATION	▼ KEY MESSAGES
PURPOSE (FOUR CAPACITIES)	
The purpose of Curriculum for Excellence is to help children and young people to become: ▸ Successful learners ▸ Confident individuals ▸ Responsible citizens ▸ Effective contributors.	Developing the **capabilities and attributes** of the four capacities is embedded across all learning.
AIM	
Curriculum for Excellence (CfE) aims to raise standards, to close the (poverty-related) attainment gap, and to prepare children and young people for their future.	Building on the messages of **Building the Curriculum 3**, the **National Improvement Framework**, **Scottish Attainment Challenge** and **Developing the Young Workforce** gives a greater focus to our aim.
VALUES	
The Scottish approach to the curriculum is values based. Wisdom, justice, compassion and integrity define the values for Scottish society.	Apply and reinforce these values at every opportunity to ensure children and young people develop understanding and respect for others and a sense of their personal and collective responsibility.
THE CURRICULUM FRAMEWORK	
The curriculum includes all that is planned for children and young people throughout their education. It includes **four contexts for learning**: ▸ curriculum areas and subjects ▸ interdisciplinary learning ▸ ethos and life of the school ▸ opportunities for personal achievement. The **Experiences and Outcomes** (Es & Os) for each curriculum area illustrate the learning within each level. Curriculum for Excellence provides flexibility for schools and settings to plan learning suitable for their own context. The school community and partners should be involved in deciding how to use this flexibility. Children's rights and **entitlements** are at the heart of the Scottish Curriculum.	The curriculum framework, as laid out in the **Building the Curriculum** Series, remains the same. Teachers and practitioners provide a curriculum that is coherent and flexible, takes account of the local context and ensures appropriate progression and levels of attainment for all children and young people. The National Improvement Framework increases the focus on literacy, numeracy and health and wellbeing and highlights the need to close the poverty-related attainment gap. The Developing the Young Workforce Programme increases the focus on recognising children's and young people's skills, the links between learning and positive destinations, and access to learning pathways that meets their needs and aspirations.

MODERATION

Moderation is the way in which practitioners arrive at a shared understanding of standards and expectations. Moderation takes place at local, regional and national levels, including:

▸ teachers and practitioners at the same curriculum level
▸ across a school or setting
▸ across a group of schools/settings
▸ within local authorities
▸ through regional groups
▸ via national groups.

Moderation is integral to planning learning, teaching and assessment.

The process of moderation is not an activity that happens only at the end of a block or year.

Teachers and practitioners, with senior leaders, regularly consider a range of assessment evidence which demonstrates how well children and young people are making progress and achieving their potential.

PRINCIPLES OF CURRICULUM DESIGN

These apply at all stages of learning with different emphases at different times.

▸ challenge and enjoyment
▸ breadth
▸ progression
▸ depth
▸ personalisation and choice
▸ coherence
▸ relevance.

The principles are taken into account when planning learning for all children and young people.

Teachers and practitioners identify what will be taught and how to best meet the needs of all learners. This is underpinned by a clear, shared understanding of progression and high quality learning and teaching.

When planning learning, teaching and assessment Experiences and Outcomes are grouped or bundled together.

Building the Ambition provides guidance to those working in the early learning and childcare sector. It should be used in parallel with CfE guidance.

RESPONSIBILITY OF ALL

▸ Literacy
▸ Numeracy
▸ Health and Wellbeing

There should be a continuous focus on these from the ages of 3 to 18.

Children and young people are entitled to two hours of quality physical education per week.

ASSESSING PROGRESS AND ACHIEVEMENT

Assessment is integral to learning and teaching. It is an ongoing process.

▸ **Achievement of a level**
Achievement of a level is based on teachers' overall professional judgement, informed by evidence

▸ **Benchmarks**
The Benchmarks are designed to support teacher professional judgement of both, progress towards, and achievement of, a level.

A range of assessment evidence is used to plan next steps in learning.

Assessment judgements should be based on the Benchmarks for each curriculum level.

The Benchmarks embed the significant aspects of learning and progression frameworks. They provide a single streamlined resource to supporting teachers' professional judgement.

INTRODUCTION TO THE EXPERIENCES & OUTCOMES (2009)

This material is for all who contribute to the education of Scotland's children and young people. The experiences and outcomes apply wherever learning is planned.

A BROAD GENERAL EDUCATION

Every child and young person in Scotland is entitled to experience a broad general education. This broad general education takes place from the early years to the end of S3 and is represented by learning across all[1] of the experiences and outcomes to the third curriculum level together with those selected for study at the fourth, as far as is consistent with each child or young person's needs. Further information on all learner entitlements can be found in *Building the Curriculum 3: A framework for learning and teaching.*

UNDERSTANDING THE CURRICULUM AS A WHOLE

By exploring the entire set of experiences and outcomes, staff will be able to see the curriculum from the early years to the end of S3 as a whole. Those who teach a particular stage will be able to see where their contributions to a child's learning and development sit in the span of progression. Secondary teachers will also see where they can make contributions to experiences and outcomes from more than one curriculum area. Staff can then plan, with colleagues, their contributions to each learner's education and also support learners in making connections in their learning. By doing this successfully, they will ensure that each learner experiences a coherent curriculum, achieves the highest possible standards, and is prepared to move successfully into the senior phase and a positive and sustained destination.

The framework is less detailed and prescriptive than previous curriculum advice. It provides professional space for teachers and other staff to use in order to meet the varied needs of all children and young people.

WHY 'EXPERIENCES AND OUTCOMES'?

The title 'experiences and outcomes' recognises the importance of the quality and nature of the learning experience in developing attributes and capabilities and in achieving active engagement, motivation and depth of learning. An outcome represents what is to be achieved.

Taken as a whole, the experiences and outcomes embody the attributes and capabilities of the four capacities.

They apply to the totality of experiences which are planned for children and young people, including the ethos and life of the school and interdisciplinary studies as well as learning within curriculum areas and subjects. This means that they apply beyond timetabled classes and into, for example, enterprise and health activities and special events.

CURRICULUM AREAS

The guidance is structured under the headings of the eight curriculum areas:

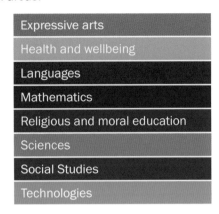

- Expressive arts
- Health and wellbeing
- Languages
- Mathematics
- Religious and moral education
- Sciences
- Social Studies
- Technologies

Some curriculum areas, for example languages, include more than one set of experiences and outcomes. The guidance also includes separate sections for literacy, numeracy and aspects of health and wellbeing, which are the responsibility of all staff.

PRINCIPLES AND PRACTICE

The principles and practice sections are essential reading for staff as they begin, and then develop, their work with the experiences and outcomes. They describe, for example, the purposes of learning within the curriculum area, how the experiences and outcomes are organised, features of effective learning and teaching, broad features of assessment, and connections with other areas of the curriculum.

Assessment is an integral part of learning and teaching. Further guidance on assessment at different stages of the journey through learning will complement the principles and practice papers, emphasising the importance of building on existing practice.

INTRODUCTORY STATEMENTS

The introductory statements within the frameworks of experiences and outcomes provide broad aims of learning within the curriculum area and act as reference points for planning from the early to the fourth levels.

STATEMENTS OF EXPERIENCES AND OUTCOMES

The statements of the experiences and outcomes themselves describe national expectations of learning and progression from the early to the fourth curriculum level, during the period from the early years to the end of S3. They do not have ceilings, to enable staff to extend the development of skills, attributes, knowledge and understanding into more challenging areas and higher levels of performance.

---

[1] The exceptions to this statement are where specific sets of experiences and outcomes are specialised: Gàidhlig, Gaelic (learners) and classical languages and religious education in Roman Catholic schools.

The experiences and outcomes are set out in lines of development which describe progress in learning. Progression is indicated through curriculum levels, which are explained in the table below.

Level	Stage
Early	The pre-school years and P1, or later for some.
First	To the end of P4, but earlier or later for some.
Second	To the end of P7, but earlier or later for some.
Third and Fourth	S1 to S3, but earlier for some. The fourth level broadly equates to SCQF level 4.
Senior phrase	S4 to S6, and college or other means of study.

APPENDICES

In most areas of the curriculum there is an appendix which provides brief explanations to help readers as they interpret the statements.

WHAT DO THE CODES MEAN?

The codes provide a unique identification for each statement, purely for ease of reference. As an example:

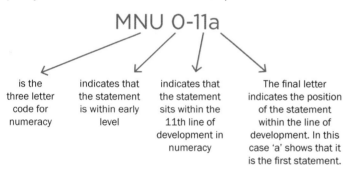

MNU 0-11a

| is the three letter code for numeracy | indicates that the statement is within early level | indicates that the statement sits within the 11th line of development in numeracy | The final letter indicates the position of the statement within the line of development. In this case 'a' shows that it is the first statement. |

WHY DO SOME STATEMENTS CROSS MORE THAN ONE LEVEL?

These describe learning which needs to be revisited, applied in new contexts and deepened over a more extended period. In all of these cases, effective planning is needed to ensure that each learner is continuing to make progress.

WHY ARE SOME STATEMENTS SHOWN IN ITALICS [WITH A YELLOW BACKGROUND]?

All staff have a responsibility to contribute to these. They include particular experiences and outcomes within health and wellbeing and all of those for literacy and numeracy. A further group of experiences and outcomes, relating to the use of information and communications technology to enhance learning, are to be found within the technologies framework.

WHY ARE SOME STATEMENTS SHOWN IN LIGHTER TEXT? [in normal text in this edition]

These are experiences and outcomes which are essential building blocks for a particular aspect of learning and development but which are to be found in a different curriculum area. To keep the frameworks as simple as possible these have been kept to a minimum.

WHY ARE THERE SOMETIMES FEWER STATEMENTS AT THIRD LEVEL THAN IN SECOND AND FOURTH?

This happens because of the particular significance of the third level as part of the entitlement for all young people. They represent a drawing together of a number of aspects of learning within that curriculum area.

TERMS USED WITHIN THE GUIDANCE

The term 'teacher' is used within the guidance to refer to those adults in teaching situations in all sectors and settings, and 'staff' or 'practitioners' to include professionals from the broader range of services to children.

EXPRESSIVE ARTS

PRINCIPLES & PRACTICE

WHAT CAN LEARNING IN THE EXPRESSIVE ARTS ACHIEVE FOR CHILDREN AND YOUNG PEOPLE?

The inspiration and power of the arts play a vital role in enabling our children and young people to enhance their creative talent and develop their artistic skills.

By engaging in experiences within the expressive arts, children and young people will recognise and represent feelings and emotions, both their own and those of others. The expressive arts play a central role in shaping our sense of our personal, social and cultural identity. Learning in the expressive arts also plays an important role in supporting children and young people to recognise and value the variety and vitality of culture locally, nationally and globally.

Learning in, through and about the expressive arts enables children and young people to:

▸ be creative and express themselves in different ways

▸ experience enjoyment and contribute to other people's enjoyment through creative and expressive performance and presentation

▸ develop important skills, both those specific to the expressive arts and those which are transferable

▸ develop an appreciation of aesthetic and cultural values, identities and ideas and, for some,

▸ prepare for advanced learning and future careers by building foundations for excellence in the expressive arts.

Building the Curriculum 1

The expressive arts are rich and stimulating, with the capacity to engage and fascinate learners of all ages, interests and levels of skill and achievement. It is therefore important that all teachers and educators look for opportunities within their own teaching approaches for interdisciplinary learning and to foster partnerships with professional arts companies, creative adults and cultural organisations.

STRUCTURE OF THE FRAMEWORK

The expressive arts experiences and outcomes will support staff in planning challenging, inspirational and enjoyable learning and teaching activities. The initial statements are closely linked to the four capacities and can be used to help to plan a wide range of learning activities, which will enable our young people to become:

▸ **successful learners,** who can express themselves, think innovatively, meet challenges positively and find imaginative solutions to problems and who have developed knowledge and skills related to the different arts and broader skills such as the use of technologies

▸ **confident individuals,** who have developed self-awareness, self-discipline, determination, commitment and confidence through drawing on their own ideas, experiences and feelings, and through successful participation

▸ **responsible citizens,** who can explore ethical questions, respond to personal and social issues, and develop stances and views, who have deepened their insight and experiences of cultural identities and who have come to recognise the importance of the arts to the culture and identities of Scotland and other societies

▸ **effective contributors,** who can develop and express their creativity, work cooperatively and communicate with others and, in so doing, show initiative, dependability, leadership and enterprise.

The framework then begins with experiences and outcomes for presentation and performance across the expressive arts, followed by the experiences and outcomes in:

▸ **art and design**

▸ **dance**

▸ **drama**

▸ **music.**

This framework provides children and young people with opportunities to be creative and imaginative, to experience inspiration and enjoyment and to develop skills in each of these areas. Participation enables children and young people to experience and enjoy the energy and excitement of performing and presenting for different audiences and of being part of an audience for others.

The experiences and outcomes from each of the lines of development are complementary and interrelated and should be considered together when planning for learning.

The experiences and outcomes do not place ceilings on aspirations for progress and development. Through them, all learners, including those with particular skills, talents and interests and those with additional support needs, will have opportunities to nurture and develop their interests and skills.

EFFECTIVE LEARNING AND TEACHING IN THE EXPRESSIVE ARTS

The framework of experiences and outcomes supports staff in meeting the needs of children and young people through providing a wide range of carefully planned, well-paced learning experiences.

Within a rich, supportive environment teachers will draw upon a skilful mix of approaches to promote a climate of creativity and innovation, including:

▸ active involvement in creative activities and performances

▸ tasks or performance opportunities which require a creative response

▸ opportunities to perform or present to an audience

▸ partnerships with professional performers or artists and other creative adults

▸ raising awareness of contemporary culture and connecting with young people's experiences

▸ appropriate, effective use of technology

▸ building on the principles of Assessment is for Learning

▸ both collaborative and independent learning

▸ establishing links within the expressive arts subjects and with the wider curriculum

▸ opportunities to analyse, explore and reflect.

The majority of activities in the expressive arts involve creating and presenting and are practical and experiential. Evaluating and appreciating are an integral part of the creative process and are linked to developing creative skills, knowledge and understanding and enhancing enjoyment.

BUILDING ON PRIOR LEARNING

Children and young people will come to their learning in the expressive arts with a range of different types and levels of experiences gained within and beyond the life of the school. Teachers will plan activities that take into account prior learning, achievement and interests.

At early to third level children and young people will enjoy activities that centre on expressing ideas, thoughts and feelings through creativity and self-expression. Development of skills is directly linked with opportunities for presenting and performing. Taken together, these experiences and outcomes from early to third level represent a broad general education in the expressive arts for all children and young people. With this in mind, the framework at the third level includes the expectation that each young person will enjoy the opportunity to contribute to a public presentation or performance in art and design, dance, drama or music, as a significant culmination of his or her broad general education. Similarly, some of the third level outcomes draw together learning from two or three related lines of development into a single outcome before expanding into the fourth level.

Fourth level experiences and outcomes provide a basis for more advanced study and further scope for depth, challenge, enjoyment, personalisation and choice. Teachers have scope to plan and organise different combinations of these experiences and outcomes, both within and between aspects of the expressive arts, to meet the varied needs and interests of young people who choose to progress beyond third level. The level of achievement at fourth level has been designed to

approximate to that associated with SCQF Level 4.

At all levels children and young people will develop new skills and consolidate prior learning. Some of these skills (such as skills of communication, evaluation and leadership) are transferable while others (such as specific performance and technical skills) are specific to one or more of the expressive arts.

Teachers are responsible for ensuring that those with particular skills, talents and interests in one or more of the expressive arts have access to and can participate in arts experiences that accelerate, challenge and enrich their learning. This will include opportunities for some learners to build skills and qualities which will lead to their employment in the creative industries sector.

BROAD FEATURES OF ASSESSMENT

Assessment in the expressive arts will focus on children and young people's skills and abilities to express themselves through creating, presenting, evaluating and appreciating. Approaches to assessment will also include a focus on their abilities to recognise, present and discuss their own feelings and emotions and those of others.

Teachers will gather evidence of progress as part of children and young people's day-to-day learning in art and design, dance, drama and music. They will also make use of specific assessment tasks in assessing some aspects of learning. From the early years through to the senior stages, children and young people will demonstrate their progress in developing their skills as they work individually and with others in creative activities including, for example, presentations to others. Discussions with learners and observations of their responses can support teachers and practitioners in the challenge of assessing learners' creative and aesthetic processes. Evidence of progress will also be demonstrated through learners' abilities and skills in communicating in different ways and settings, solving problems creatively, and justifying their opinions of their own and others' work.

Approaches to assessment should identify the extent to which children and young people can apply these skills in their learning and their daily lives and in preparing for the world of work. For example:

▸ How well do they demonstrate appreciation and understanding of cultural identity?

▸ Do they show awareness of the role and impact of creative arts on people's lifelong interest and enjoyment of the expressive arts?

Children and young people can demonstrate their progress in skills, knowledge and understanding as they develop their practical skills and express increasingly complex concepts and ideas. For example, they:

▸ apply their creative skills to produce and perform more

- complex pieces of work and to recognise creativity and skill in the work of other people
- demonstrate increasing skills and confidence in presentations and performances, and in appreciation of how the expressive arts relate to the wider world and different cultures
- show enjoyment of the expressive arts, for example through evaluating constructively their own work and that of others, and suggesting how it can be improved.

Assessment should also link with other areas of the curriculum within and outside the classroom and, for example, offer children and young people opportunities to become aware of the role of professional arts companies and cultural organisations in society and the economy.

LINKS WITH REST OF THE CURRICULUM

Learning in the expressive arts offers rich and exciting opportunities for interdisciplinary work across art and design, dance, drama and music and with other areas of the curriculum. Ready examples include the opportunities for collaboration with technologies afforded by the study of design in a variety of contexts. As participation in dance activities contributes to children and young people's physical activity, experiences and outcomes in dance can be readily linked with those for physical education. Moving image media provides opportunities to explore dance, drama, music, art and design within another narrative medium and to combine these traditional expressive arts in film-making work.

Children and young people will develop, enhance and apply skills gained in the expressive arts in a very broad range of activities including role play, participation in whole school events, community events and outdoor learning. Such activities promote the development of skills in areas such as talking and working with others, and contribute greatly to children and young people's mental, emotional, social and physical wellbeing.

PROVIDING INSIGHTS AND EXPERIENCES OF SCOTLAND'S DISTINCTIVE CULTURAL IDENTITES

Learning in the expressive arts helps learners develop their knowledge, understanding and appreciation of contemporary and historical arts within their own communities, within Scotland and beyond. Children and young people will enjoy numerous and diverse opportunities to contribute to, reflect on and respond to the arts within their own and other cultures.

INSPIRATION AND ENJOYMENT

One of the main purposes of learning in the expressive arts is to develop lifelong appreciation of, and participation in, expressive arts and cultural activities. The framework therefore includes not only statements of the intended outcomes of learning but also statements of experiences which provide opportunities for inspiration and enjoyment.

Judgements about learning will be based on evidence derived from a broad range of sources and across a range of activities and will refer to the learner's progress over time. High quality learning experiences will generate inspiration and enjoyment which will motivate and support effective learning.

CONTRIBUTING TO THE CURRICULUM IN ITS BROADEST SENSE?

Through their involvement in the expressive arts, all children and young people can express themselves in innovative, motivating ways, and experience enjoyment and enrichment in their lives.

The framework acknowledges that many children and young people will engage with the expressive arts in what were formerly seen as extra-curricular activities, and that the expressive arts can and should play an important part in the life of the school or early years centre. The experiences and outcomes relate to all aspects of participation in the expressive arts.

EXPERIENCES & OUTCOMES

Experiences in the expressive arts involve creating and presenting and are practical and experiential. Evaluating and appreciating are used to enhance enjoyment and develop knowledge and understanding.

My learning in, through and about the expressive arts:

▸ enables me to experience the inspiration and power of the arts

▸ recognises and nurtures my creative and aesthetic talents

▸ allows me to develop skills and techniques that are relevant to specific art forms and across the four capacities

▸ provides opportunities for me to deepen my understanding of culture in Scotland and the wider world

▸ is enhanced and enriched through partnerships with professional arts companies, creative adults and cultural organisations.

GLOSSARIES

[An appendix of explanations and glossaries is included for Art and Design, Dance, Drama and Music.] The explanations of specific language are intended to help educators, parents, children and young people interpret the outcomes.

PARTICIPATION IN PERFORMANCES AND PRESENTATIONS

All aspects of learning in expressive arts include opportunities to present and perform, for example through preparation of artwork for display, presentation of a short improvised drama to members of the class or performance of dance or music to parents or in the community. At third level, as a culmination of learning within their broad general education each young person should have the opportunity to contribute to a significant presentation (such as an exhibition) or performance in at least one area of the expressive arts.

EXA 0-01a / 1-01a / 2-01a I have experienced the energy and excitement of presenting/performing for audiences and being part of an audience for other people's presentations/performances.	
EXA 3-01a I have used the skills I have developed in the expressive arts to contribute to a public presentation/performance.[1]	There are no benchmarks for these Experiences & Outcomes
EXA 3-01b I have experienced the energy and excitement of being part of an audience for other people's presentations/performances.	
EXA 4-01a I have experienced the energy and excitement of presenting/performing for different audiences.	

E
1
2
3
4

Design: © Harold Raitt / SeeHearTeach.scot (2019)   Content: © Crown copyright (2017)

[1]   Participation in this experience should occur in at least one area of the expressive arts. According to the context this will be either a performance or a presentation.

ART AND DESIGN

Through art and design, learners have rich opportunities to be creative and to experience inspiration and enjoyment. They explore a wide range of two- and three-dimensional media and technologies through practical activities, and create, express, and communicate ideas. Their studies of the works of artists and designers enhance their enjoyment and deepen their knowledge and understanding.

E

EXA 0-02a I have the freedom to discover and choose ways to create images and objects using a variety of materials.

EXA 0-04a / 1-04a I can create a range of visual information through observing and recording from my experiences across the curriculum.

EXA 0-05a / 1-05a / 2-05a Inspired by a range of stimuli, I can express and communicate my ideas, thoughts and feelings through activities within art and design.

EXA 0-06a Working on my own and with others, I use my curiosity and imagination to solve design problems.

EXA 0-07a / 1-07a / 2-07a I can respond to the work of artists and designers by discussing my thoughts and feelings. I can give and accept constructive comment on my own and others' work.

- Records from experiences across the curriculum, for example, through observing and remembering, makes a model or drawing based on an aspect of the natural environment such as natural items from the sea shore, the countryside, a forest.
- Solves simple design problems, working on their own and with others, using a degree of trial and error, for example, designs a simple container for an agreed purpose.
- Recognises colour, line, shape and at least one more of the visual elements: form, tone, pattern, texture.
- Shares thoughts and feelings in response to the work of at least one artist and one designer, giving reasons for likes and dislikes.
- Shares views and listens appropriately to the views of others on their own or others' work.

When creating images and objects to express ideas, thoughts and feelings:
- uses a variety of available materials and technology;
- shows understanding that line can have different qualities, for example, thick, thin, broken, wavy.

1

EXA 1-02a I have the opportunity to choose and explore a range of media and technologies to create images and objects, discovering their effects and suitability for specific tasks.

EXA 1-03a I can create and present work using the visual elements of line, shape, form, colour, tone, pattern and texture.

EXA 0-04a / 1-04a I can create a range of visual information through observing and recording from my experiences across the curriculum.

EXA 0-05a / 1-05a / 2-05a Inspired by a range of stimuli, I can express and communicate my ideas, thoughts and feelings through activities within art and design.

EXA 1-06a I can use exploration and imagination to solve design problems related to real-life situations.

EXA 0-07a / 1-07a / 2-07a I can respond to the work of artists and designers by discussing my thoughts and feelings. I can give and accept constructive comment on my own and others' work.

- Records directly from experiences across the curriculum, for example, observes and sketches a view from a window, features of the built environment, pets, self or others.
- Presents images and objects created, for example, positions a simple frame over a picture or arranges an object on a simple stand and observes from different angles.
- Solves at least one design problem related to real-life, showing some evidence of planning, for example, designs a simple item to be worn on the head or body.
- Recognises and names most of the visual elements: line, shape, form, colour, tone, pattern, texture.
- Shares thoughts and feelings by expressing personal views in response to the work of at least one artist and one designer.
- Shares views and listens appropriately to views of others, suggesting what works well and what could be improved in their own and others' work, using some art and design vocabulary.

When creating images and objects to express ideas, thoughts and feelings:
- chooses and uses technology and a range of media;
- shows understanding of basic colour theory, for example, which secondary colours are made from mixing primary colours;
- shows some understanding of the qualities and limitations of selected media, for example, uses pencil instead of a large brush to make fine marks, uses chalks instead of pencil to fill larger spaces;
- shows understanding of the concept of scale, for example, represents mountains as bigger than people.

2

EXA 2-02a I have the opportunity to choose and explore an extended range of media and technologies to create images and objects, comparing and combining them for specific tasks.

EXA 2-03a I can create and present work that shows developing skill in using the visual elements and concepts.

EXA 2-04a Through observing and recording from my experiences across the curriculum, I can create images and objects which show my awareness and recognition of detail.

EXA 0-05a / 1-05a / 2-05a Inspired by a range of stimuli, I can express and communicate my ideas, thoughts and feelings through activities within art and design.

EXA 2-06a I can develop and communicate my ideas, demonstrating imagination and presenting at least one possible solution to a design problem.

EXA 0-07a / 1-07a / 2-07a I can respond to the work of artists and designers by discussing my thoughts and feelings. I can give and accept constructive comment on my own and others' work.

- Records from experiences across the curriculum, showing recognition of detail, for example, observes and captures the detail seen in a natural form, such as a feather or a plant or an interesting personal item, such as a bicycle.
- Creates a simple plan that explains how they will investigate and develop ideas in response to a design brief.
- Follows a step-by-step process to develop and communicate ideas in response to a design brief.
- Recognises and describes the visual elements in their own and others' work.
- Selects, presents and discusses relevant information, from a range of sources, about the work of chosen artists and designers, for example, in relation to how and why they have used colour or shape in their work.
- Explains, with supporting reasons, what works well and what could be improved in their own or others' work, using appropriate art and design vocabulary.

When creating images and objects to express ideas, thoughts and feelings:
- uses a range of drawing implements to produce specific effects, for example, uses different grades of pencil to create tone or uses pen and ink to create bold line;
- shows understanding of the properties of different types of paint such as watercolour, acrylic, poster paint;
- shows understanding of the properties of a range of modelling media, through practical exploration;
- applies a printmaking process, for example, makes prints from polystyrene;
- shows understanding of the differences between media and how media can be combined to create effects, for example, combines wax crayon with water-based paint in a picture;
- shows understanding of the concept of depth, for example, shows a foreground, a middle ground and a background in a picture.

DANCE

Through dance, learners have rich opportunities to be creative and to experience inspiration and enjoyment. Creating and performing will be the core activities for all learners, and taking part in dance contributes to their physical education and physical activity. Learners develop their technical skills and the quality of their movement, and use their imagination and skills to create and choreograph dance sequences. They further develop their knowledge and understanding and their capacity to enjoy dance through evaluating performances and commenting on their work and the work of others.

Experiences and outcomes	Benchmarks	Level
EXA 0-08a I have the opportunity and freedom to choose and explore ways that I can move rhythmically, expressively and playfully. **EXA 0-09a / 1-09a / 2-09a** Inspired by a range of stimuli, I can express my ideas, thoughts and feelings through creative work in dance. **EXA 0-10a** I have opportunities to enjoy taking part in dance experiences. **EXA 0-11a / 1-11a / 2-11a** I can respond to the experience of dance by discussing my thoughts and feelings. I can give and accept constructive comment on my own and others' work.	• Performs a range of simple, repeated, intentional movements and gestures. • Uses space and resources creatively. • Chooses and explores ways of moving rhythmically, expressively and playfully. • Participates in dance that is taught and/or creative movement invented by peers. • Shows understanding that dance consists of combined movements and gestures, usually performed with music or a beat. • Shares their responses to stimuli through movement with, for example, peers or practitioner. • Shares thoughts and feelings in response to dance experiences, either as a performer or as part of an audience, giving reasons for likes and dislikes. • Shares views and listens appropriately to the views of others on their own or others' work.	E
EXA 1-08a I enjoy creating short dance sequences, using travel, turn, jump, gesture, pause and fall, within safe practice. **EXA 0-09a / 1-09a / 2-09a** Inspired by a range of stimuli, I can express my ideas, thoughts and feelings through creative work in dance. **EXA 1-10a** I am becoming aware of different features of dance and can practise and perform steps, formations and short dance. **EXA 0-11a / 1-11a / 2-11a** I can respond to the experience of dance by discussing my thoughts and feelings. I can give and accept constructive comment on my own and others' work.	• Identifies and performs the body actions of turn, jump, gesture, pause and fall, with some degree of control. • Creates, rehearses and performs short dance sequences, working on their own and with others. • Creates new dance movements and sequences using their dance repertoire, incorporating different speeds and levels, characters and emotions to add interest and variety. • Explores rhythm, movement and space, and increases possibilities for expression through movement. • Understands some of the different forms of dance, for example, Scottish, Irish, Bollywood, tap, ballet, jazz, hip hop and ballroom. • Demonstrates understanding of simple formations, such as circles or squares, through taking in part in group dance. • Demonstrates safe practice in dance, for example, being aware of personal space, planned landings. • Shares thoughts and feelings by expressing personal views in response to experiencing live or recorded dance performance. • Shares views and listens appropriately to views of others, suggesting what works well and what could be improved in their own and others' work, using some dance vocabulary.	1
EXA 2-08a I can explore and choose movements to create and present dance, developing my skills and techniques. **EXA 0-09a / 1-09a / 2-09a** Inspired by a range of stimuli, I can express my ideas, thoughts and feelings through creative work in dance. **EXA 2-10a** I have taken part in dance from a range of styles and cultures, demonstrating my awareness of the dance features. **EXA 0-11a / 1-11a / 2-11a** I can respond to the experience of dance by discussing my thoughts and feelings. I can give and accept constructive comment on my own and others' work.	• Shows understanding of the key features of dance from a range of styles and cultures, through dance performance. • Demonstrates coordination and some control in a range of dance actions and sequences. • Creates, rehearses and performs a short original dance piece, comprising several sequences, to music or a rhythm. • Develops and refines own dance repertoire through continued exploration and practice. • Selects and applies dance skills to create dance that shows variation, for solo or group performance. • Justifies own creative choices using appropriate dance vocabulary, for example, explains explosive movement inspired by fireworks in terms of speed and levels. • Explains, with supporting reasons, what works well and what could be improved in their own or others' work, using appropriate dance vocabulary.	2

ART AND DESIGN: EXPLANATIONS & GLOSSARY

Opportunities to study design in the following contexts: graphic, product, fashion/textile, architecture, interior and jewellery should be made available across the five levels, taking balance and previous learning into consideration.

Art and design concepts For example, space, scale, proportion and perspective.

Art and design technology For example, computer software, photography, moving image media and screen printing.

Design brief A written plan that identifies a problem to be solved, its criteria and its constraints. The design brief is used to encourage consideration of all aspects of a problem before attempting a solution.

Design process A systematic problem-solving strategy, with criteria and constraints, used to develop many possible solutions to solve a problem. The process involves: investigation, development of ideas, production of solution and evaluation of solution.

Expressive Activities involving the expression of personal ideas, thoughts and feelings in visual terms. This could include drawing, painting, sculpture, printmaking and photography.

Form External three-dimensional outline, appearance or configuration of something that could be, for example, solid, transparent, rigid, flexible.

Medium/Media Tool(s) for creating and presenting in art and design, such as chalks, drawing inks, gouache, acrylics, fabric dyes, printing inks, sculpting materials, jewellery metals and materials, and digital media, including photographs and moving image media.

Visual elements The basic elements (building blocks) in art and design activities – line, shape, form, colour, tone, pattern, texture.

DANCE: EXPLANATIONS & GLOSSARY

Choreographic form Ways of creating dance, for example repeating phrases of movement.

Dance motif A short pattern of movement that expresses and communicates a mood, a feeling, an activity or an idea.

Dance sequences Routines which may contain the body actions of travel, turn, jump, gesture, pause and fall within safe practice.

Theatre arts technology For example lighting and sound equipment used to enhance performances.

DRAMA

Through drama, learners have rich opportunities to be creative and to experience inspiration and enjoyment. Creating and presenting are prominent activities for all learners. Their acting and presenting skills are developed through participating in scripted or improvised drama. Exploring real and imaginary situations helps learners to understand and share their world. They develop their capacity to enjoy drama and their knowledge and understanding through evaluating technical aspects and scripts, and commenting on their work and the work of others.

E	
EXA 0-12a I have the freedom to choose and explore how I can use my voice, movement, and expression in role play and drama. **EXA 0-13a / 1-13a / 2-13a** Inspired by a range of stimuli, I can express and communicate my ideas, thoughts and feelings through drama. **EXA 0-14a** I use drama to explore real and imaginary situations, helping me to understand my world. **EXA 0-15a / 1-15a / 2-15a** I can respond to the experience of drama by discussing my thoughts and feelings. I can give and accept constructive comment on my own and others' work.	• Takes on a role within a play or dramatised situation, for example, a puppet show, a real or imagined situation, re-enactment of a story or traditional tale. • Communicates ideas and feelings using aspects of voice, such as volume, expression and clarity. • Communicates ideas and feelings using movement, for example, through body language, gestures, actions and posture. • Communicates ideas and feelings using facial expressions, for example, to show happy, sad, surprised, angry, scared. • Conveys through drama what characters in real or imaginary situations might say, do or feel, for example, being upset about losing a toy, what a character in a well-known fairy tale might say or how they might feel. • Communicates their ideas through improvised drama i.e. making it up as they go along. • Shares thoughts and feelings about drama experiences, for example, during a discussion about characters or events in a drama, giving reasons for likes and dislikes. • Shares views and listens appropriately to the views of others on their own or others' work.
1	
EXA 1-12a I enjoy creating, choosing and accepting roles, using movement, expression and voice. **EXA 0-13a / 1-13a / 2-13a** Inspired by a range of stimuli, I can express and communicate my ideas, thoughts and feelings through drama. **EXA 1-14a** I have developed confidence and skills in creating and presenting drama which explores real and imaginary situations, using improvisation and script. **EXA 0-15a / 1-15a / 2-15a** I can respond to the experience of drama by discussing my thoughts and feelings. I can give and accept constructive comment on my own and others' work.	• Creates, chooses and takes on a role within a drama such as a real or imagined situation, re-enactment of a story, a traditional tale. • Uses voice, considering use of volume, expression, clarity and pace to convey a character. • Uses movement in roles, conveying a character through gestures, actions and posture. • Uses expression in role, conveying a character through body language, for example, facial expression. • Creates a short drama using improvisation, from a given stimulus, and working collaboratively. • Shows understanding of how to work from a script by acting or speaking at the appropriate time, for example, in a nativity play, a sound story or a poem. • Contributes towards the development of a drama, for example, by discussing aspects such as character, performance, or script, for example, what a character in a well-known story might say to another. • Shares views and listens appropriately to the views of others about what works well and what could be improved in their own and others' work, using some drama vocabulary.
2	
EXA 2-12a I can create, adapt and sustain different roles, experimenting with movement, expression and voice and using theatre arts technology. **EXA 0-13a / 1-13a / 2-13a** Inspired by a range of stimuli, I can express and communicate my ideas, thoughts and feelings through drama. **EXA 2-14a** I have created and presented scripted or improvised drama, beginning to take account of audience and atmosphere. **EXA 0-15a / 1-15a / 2-15a** I can respond to the experience of drama by discussing my thoughts and feelings. I can give and accept constructive comment on my own and others' work.	• Conveys a character using characterisation techniques such as hot seating, role on the wall, thought tracking. • Chooses voice appropriately for role, considering volume, tone, clarity, pace, characterisation, and emotion. • Chooses appropriate movement for role, for example, to convey the character's setting, physical features, the character's feelings. • Chooses relevant expression in role, showing how the character might interact with others, for example, through body language. • Uses movement, expression and voice to create atmosphere, for example, a high pitched voice, wide eyes and crouched body to suggest a frightening situation. • Creates a short drama, as part of a group or individually, using improvisation or a published script. • Builds on the contributions of others in developing ideas for a shared drama, with regard to plot, characters and theatre arts. • Presents a short drama, as part of a group, using improvisation or a script. • Uses theatre arts technology such as props, basic lighting and sound to enhance a performance effectively, for example, chooses appropriate music or makes sound effects to create atmosphere. • Gives a personal response to drama experiences, with appropriate justification. • Explains, with supporting reasons, what works well and what could be improved in their own and others' work, using appropriate drama vocabulary.

DRAMA: EXPLANATIONS & GLOSSARY

Drama forms For example a play, comedy or pantomime.

Drama conventions Alternative ways of presenting parts of a drama, for example mime, voice over, freeze frame.

Theatre arts technology For example lighting and sound equipment used to enhance performances.

MUSIC

Through music, learners have rich opportunities to be creative and to experience inspiration and enjoyment. Performing and creating music will be the prominent activities for all learners. Through these activities they develop their vocal and instrumental skills, explore sounds and musical concepts, and use their imagination and skills to create musical ideas and compositions. They can further develop their understanding and capacity to enjoy music through listening to musical performances and commenting on them. They use ICT to realise or enhance their composition and performance, and to promote their understanding of how music works.

EXA 0-16a I enjoy singing and playing along to music of different styles and cultures. **EXA 0-17a** I have the freedom to use my voice, musical instruments and music technology to discover and enjoy playing with sound and rhythm. **EXA 0-18a / 1-18a / 2-18a** Inspired by a range of stimuli, and working on my own and/or with others, I can express and communicate my ideas, thoughts and feelings through musical activities. **EXA 0-19a** I can respond to music by describing my thoughts and feelings about my own and others' work.	• Participates actively and uses his/her voice in singing activities from a range of styles and cultures, for example, nursery rhymes and songs with actions. • Uses instruments such as drum, claves, chime bar to play along to a range of music styles. • Shares thoughts and feelings about music experiences such as live and/or recorded music, peer nursery rhyme performances, school concerts, giving reasons for likes and dislikes. • Shares views and listens appropriately to the views of others, for example, states if the music is fast/slow or loud/quiet. When communicating ideas and feelings through creative music activities: • uses voice to explore sound and rhythm, for example, hums, whispers, sings; • chooses different musical instruments to play such as chime bar, drum or body percussion, exploring sound and rhythm by, for example, clapping, tapping; • uses technology to capture sound, for example, audio recorders, microphones, apps and other software. **E**
EXA 1-16a I can sing and play music from other styles and cultures, showing growing confidence and skill while learning about musical notation and performance directions. **EXA 1-17a** I can use my voice, musical instruments and music technology to discover and enjoy playing with sound, rhythm, pitch and dynamics. **EXA 0-18a / 1-18a / 2-18a** Inspired by a range of stimuli, and working on my own and/or with others, I can express and communicate my ideas, thoughts and feelings through musical activities. **EXA 1-19a / 2-19a** I have listened to a range of music and can respond by discussing my thoughts and feelings. I can give and accept constructive comment on my own and others' work.	• Performs songs with enthusiasm, from a range of styles and cultures, demonstrating a variety of basic singing techniques such as accurate pitch, good diction and appropriate dynamics, for example, loud or quiet. • Performs a simple rhythm part on a range of instruments, for example, keeps the beat using body/untuned percussion. • Performs simple melodic parts, for example, on tuned percussion, tin whistle, recorder. • Follows performance directions, for example, follows the group leader. • Follows simple music notation, for example, in the form of pictures, graphics, treble clef. • Shares thoughts and feelings by expressing personal views in response to musical experiences such as performances, school shows and music from different styles and cultures. • Shares views and listens appropriately to views of others, suggesting what works well and what could be improved in their own and others' work, using some music vocabulary. When communicating ideas and feelings through creative musical activities, working on their own and/or with others: • uses voice, instruments and technology to create musical ideas using sound, rhythm, pitch and dynamics, for example, by creating a soundscape or by adding tuned/untuned percussion to enhance a story or a song. **1**
EXA 2-16a I can sing and play music from a range of styles and cultures, showing skill and using performance directions, and/or musical notation. **EXA 2-17a** I can use my voice, musical instruments and music technology to experiment with sounds, pitch, melody, rhythm, timbre and dynamics. **EXA 0-18a / 1-18a / 2-18a** Inspired by a range of stimuli, and working on my own and/or with others, I can express and communicate my ideas, thoughts and feelings through musical activities. **EXA 1-19a / 2-19a** I have listened to a range of music and can respond by discussing my thoughts and feelings. I can give and accept constructive comment on my own and others' work.	• Performs songs in unison and in parts, individually or as part of a group, and communicates the mood and character of songs from a range of styles and cultures, such as folk songs or songs from musicals, using appropriate performance directions, for example, gradually getting louder/ quieter, and/or musical notation. • Performs on instruments, individually or as part of a group, to communicate the mood and character of a piece of music through, for example, the use of appropriate dynamics and expression. • Applies verbal and non-verbal techniques whilst giving and/or following performance directions, for example, eye contact and/or body language. • Uses voice, instruments and technology to create music, experimenting with timbre, for example, uses tuned/untuned percussion instruments to create simple melodies and rhythms. • Explains preference for music pieces listened to, live and/or recorded, using appropriate music concepts. • Recognises a range of music styles and identifies some of the main instruments used in, for example, classical music, jazz music, rock and pop music. • Explains, with supporting reasons, what works well and what could be improved in their own and others' work, using appropriate music vocabulary. **2**

MUSIC: EXPLANATIONS & GLOSSARY

Dynamics The varying degrees of loudness and quietness in sound.

Music concepts Terms that describe the ingredients of music, such as repetition, harmony, major key, syncopation.

Music technology The use of electronic devices and computer software in music compositions and performance.

Pitch The term used to describe how high or low/deep a note or sound is.

Timbre The tone colour or quality of tone which distinguishes one instrument from another.

HEALTH & WELLBEING

PRINCIPLES & PRACTICE

The Principles & Practice statements for 'Health & Wellbeing: Responsibility of All Practitioners' (from the front of the original CfE document) and the statements for Health & Wellbeing as the responsibilty of teachers (in primary) and Health & Wellbeing specialists (in primary and secondary) have been combined here.

Dark green shading in this column denotes that the text appears in the Principles & Practice statements for Health & Wellbeing: Responsibility of All on pages 8-11 of the original CfE document.

Lighter shading in this column denotes text appearing in the Principles & Practice for Health & Wellbeing on pages 72-78 of that document.

HWB: RoA

HWB

Learning through health and wellbeing promotes confidence, independent thinking and positive attitudes and dispositions. Because of this, it is the responsibility of every teacher to contribute to learning and development in this area.

Building the Curriculum 1

Curriculum for Excellence has an important role to play in promoting the health and wellbeing of children and young people and of all of those in the educational communities to which they belong. This paper is intended to support discussion and planning between practitioners in all sectors and services and in local authorities.

This paper is closely related to the Guidance on the Schools (Health Promotion and Nutrition) (Scotland) Act 2007 (http://www.scotland.gov.uk/Topics/Education/Schools/HLivi/foodnutrition). Together, these documents describe the expectations upon individuals, schools and local authorities for promoting the health and wellbeing of children and young people.

MAIN PURPOSES OF LEARNING

Learning in health and wellbeing ensures that children and young people develop the knowledge and understanding, skills, capabilities and attributes which they need for mental, emotional, social and physical wellbeing now and in the future. Learning through health and wellbeing enables children and young people to:

▶ make informed decisions in order to improve their mental, emotional, social and physical wellbeing
▶ experience challenge and enjoyment
▶ experience positive aspects of healthy living and activity for themselves
▶ apply their mental, emotional, social and physical skills to pursue a healthy lifestyle
▶ make a successful move to the next stage of education or work
▶ establish a pattern of health and wellbeing which will be sustained into adult life, and which will help to promote the health and wellbeing of the next generation of Scottish children.

It also enables some to perform at high levels in sport or prepare for careers within the health and leisure industries.

PRACTITIONERS' ROLES AND RESPONSIBILITIES

Children and young people should feel happy, safe, respected and included in the school environment and all staff should be proactive in promoting positive behaviour in the classroom, playground and the wider school community. Robust policies and practice which ensure the safety and wellbeing of children should already be in place.

Good health and wellbeing is central to effective learning and preparation for successful independent living. This aspiration for every child and young person can only be met through a concerted approach; schools and their partners working together closely to plan their programmes for health and wellbeing explicitly, taking account of local circumstances and individual needs. The diagram on page 19 illustrates this shared vision and common goal.

WHAT THE FRAMEWORK MEANS FOR PRACTITIONERS

The statements of experiences and outcomes in health and wellbeing reflect a holistic approach to promoting the health and wellbeing of all children and young people. They are consistent with the United Nations Convention on the Rights of the Child, which sets out the right for all children and young people to have access to appropriate health services and to have their health and wellbeing promoted. They build on the considerable work of Health Promoting Schools and the publication of Being Well, Doing Well which underlines the importance of a 'health enhancing' school ethos – one characterised by care, respect, participation, responsibility and fairness for all. The framework complements the duty in the Schools (Health Promotion and Nutrition) (Scotland) Act 2007 for Scottish Ministers and local authorities to endeavour to ensure that all schools are health promoting.

Children and young people should feel happy, safe, respected and included in the school environment and all staff should be proactive in promoting positive behaviour in the classroom, playground and the wider school community. Robust policies and practice which ensure the safety and wellbeing of children should already be in place. In addition, there are many ways in which establishments can assist young people. These include peer support, buddies, breakfast or lunch clubs, safe areas, mentors, pupil support staff and extended support teams.

Good health and wellbeing is central to effective learning and preparation for successful independent living. This aspiration for every child and young person can only be met through a concerted approach: schools and their partners working together closely to plan their programmes for health and wellbeing explicitly, taking account of local circumstances and individual needs. Planning to provide and manage the many different and complementary contributions may be challenging but is needed. Each individual practitioner must be aware of his or her roles and responsibilities. The diagram below illustrates this shared vision and common goal.

STRUCTURE OF THE FRAMEWORK

The framework begins by describing features of the environment for learning which will support and nurture the health and wellbeing of children and young people, including a positive ethos and relationships, and participation in activities which promote a healthy lifestyle. These statements are intended to help to inform planning and practice within establishments or clusters and also by individual practitioners.

In the version which summarises those aspects which are the responsibility of all practitioners, the framework continues with experiences and outcomes which include those in mental, emotional, social and physical wellbeing, aspects of planning for choices and changes, and relationships.

The framework begins by describing features of the environment for learning which will support and nurture the health and wellbeing of children and young people, including a positive ethos and relationships, and participation in activities which promote a healthy lifestyle. These statements are intended to help to inform planning and practice within establishments or clusters and also by individual practitioners.

The statements of experiences and outcomes are then structured into the following organisers:

- Mental, emotional, social and physical wellbeing
- Planning for choices and changes
- Physical education, physical activity and sport
- Food and health
- Substance misuse
- Relationships, sexual health and parenthood.

The aspects of the health and wellbeing framework which are the responsibility of all adults who are working together to support the learning and development of children and young people are identified through the use of italics [and a yellow background].

Many of the experiences and outcomes span two or more levels; some are written to span from early to fourth because they are applicable throughout life. All of these should be revisited regularly in ways which take account of the stage of development and understanding of each child and young person and are relevant and realistic for them.

PRACTITIONERS' ROLES AND RESPONSIBILITIES

Some contributions are the responsibility of all, while other contributions relate to specific stages or are more specialised.

HEALTH AND WELLBEING ACROSS LEARNING:
THE RESPONSIBILITY OF ALL PRACTITIONERS

Everyone within each learning community, whatever their contact with children and young people may be, shares the responsibility for creating a positive ethos and climate of respect and trust – one in which everyone can make a positive contribution to the wellbeing of each individual within the school and the wider community. There are many ways in which establishments can assist young people. These include peer support, buddies, breakfast or lunch clubs, safe areas, mentors, pupil support staff, and extended support teams.

The responsibilities include individuals' contributions to the features set out in the introductory statements, and experiences and outcomes in mental, emotional, social and physical wellbeing, planning for choices and changes, and relationships.
The [responsibilities of all]* include each practitioner's role in establishing open, positive, supportive relationships across the school community, where children and young people will feel that they are listened to, and where they feel secure in their ability to discuss sensitive aspects of their lives; in promoting a climate in which children and young people feel safe and secure; in modelling behaviour which promotes health and wellbeing and encouraging it in others[;]* through using learning and teaching methodologies which promote effective learning; and by being sensitive and responsive to the wellbeing of each child and young person. Practical responsibilities include understanding of anti-discriminatory, anti-bullying and child protection policies by all staff and knowledge of the steps to be taken in any given situation, including appropriate referral.

FOCUSED PROGRAMMES

Children will experience certain aspects of health and wellbeing through focused programmes such as personal and social education programmes. Within these programmes, schools will often draw on the expertise of others. For example, when substance misuse is being considered, specialists within and outwith the learning community working together are able to ensure that children and young people learn in the most effective ways. Subject teachers, including teachers of home economics and physical education, play a very important role in the teaching and learning of health and wellbeing through the experiences and outcomes for food and health, and physical education, physical activity and sport. Sports specialists play an important part in physical activity and sport provision.

PARTNERSHIP WORKING ACROSS SECTORS AND SERVICES

Children's and young people's learning in health and wellbeing benefits strongly from [close involvement with children and young people and their parents or carers and]* partnership [working]† between teachers and colleagues such as home link staff, health professionals, educational psychologists and sports coaches. Partners can make complementary contributions through their specialist expertise and knowledge.

Effective partnership working:

- engages the active support of parents and carers
- reinforces work across transitions and planning across sectors
- maximises the contributions of the wider community
- draws upon specialist expertise
- ensures, through careful planning and briefing, that all contributions come together in ways which achieve coherence and progression.

PERSONAL SUPPORT FOR CHILDREN AND YOUNG PEOPLE

The health and wellbeing of every child and young person is greatly enhanced through the individual support and pastoral care which they receive through having an identified member of staff who knows and understands them and can support them in facing changes and challenges and in making choices. Members of staff are often best placed to identify even minor changes of mood in a child or young person which could reflect an important emotional, social or mental health issue with which that child or young person needs help or support. It is important that children and young people feel that they can share their anxieties with an appropriate individual who has the skills, rapport, responsibility and the time to listen and to help, or can identify appropriate sources of support.

FACTORS TO TAKE INTO ACCOUNT IN PLANNING

Children's capacities to learn are shaped by their background and home circumstances as well as by their individual development. Exposure to different social and environmental influences contributes to the way that attitudes, values and behaviours are formed. These in turn affect their ability to make and take decisions.

Progression and development in many aspects of health and wellbeing will depend upon the stage of growth, development and maturity of the individual, upon social issues and upon the community context. Teachers and other practitioners in planning together will take account of these factors, ensuring that experiences are relevant and realistic for the child or young person in his or her circumstances. Particularly within experiences and outcomes which span more than one level, careful planning will be required to ensure appropriate pace and coverage, and teachers and other practitioners will need to decide when and how the experiences and outcomes are introduced. The planning arrangements within which local authorities, schools and teachers work must ensure that these decisions are taken in the best interests of each child and young person and take account of his or her social and personal circumstances as necessary.

The knowledge, skills and attitudes identified within the various aspects of the health and wellbeing experiences and outcomes are interrelated; teachers and other practitioners will plan and present learning in ways that enable learners to see them as closely linked.

The experiences and outcomes support learning which is challenging and enjoyable; they provide the necessary breadth and depth to meet the needs of all learners; they ensure that account is taken of individual and/or community contexts. The experiences and outcomes thus offer flexibility to allow school staff and partner agencies to plan health and wellbeing programmes which take account of local needs and are innovative, use relevant learning contexts and ensure coherence and progression. It is important that all aspects of health and wellbeing, including events, are planned as part of a whole school strategy, to ensure that they have sustained impact.

FEATURES OF EFFECTIVE LEARNING & TEACHING
FEATURES OF EFFECTIVE PROMOTION

Effective learning through health and wellbeing which promotes confidence, independent thinking and positive attitudes and actions requires:

Leadership which:

▸ establishes a shared vision of health and wellbeing for all

▸ is open, collaborative and responsive

▸ engages and works with parents and carers and all stakeholders to provide children and young people with coherent and positive experiences which promote and protect their health

▸ promotes the health of all within the school community and develops arrangements to support their mental, social, emotional and physical wellbeing

▸ responds sensitively and appropriately if a critical incident takes place within the school community, and has contingency plans in place to enable this to happen.

Partnership working which:

▸ engages the active support of parents and carers

▸ reinforces work across transitions and cluster planning across sectors

▸ maximises the contributions of the wider community

▸ draws upon specialist expertise

▸ ensures, through careful planning and briefing, that all contributions come together in ways which ensure coherence and progression.

*   in 'Responsibility of all' text only
†   in non-'Responsibility of all' text only

Learning and teaching which:

▸ engages children and young people and takes account of their views and experiences, particularly where decisions are to be made that may impact on life choices

▸ takes account of research and successful practice in supporting the learning and development of children and young people, particularly in sensitive areas such as substance misuse

▸ uses a variety of approaches including active, cooperative and peer learning and effective use of technology

▸ encourages and capitalises on the potential to experience learning and new challenges in the outdoor environment

▸ encourages children and young people to act as positive role models for others within the educational community

▸ leads to a lasting commitment in children and young people to follow a healthy lifestyle by participation in experiences which are varied, relevant, realistic and enjoyable

▸ helps to foster health in families and communities through work with a range of professions, parents and carers, and children and young people, and enables them to understand the responsibilities of citizenship

▸ harnesses the experience and expertise of different professions, including developing enterprise and employability skills.

BROAD FEATURES OF ASSESSMENT

As important aspects of health and wellbeing are the responsibility of all staff in educational establishments in partnership with others, and because of the importance of health and wellbeing to learning and development, everyone should be clear about their areas of responsibility and their roles in assessment. In health and wellbeing, assessment has to take account of the breadth and purpose of the wide range of learning experienced by children and young people within this curriculum area. It will focus on children and young people's knowledge and understanding, skills and attributes in relation to physical education, food and health, substance misuse, relationships, sexual health and parenthood, and their social and life skills.

Teachers and learners can gather evidence of progress as part of day-to-day learning inside and outside the classroom and, as appropriate, through specific assessment tasks. From the early years through to the senior stages, children and young people's progress will be seen in how well they are developing and applying their knowledge, understanding and skills in, for example, key features of healthy living and relationships, and in approaches to personal planning, assessing risk and decision making. For example:

▸ To what extent do they understand the role of healthy eating and physical fitness in contributing to their wellbeing?

▸ How well are they applying personal and interpersonal skills as part of their daily lives, and developing them as they grow and mature?

▸ Through their involvement in planning, managing and participating in individual and group activities in school and in the community, do they demonstrate skills, attitudes and attributes which will be important for the world of work, such as judgement, resilience and independence?

Progression in knowledge, understanding and skills can be seen as children and young people demonstrate that they are:

▸ applying their knowledge and skills with increasing confidence and competence in dealing with familiar circumstances and new challenges

▸ developing an increasing depth of understanding of their own and others' motivations, attitudes, beliefs and behaviours

▸ extending the range of their relationships within and outwith the school.

Assessment should also link with other areas of the curriculum, within and beyond the classroom, offering children and young people opportunities to apply their knowledge and skills in more complex, demanding or unfamiliar learning or social contexts.

PERSONAL SAFETY

Each organiser includes statements of experiences and outcomes relating to relevant aspects of personal safety: for example travelling safely, responses in emergencies, food safety, substance misuse and safety in relationships.

CONTRIBUTION OF PHYSICAL EDUCATION, PHYSICAL ACTIVITY AND SPORT TO HEALTH AND WELLBEING

Regular physical activity is essential for good health. Physical education should inspire and challenge children and young people to experience the joy of movement, to develop positive attitudes both individually and as part of a group and to enhance their quality of life through active living. This will give children and young people an important foundation for participation in experiences in physical activities and sport and in preparation for a healthy and fulfilling lifestyle. Children and young people will participate in and enjoy physical activity and sport, in addition to planned physical education sessions, at break times and lunchtimes, during travel and beyond the school day. Outdoor learning can contribute to physical activity and enhance learning in different areas of the curriculum.

Taken together, the experiences and outcomes in physical education, physical activity and sport aim to establish the pattern of daily physical activity which, research has shown, is most likely to lead to sustained physical activity in adult life.

A WHOLE SCHOOL APPROACH TO FOOD AND HEALTH

Schools contribute to improving children's diets through the promotion of consistent healthy eating messages enabling them to make healthy food choices and to develop lifelong healthy eating habits. A good diet is essential for good health. Research shows that many children fall short of national dietary recommendations. A poorly balanced diet can contribute to the risk of developing a number of diseases and conditions including tooth decay, obesity, certain cancers, diabetes, coronary heart disease and stroke.

Hungry for Success encouraged the adoption of a whole school approach to food and health. This approach is now reinforced through the Schools (Health Promotion and Nutrition) (Scotland) Act 2007 and forms the basis of this framework for food and health.

Practical food activities feature across the food and health experiences and outcomes so that children and young people will enjoy a variety of opportunities to apply their knowledge and skills to plan and safely prepare dishes for a healthy balanced diet to meet their own needs and the needs of others. In this way they will gain an appreciation that preparing and eating food can be a pleasant, enjoyable and social experience.

CONNECTIONS WITHIN AND BEYOND HEALTH AND WELLBEING

Whatever their contributions to the curriculum as a whole, all practitioners can make connections between the health and wellbeing experiences and outcomes and their learning and teaching in other areas of the curriculum.

Within health and wellbeing, physical education can build learners' physical competences, improve aspects of fitness, and develop personal and interpersonal skills and attributes in preparation for leading a fulfilling, active and healthy lifestyle. The Scottish Government expects schools to continue to work towards the provision of at least two hours of good quality physical education for every child, every week.

The health and wellbeing experiences and outcomes are designed to encourage links with all other areas of the curriculum, to reinforce learning and to provide relevant, enjoyable and active experiences.

▶ The health and wellbeing experiences and outcomes provide valuable opportunities to develop skills in literacy and numeracy.

▶ There are important links between health and wellbeing, and religious and moral education and religious education in Roman Catholic schools in the establishment of values and growth of spiritual wellbeing, and in considering relationships.

▶ Participation in expressive arts activities can make an important contribution to a child's or young person's sense of wellbeing and can bring learning to life. Using the expressive arts as a medium for learning, for example through role play, can engage learners in issues such as bullying, in more engaging and accessible ways.

▶ There are very close connections between dance and physical education, in particular through the shared outcomes in evaluating and appreciating.

▶ There are clear connections between science and several aspects of health and wellbeing; between the technologies and, for example, food and health; and between the social studies and the aspects relating to citizenship and participation.

In all of these cases staff have the scope to group experiences and outcomes together in different and imaginative ways which enrich, consolidate and enhance progression in learning.

EXPERIENCES & OUTCOMES[1]

Learning in health and wellbeing ensures that children and young people develop the knowledge and understanding, skills, capabilities and attributes which they need for mental, emotional, social and physical wellbeing now and in the future.

Learning through health and wellbeing promotes confidence, independent thinking and positive attitudes and dispositions. Because of this, it is the responsibility of every teacher to contribute to learning and development in this area.

Building the Curriculum 1

Each establishment, working with partners, should take a holistic approach to promoting health and wellbeing, one that takes account of the stage of growth, development and maturity of each individual, and the social and community context.

I can expect my learning environment to support me to:

▸ develop my self-awareness, self-worth and respect for others

▸ meet challenges, manage change and build relationships

▸ experience personal achievement and build my resilience and confidence

▸ understand and develop my physical, mental and spiritual wellbeing and social skills

▸ understand how what I eat, how active I am and how decisions I make about my behaviour and relationships affect my physical and mental wellbeing

▸ participate in a wide range of activities which promote a healthy lifestyle

▸ understand that adults in my school community have a responsibility to look after me, listen to my concerns and involve others where necessary

▸ learn about where to find help and resources to inform choices

▸ assess and manage risk and understand the impact of risk-taking behaviour

▸ reflect on my strengths and skills to help me make informed choices when planning my next steps

▸ acknowledge diversity and understand that it is everyone's responsibility to challenge discrimination.

| *Responsibility of All* | Es & Os in *italics* on a yellow background are the Responsibility of All practitioners. |

---

[1] Because of the nature of development and learning in health and wellbeing, many of the experiences and outcomes are written to span two or more levels. They should be regularly revisited through a wide range of relevant and realistic learning experiences to ensure that every child and young person is progressing in his or her development and learning.

PERSONAL & SOCIAL EDUCATION

MENTAL, EMOTIONAL, SOCIAL AND PHYSICAL WELLBEING

Mental, emotional, social and physical wellbeing are essential for successful learning.

The mental, emotional, social and physical wellbeing of everyone within a learning community should be positively developed by fostering a safe, caring, supportive, purposeful environment that enables the development of relationships based on mutual respect. The four aspects of wellbeing are inextricably linked and are only separated here for practical purposes.

MENTAL AND EMOTIONAL WELLBEING	*HWB 0-01a / 1-01a / 2-01a* I am aware of and able to express my feelings and am developing the ability to talk about them.	E 1 2
	HWB 0-02a / 1-02a / 2-02a I know that we all experience a variety of thoughts and emotions that affect how we feel and behave and I am learning ways of managing them.	
	HWB 0-03a / 1-03a / 2-03a I understand that there are people I can talk to and that there are a number of ways in which I can gain access to practical and emotional support to help me and others in a range of circumstances.	
	HWB 0-04a / 1-04a / 2-04a I understand that my feelings and reactions can change depending upon what is happening within and around me. This helps me to understand my own behaviour and the way others behave.	
	HWB 0-05a / 1-05a / 2-05a I know that friendship, caring, sharing, fairness, equality and love are important in building positive relationships. As I develop and value relationships, I care and show respect for myself and others.	
	HWB 0-06a / 1-06a / 2-06a I understand the importance of mental wellbeing and that this can be fostered and strengthened through personal coping skills and positive relationships. I know that it is not always possible to enjoy good mental health and that if this happens there is support available.	
	HWB 0-07a / 1-07a / 2-07a I am learning skills and strategies which will support me in challenging times, particularly in relation to change and loss.	
	HWB 0-08a / 1-08a / 2-08a I understand that people can feel alone and can be misunderstood and left out by others. I am learning how to give appropriate support.	
SOCIAL WELLBEING	*HWB 0-09a / 1-09a / 2-09a* As I explore the rights to which I and others are entitled, I am able to exercise these rights appropriately and accept the responsibilities that go with them. I show respect for the rights of others.	HWB Es & Os which are the 'Responsibility of All Practitioners' have no benchmarks[1]
	HWB 0-10a / 1-10a / 2-10a I recognise that each individual has a unique blend of abilities and needs. I contribute to making my school community one which values individuals equally and is a welcoming place for all.	
	HWB 0-11a / 1-11a / 2-11a I make full use of and value the opportunities I am given to improve and manage my learning and, in turn, I can help to encourage learning and confidence in others.	E 1 2
	HWB 0-12a / 1-12a / 2-12a Representing my class, school and/or wider community encourages my self-worth and confidence and allows me to contribute to and participate in society.	
	HWB 0-13a / 1-13a / 2-13a Through contributing my views, time and talents, I play a part in bringing about positive change in my school and wider community.	
	HWB 0-14a / 1-14a / 2-14a I value the opportunities I am given to make friends and be part of a group in a range of situations.	
PHYSICAL WELLBEING	*HWB 0-15a / 1-15a / 2-15a* I am developing my understanding of the human body and can use this knowledge to maintain and improve my wellbeing and health.	
	HWB 0-16a / 1-16a / 2-16a I am learning to assess and manage risk, to protect myself and others, and to reduce the potential for harm when possible.	E 1 2
	HWB 0-17a / 1-17a / 2-17a I know and can demonstrate how to keep myself and others safe and how to respond in a range of emergency situations.	
	HWB 0-18a / 1-18a / 2-18a I know and can demonstrate how to travel safely.	

[1] [See Frequently Asked Question 15 on page 129.]

PLANNING FOR CHOICES AND CHANGE

Learners need to experience opportunities which are designed not only to raise their awareness of future choices but also raise their expectations and aspirations. They develop the skills for personal planning and making decisions in the context of curriculum, learning and achievement which will prepare them for next stages in life.

Learners should experience activities which enable them to develop the skills and attributes they will need if they are to achieve and sustain positive destinations beyond school. Demands and employment patterns are changing, so it is particularly important for all young people to develop high levels of skill and also an understanding of the world of work, training and lifelong learning so that they can embrace opportunities.

E	**HWB 0-19a** *In everyday activity and play, I explore and make choices to develop my learning and interests. I am encouraged to use and share my experiences.*	
1	**HWB 1-19a** *Through taking part in a variety of events and activities, I am learning to recognise my own skills and abilities as well as those of others.*	HWB Es & Os which are the 'Responsibility of All Practitioners' have no benchmarks[1]
2	**HWB 2-19a** *Opportunities to carry out different activities and roles in a variety of settings have enabled me to identify my achievements, skills and areas for development. This will help me to prepare for the next stage in my life and learning.*	

EXPECTATIONS AND ASPIRATIONS and
RELEVANCE OF LEARNING TO FUTURE CHOICES

E	**HWB 0-20a / 1-20a** I can describe some of the kinds of work that people do and I am finding out about the wider world of work.	**Early Level** • Shares aspirations and goals for the future. • Talks about own learning, strengths and next steps. • Discusses some of the rewards that a job brings, for example, meeting new people, money, helping others. • Communicates with others about different jobs in the community.
1		**1st Level** • Talks about own strengths, interests and skills and links these to career ambitions. • Sets learning goals and works towards achieving them. • Talks about the world of work, for example, from visits, visitors and interdisciplinary learning. • Describes skills needed for different jobs in the community.
2	**HWB 2-20a** I am investigating different careers/occupations, ways of working, and learning and training paths. I am gaining experience that helps me recognise the relevance of my learning, skills and interests to my future life.	• Explains own ambitions and identifies ways to achieve them. • Manages personal profile and uses it to discuss interests, strengths and skills. • Identifies connections between skills and the world of work. • Uses investigative skills to gain more information about jobs / careers.

[1] [See Frequently Asked Question 15 on page 129.]

PHYSICAL EDUCATION, PHYSICAL ACTIVITY & SPORT:
PHYSICAL ACTIVITY AND SPORT[1]

In addition to planned physical education sessions, physical activity and sport take place in the classroom, in the school, during travel such as walking and cycling, in the outdoor environment and in the community. Learning in, through and about physical activity and sport is enhanced by participating in a wide range of purposeful and enjoyable physical pursuits at break times, lunchtimes, within and beyond the place of learning.

The experiences and outcomes are intended to establish a pattern of daily physical activity which, research has shown, is most likely to lead to sustained physical activity in adult life. Experiences and outcomes should also open up opportunities for learners to participate and perform at their highest level in sport and, if interested, pursue careers in the health and leisure industries.

PHYSICAL EDUCATION, PHYSICAL ACTIVITY & SPORT:
PHYSICAL ACTIVITY AND HEALTH

Learners develop an understanding of their physical health and the contribution made by participation in physical education, physical activity and sport to keeping them healthy and preparing them for life beyond school. They investigate the relationship between diet and physical activity and their role in the prevention of obesity.

The experiences and outcomes are intended to establish a pattern of daily physical activity which, research has shown, is most likely to lead to sustained physical activity in adult life. Physical activity and sport take place in addition to planned physical education sessions, at break times and lunchtimes in and beyond the place of learning.

[ACTIVITY,][2] DIET, REST AND SLEEP

HWB 0-25a I am enjoying daily opportunities to participate in different kinds of energetic play, both outdoors and indoors.	HWB Es & Os which are the 'Responsibility of All Practitioners' have no benchmarks	E
HWB 0-27a I know that being active is a healthy way to be. HWB 0-28a I can describe how I feel after taking part in energetic activities and I am becoming aware of some of the changes that take place in my body.	• Demonstrates different ways of being active, for example, energetic play. • Identifies how being active affects their body, for example, raised heartbeat, getting hot. • Gives reasons why being active is good for health.	
HWB 1-25a Within and beyond my place of learning I am enjoying daily opportunities to participate in physical activities and sport, making use of available indoor and outdoor space.	HWB Es & Os which are the 'Responsibility of All Practitioners' have no benchmarks	1
HWB 1-27a I am aware of the role physical activity plays in keeping me healthy and know that I also need to sleep and rest, to look after my body. HWB 1-28a I understand that my body needs energy to function and that this comes from the food I eat. I am exploring how physical activity contributes to my health and wellbeing.	• Suggests different ways of being active and the positive effect this can have on health. • Articulates how much sleep is needed in childhood and why this is important. • Explains that food is the fuel that gives the body energy.	
HWB 2-25a I am experiencing enjoyment and achievement on a daily basis by taking part in different kinds of energetic physical activities of my choosing, including sport and opportunities for outdoor learning, available at my place of learning and in the wider community.	• Participates daily in moderate to vigorous physical activity.	2
HWB 2-26a I have investigated the role of sport and the opportunities it may offer me. I am able to access opportunities for participation in sport and the development of my performance in my place of learning and beyond.	• Identifies and accesses opportunities for sport and/or outdoor learning within place of learning and community.	
HWB 2-27a I can explain why I need to be active on a daily basis to maintain good health and try to achieve a good balance of sleep, rest and physical activity.	• Explains the interrelationship of daily physical activity, diet, rest and sleep on health and wellbeing.	
HWB 2-28a I can explain the links between the energy I use while being physically active, the food I eat, and my health and wellbeing.	• Identifies a range of activities at different intensities and explains how these may influence food/energy requirements, for example, 100m sprint – higher energy requirement; recreational bike ride – lower energy requirement.	

---

1. [The *Benchmarks* place HWB 25-28 under a heading of 'Physical Activity and Health'. The *Es & Os* place them under two headings, 'Physical Activity and Sport' (HWB 25/26) and 'Physical Activity and Health' (HWB 27/28).]

2. [The *Benchmarks* call this section 'Diet, Rest and Sleep', which ignores the great importance of physical activity in the Es & Os / Benchmarks given.]

SUBSTANCE MISUSE [AND EMERGENCIES][3]

Learners develop their understanding of the use and misuse of a variety of substances including over the counter and prescribed medicines, alcohol, drugs, tobacco and solvents. They explore and develop their understanding of the impact of risk-taking behaviour on their life choices. The experiences and outcomes will enable learners to make informed personal choices with the aim of promoting healthy lifestyles.
[Learners develop an understanding of the role of the emergency services and how/when to use them][3].

E	USE OF SUBSTANCES	HWB 0-38a I understand there are things I should not touch or eat and how to keep myself safe, and I am learning what is meant by medicines and harmful substances.	• Identifies which substances may be helpful and which may be harmful in given situations.
	ACTION IN UNSAFE SITUATIONS	HWB 0-42a I can show ways of getting help in unsafe situations and emergencies.	• Suggests ways to get help in unsafe and emergency situations, for example, seeking out an adult. • Names the emergency services.
1	USE OF SUBSTANCES	HWB 1-38a I know that there are medicines and some other substances that can be used in a safe way to improve health and I am becoming aware of how choices I make can affect my health and wellbeing.	• Identifies conditions which require medication and how it benefits health.
	ACTION IN UNSAFE SITUATIONS	HWB 1-42a I know how to react in unsafe situations and emergencies.	• Identifies why misusing medication can be harmful. • Links personal actions to health and wellbeing, using role play for example. • Describes when and how to contact emergency services. • Shares key information about an emergency situation.
2	USE OF SUBSTANCES	HWB 2-38a I understand the effect that a range of substances including tobacco and alcohol can have on the body.	• Gives examples of what can happen to the body as a result of smoking tobacco or drinking alcohol. • Knows the recommended alcohol intake advice.
	INFORMED CHOICES	HWB 2-39a I know that popular culture, the media and peer groups as well as my own attitudes and values can influence how I feel about substance use and recognise the impact this may have on my actions.	• Gives examples of how peer, media and other pressures can influence decision making.
	RISK-TAKING BEHAVIOUR	HWB 2-40a I know that alcohol and drugs can affect people's ability to make decisions. HWB 2-41a I can identify the different kinds of risks associated with the use and misuse of a range of substances. HWB 2-43a I understand the impact that misuse of substances can have on individuals, their families and friends.	• Identifies risks associated with the use of substances, for example, overdose, impaired judgement / vision. • Identifies the impact of risk taking behaviours on life choices and relationships, for example, job prospects, limited foreign travel, loss of driving licence, family.
	ACTION IN UNSAFE SITUATIONS	HWB 2-42a I know of actions I can take to help someone in an emergency.	• Performs basic first aid procedures, for example, minor bleeding and burns, recovery position. • Explains how to contact the appropriate emergency services giving full details of the incident and location.

RELATIONSHIPS, SEXUAL HEALTH AND PARENTHOOD

Learners develop an understanding of how to maintain positive relationships with a variety of people and are aware of how thoughts, feelings, attitudes, values and beliefs can influence decisions about relationships, and sexual health. They develop their understanding of the complex roles and responsibilities of being a parent or carer.

E		*HWB 0-44a / 1-44a I am aware of how friendships are formed and that likes, dislikes, special qualities and needs can influence relationships.* *HWB 0-44b / 1-44b I understand positive things about friendships and relationships but when something worries or upsets me I know who I should talk to.*	HWB Es & Os which are the 'Responsibility of All Practitioners' have no benchmarks
	PHYSICAL CHANGES	HWB 0-47a / 1-47a I recognise that we have similarities and differences but are all unique.	• Identifies body differences and similarities.
	SEXUAL HEALTH AND SEXUALITY	HWB 0-47b / 1-47b I am aware of my growing body and I am learning the correct names for its different parts and how they work. [See also SCN 0-12a]	• Describes how bodies change as they grow. Identifies body parts using correct names, for example, penis, testicles, vulva and nipples.
		HWB 0-48a / 1-48a I am learning what I can do to look after my body and who can help me.	• Demonstrates modesty and privacy through, for example, closing toilet doors. • Manages personal space with respect towards self and others.
		HWB 0-49a / 1-49a I am learning about respect for my body and what behaviour is right and wrong. I know who I should talk to if I am worried about this.	• Demonstrates an understanding of the concept, 'my body belongs to me'. • Recognises and communicates uncomfortable feelings in relation to a person or situation using, for example, the 3-step model: say no, go away, talk to someone you trust.
		HWB 0-45a / 1-45a I know that there are people in our lives who care for and look after us and I am aware that people may be cared for by parents, carers or other adults.	• Identifies people who can help, for example, teachers, family members. • Recognises that care can come from a variety of different people. • Identifies that families may be made up of different people.
		HWB 0-45b / 1-45b / 2-45b I am aware of the need to respect personal space and boundaries and can recognise and respond appropriately to verbal and non-verbal communication.	No benchmarks

ROLE OF PARENT/ CARER	HWB 0-50a / 1-50a I am learning about where living things come from and about how they grow, develop and are nurtured.	• Gives examples of where living things come from, for example, plants from seeds, fish from eggs. • Explains that living things need food, water and care to grow and survive.	E
	HWB 0-51a / 1-51a I am able to show an awareness of the tasks required to look after a baby.	• Describes the basic needs of a baby, for example, eye contact, cuddling, washing, changing, feeding, sleeping.	
PHYSICAL CHANGES SEXUAL HEALTH AND SEXUALITY ROLE OF PARENT/ CARER	*HWB 0-44a / 1-44a I am aware of how friendships are formed and that likes, dislikes, special qualities and needs can influence relationships.*	HWB Es & Os which are the 'Responsibility of All Practitioners' have no benchmarks	1
	HWB 0-44b / 1-44b I understand positive things about friendships and relationships but when something worries or upsets me I know who I should talk to.		
	HWB 0-47a / 1-47a I recognise that we have similarities and differences but are all unique.	• Recognises that everyone is unique and identifies similarities and differences. • Explains that development and growth of each individual is different.	
	HWB 0-47b / 1-47b I am aware of my growing body and I am learning the correct names for its different parts and how they work.	• Identifies the correct words for body parts and their functions, for example, womb, scrotum, ovaries, vagina.	
	HWB 0-48a / 1-48a I am learning what I can do to look after my body and who can help me.	• Explains about own and others' needs for privacy. • Expresses feelings through appropriate closeness to others.	
	HWB 0-49a / 1-49a I am learning about respect for my body and what behaviour is right and wrong. I know who I should talk to if I am worried about this.	• Articulates the right to respond to inappropriate behaviours, for example, using the 3-step model: say no, go away, talk to someone you trust. • Identifies who to talk to if worried or concerned.	
	HWB 0-45a / 1-45a I know that there are people in our lives who care for and look after us and I am aware that people may be cared for by parents, carers or other adults.	• Explains ways in which families may differ and that there are a variety of people who may care for us. • Explains changes to the body at different stages of life.	
	HWB 0-45b / 1-45b / 2-45b I am aware of the need to respect personal space and boundaries and can recognise and respond appropriately to verbal and non-verbal communication.	No benchmarks	
	HWB 0-50a / 1-50a I am learning about where living things come from and about how they grow, develop and are nurtured.	• Identifies what is needed for growth and development of animals, plants and humans.	
	HWB 0-51a / 1-51a I am able to show an awareness of the tasks required to look after a baby.	• Explains how to meet the basic needs of a baby, for example, eye contact, cuddling, washing, changing, feeding.	
POSITIVE RELATION-SHIPS PHYSICAL CHANGES SEXUAL HEALTH AND SEXUALITY ROLE OF PARENT/ CARER	HWB 2-44a I understand that a wide range of different kinds of friendships and relationships exist.	• Identifies different kinds of friendships and relationships.	2
	HWB 2-44b I am aware that positive friendships and relationships can promote health and the health and wellbeing of others.	No benchmarks	
	HWB 2-45a I am identifying and practising skills to manage changing relationships and I understand the positive impact this can have on my emotional wellbeing.	• Identifies the skills required to manage changing relationships, for example, tolerance, empathy, loyalty, kindness, resilience, mutual trust and respect. • Explains the impact of positive relationships on emotional wellbeing.	
	HWB 0-45b / 1-45b / 2-45b I am aware of the need to respect personal space and boundaries and can recognise and respond appropriately to verbal and non-verbal communication.	No benchmarks	
	HWB 2-47a I recognise that how my body changes can affect how I feel about myself and how I may behave.	• Identifies positive things about own body image and appearance. • Identifies strategies to manage emotions, for example, relaxation techniques, speaking to someone, taking time out.	
	HWB 2-48a I can describe the physical and emotional changes during puberty, understand why they are taking place and the importance of personal hygiene.	• Uses correct terminology for all private body parts and reproductive organs, for example, breasts, clitoris. • Describes the physical and emotional changes during puberty including erections, wet dreams, pubic hair, masturbation, menstruation, hormones, mood swings. • Demonstrates an understanding of diversity in sexuality and gender identity. • Describes ways of keeping hygienic during puberty.	
	HWB 2-49a I know that all forms of abuse are wrong and I am developing the skills to keep myself safe and get help if I need it.	• Identifies abusive and bullying behaviour, for example, on-line, face to face and knows where to go for help. • Explains own rights and responsibilities in relation to abuse. • Describes the concept of consent.	
	HWB 2-50a I am able to describe how human life begins and how a baby is born.	• Describes human conception and birth, for example, sexual intercourse, egg and sperm, giving birth. • Gives reasons why contraception may be used, for example, to prevent pregnancy and infection. • Describes some symptoms of pregnancy.	
	HWB 2-51a I can describe the role of a parent/carer and the skills, commitment and qualities the role requires.	• Describes skills and qualities required to be a parent/carer, for example, commitment, love, patience, sense of humour.	

3   [The title in the *Es & Os* and *Benchmarks* is simply 'Substance misuse'. However, this understates the importance accorded to general emergencies at Early, First and Second Level, and to emergencies which fall under the remit of all of the emergency services.]

PHYSICAL EDUCATION

The following Experiences & Outcomes / Benchmarks from 'Health & Wellbeing: Personal & Social Education' are also relevant here:

▸ **Physical Wellbeing** (from 'Mental, Social, Emotional and Physical Wellbeing' on page 25)
▸ **[Activity,] Diet, Rest and Sleep** (from 'Physical Activity and Sport' / 'Physical Activity and Health' on page 27)

PHYSICAL EDUCATION, PHYSICAL ACTIVITY AND SPORT:
PHYSICAL EDUCATION

Physical education provides learners with a platform from which they can build physical competences, improve aspects of fitness, and develop personal and interpersonal skills and attributes. It enables learners to develop the concepts and skills necessary for participation in a wide range of physical activity, sport, dance and outdoor learning, and enhances their physical wellbeing in preparation for leading a fulfilling, active and healthy lifestyle.

They encounter a variety of practical learning experiences, including working on their own, with a partner and in small and large groups, and using small and large equipment and apparatus, both outdoors and indoors.

Learning in, through and about physical education is enhanced by participating on a regular basis in a wide range of purposeful, challenging, progressive and enjoyable physical activities with choice built in for all learners. The Scottish Government expects schools to continue to work towards the provision of at least two hours of good quality physical education for every child, every week.

PHYSICAL COMPETENCIES

KINAESTHETIC AWARENESS	**HWB 0-21a** I am learning to move my body well, exploring how to manage and control it and finding out how to use and share space. **HWB 0-22a** I am developing my movement skills through practice and energetic play.	• Shows awareness of personal space (i.e. where body ends and space begins). • Moves at different speeds, levels and directions with others in a designated space. • Shows awareness of body parts and body positions when performing a range of different movements.
BALANCE AND CONTROL		• Shows control of personal space and body parts when moving. • Holds balance in various shapes and maintains balance when moving. • Is beginning to manipulate objects as part of energetic play.
COORDINATION AND FLUENCY		• Links movements together (moves body or parts of body in order). • Is beginning to move with purpose. • Is beginning to develop knowledge and understanding of what a quality movement looks like and feels like.
RHYTHM AND TIMING		• Demonstrates how to use repeated patterns of movement to create simple sequences, for example, one foot to two feet jumping. • Responds with movement, for example, jump-clap-turn to recognised rhythm, beat, music, words.
GROSS AND FINE MOTOR SKILLS		• Performs basic components of movement, for example, run, jump, gallop, transfer of weight from one foot to another. • Is beginning to perform movement skills in sequence, for example, catch an object with two hands. • Is beginning to demonstrate eye/hand and eye/foot co-ordination required for movement skills, for example, pass object from one hand to the other.
KINAESTHETIC AWARENESS	**HWB 1-21a** I am discovering ways that I can link actions and skills to create movement patterns and sequences. This has motivated me to practise and improve my skills to develop control and flow. **HWB 1-22a** I am developing skills and techniques and improving my level of performance and fitness.	• Shows awareness of the space around them and the space of others, and is beginning to use this information to control movements. • Shows control over movement in personal and shared space which includes adapting to changes in speed, direction and level. • Shows awareness of body parts and body positions when performing a range of different movements.
BALANCE AND CONTROL		• Manipulates parts of the body when moving with purpose. • Holds balances in various shapes with and without equipment and describes what helps to maintain balance. • Manipulates objects while maintaining balance, for example, receiving and sending a ball with the preferred foot.
COORDINATION AND FLUENCY		• Links and orders a series of movements with and without equipment to perform a sequence, for example, hopscotch. • Moves with purpose demonstrating balance, control and rhythm. • Demonstrates knowledge and understanding of what a quality movement looks like, and feels like.
RHYTHM AND TIMING		• Demonstrates how to use repeated patterns of movement to create simple sequences, for example, one foot to two feet jumping. • Moves the body/parts of the body or objects in response to given cues to create an appropriate tempo, for example, 1-2-3 hop sequence.
GROSS AND FINE MOTOR SKILLS		• Performs movement skills in simple activities, for example, skipping. • Performs movement skills in sequence, for example, jump from bench and cushion the landing while staying in balance. • Demonstrates eye/hand and eye/foot co-ordination required for movement skills, for example, track the flight of the ball with the eyes, then catch it.

KINAESTHETIC AWARENESS	**HWB 2-21a** As I encounter new challenges and contexts for learning, I am encouraged and supported to demonstrate my ability to select, adapt and apply movement skills and strategies, creatively, accurately and with control.	• Moves efficiently in personal and shared space. • Performs and refines movement with a focus on quality, using different speeds/pathways/levels. • Is internally aware of body parts and adopts body positions effectively in a variety of challenging situations.
BALANCE AND CONTROL		• Differentiates between movements of different parts of the body, with a focus on quality, for example, rolling segmentally, leading first with the head, followed by the shoulders and then the pelvis. • Combines and applies static and dynamic balance with and without equipment at different speeds, directions and levels, for example, dodging and feinting. • Manipulates objects while maintaining balance to result in desired outcomes, for example, baton changeover in relay race.
COORDINATION AND FLUENCY		• Performs a sequence of movements with a clear beginning, middle and end with increasing fluency, for example, a cartwheel followed by a forward roll. • Moves with purpose and confidence, demonstrating balance, control and rhythm. • Explains what a quality movement looks like and feels like, to help modify and improve performance.
RHYTHM AND TIMING	**HWB 2-22a** I practise, consolidate and refine my skills to improve my performance. I am developing and sustaining my levels of fitness.	• Creates sequences of movement using a variety of stimuli with a focus on quality. • Maintains rhythm with or without equipment, for example, pass and move, keeping possession of the ball. • Performs actions that involve a transition from one phase to another, for example, forward roll into straight jump.
GROSS AND FINE MOTOR SKILLS		• Performs movement skills with confidence, for example, using active footwork to move to a space to receive the netball. • Performs movement skills in sequence with confidence, for example, keeping the ball up with bat/racquet. • Demonstrates eye/hand and eye/foot co-ordination to execute movement skills, for example, striking a ball with a bat or kicking a ball towards a target.

COGNITIVE SKILLS

FOCUS AND CONCENTRATION		• Focuses on task and pays attention to stimuli, for example, instructions from a practitioner.
CUE RECOGNITION	**HWB 0-21a** I am learning to move my body well, exploring how to manage and control it and finding out how to use and share space.	• Recognises external cues that need an immediate response, for example, starting and stopping.
SEQUENTIAL THINKING		• Remembers two-step simple instructions, for example, bounce the ball and then change direction.
PRIORITISING		• Works out the order for dealing with information (or tasks). • Repeats tasks in the correct sequence.
DECISION MAKING	**HWB 0-22a** I am developing my movement skills through practice and energetic play.	• Makes decisions in response to simple tasks, for example, knowing when to start and stop.
MULTI-PROCESSING		• Listens to and makes sense of two/three pieces of information, for example, bounce the ball when moving forwards.
PROBLEM SOLVING		• Uses prior knowledge, and identifies key information to help form a solution.
CREATIVITY		• Moves in response to a variety of stimuli. • Demonstrates imagination through energetic play.
FOCUS AND CONCENTRATION		• Focuses attention in more demanding situations, for example, working with a partner or in a small group.
CUE RECOGNITION	**HWB 1-21a** I am discovering ways that I can link actions and skills to create movement patterns and sequences. This has motivated me to practise and improve my skills to develop control and flow.	• Recognises and responds to both internal and external cues at the same time, for example, follow the leader.
SEQUENTIAL THINKING		• Plans and creates a sequence of actions, for example, bounce the ball three times, then change direction and change how you travel with the ball.
PRIORITISING		• Draws on some prior knowledge to work out the order for dealing quickly with information (or tasks). Repeats tasks in the correct sequence with more precision.
DECISION MAKING		• Makes decisions when presented with two or three different options and can explain why.
MULTI-PROCESSING	**HWB 1-22a** I am developing skills and techniques and improving my level of performance and fitness.	• Takes in and makes sense of two or three pieces of information at the same time from external and/or internal sources, for example, 'Simon Says'.
PROBLEM SOLVING		• Demonstrates adaptability when finding different solutions to solve problems.
CREATIVITY		• Combines actions to create movement sequences independently and with others in response to stimuli, for example, music, words. • Demonstrates flair, originality, and imagination when performing.

COGNITIVE SKILLS (CONT.)

FOCUS AND CONCENTRATION	HWB 2-21a As I encounter new challenges and contexts for learning, I am encouraged and supported to demonstrate my ability to select, adapt and apply movement skills and strategies, creatively, accurately and with control.	• Manages impulsive responses to stay focused on task and filter out distractions, for example, taking a shot in netball with defender in front of the net.
CUE RECOGNITION		• Recognises a range of cues and begins to prioritise those that need to be responded to first.
SEQUENTIAL THINKING		• Plans a series of three or more actions in order to address simple movement challenges.
PRIORITISING		• Recognises the importance of particular moments, or actions in a sequence. Draws on prior knowledge to select an effective order that contributes to successful performance.
DECISION MAKING		• Makes decisions when presented with a greater variety of options and can explain why.
MULTI-PROCESSING	HWB 2-22a I practise, consolidate and refine my skills to improve my performance. I am developing and sustaining my levels of fitness.	• Takes in and makes sense of several pieces of information at the same time, from a number of different sources which contribute to successful performance.
PROBLEM SOLVING		• Adapts previous plans, movement skills and strategies to generate a solution and explains why it is the most effective.
CREATIVITY		• Creates and adapts movement sequences independently and with others in response to stimuli. • Demonstrates flair, originality and imagination that contributes to a quality performance.

(2)

PERSONAL QUALITIES

MOTIVATION	HWB 0-22a I am developing my movement skills through practice and energetic play.	• Participates with enthusiasm. Enjoys being challenged. • Sets targets in simple tasks. • Describes why people participate in physical activity, for example, to have fun.
CONFIDENCE AND SELF-ESTEEM		• Is developing an awareness of self and an increasing self-reliance in dealing with new situations. • Discusses learning with adult support, and describes likes and dislikes. • Responds and contributes to self and peer assessment with respect. • Celebrates, values and uses achievements to build next steps.
DETERMINATION AND RESILIENCE	HWB 0-23a I am aware of my own and others' needs and feelings especially when taking turns and sharing resources. I recognise the need to follow rules.	• Is learning how to be a good winner and cope appropriately with losing. • Stays on task that may at first seem challenging, to achieve success. • Identifies and expresses some emotions appropriately, for example, happy/sad and understands how they can affect behaviour.
RESPONSIBILITY AND LEADERSHIP		• Accepts direction from an adult or peer. • Seeks appropriate help. • Is beginning to use self-control when carrying out simple tasks. • Adopts different roles when working individually or as part of a group. • Makes choices about learning and playing in a variety of contexts.
RESPECT AND TOLERANCE	HWB 0-24a By exploring and observing movement, I can describe what I have learned about it.	• Shares with others and shows consideration during energetic play. • Is aware of ideas, thoughts and feelings of others. • Takes turns with others to use equipment safely.
COMMUNICATION		• Is developing the ability to know when to listen and when to talk when interacting with others. • Uses words and/or body language to express ideas, thoughts and feelings.

(E)

MOTIVATION	**HWB 1-22a** I am developing skills and techniques and improving my level of performance and fitness. **HWB 1-23a** I can follow and understand rules and procedures, developing my ability to achieve personal goals. I recognise and can adopt different roles in a range of practical activities. **HWB 1-24a** I can recognise progress and achievement by discussing my thoughts and feelings and giving and accepting feedback.	• Shows an enthusiasm to participate. Enjoys being challenged. • Recognises and responds to both internal and external motivation to: – set targets – achieve personal goals – improve performance. • Identifies and describes reasons why people participate in physical activity, for example, to have fun, to be healthy, to set individual goals or to belong to a group.
CONFIDENCE AND SELF-ESTEEM		• Has a positive awareness of self as physical competencies improve. • Discusses learning and identifies strengths and next steps. • Responds and contributes to self and peer assessment with respect. • Celebrates, values and uses achievements as part of improving performance.
DETERMINATION AND RESILIENCE		• Identifies and discusses how to be a good winner and cope appropriately with losing. • Demonstrates persistence when facing a challenge and works to achieve a successful outcome. • Recognises a variety of emotions and is developing the ability to manage them appropriately.
RESPONSIBILITY AND LEADERSHIP		• Demonstrates a continuing readiness to learn and is developing planning and organisational skills. • Develops a range of strategies to increase self-control when performing independently and/or with others. • Adopts a variety of roles that lead to successful outcomes. • Identifies and discusses the role of leader and the associated responsibilities.
RESPECT AND TOLERANCE		• Demonstrates how to include others when completing movement tasks. • Engages positively with others to use equipment safely and fairly. • Listens to and responds to the ideas, thoughts and feelings of others with respect. Responds appropriately, for example, nodding or agreeing, asking and answering questions.
COMMUNICATION		• Demonstrates knowledge and understanding of a range of verbal and non-verbal communication skills and is beginning to apply them when interacting with or presenting to others, for example, uses eye contact, body language and gestures.
MOTIVATION	**HWB 2-22a** I practise, consolidate and refine my skills to improve my performance. I am developing and sustaining my levels of fitness. **HWB 2-23a** While working and learning with others, I improve my range of skills, demonstrate tactics and achieve identified goals. **HWB 2-24a** (see below)	• Is self-motivated in movement challenges and demonstrates positive effort. • Sets and acts upon personal goals based on knowledge and understanding of what it means to perform well. • Explains factors that affect and influence participation in physical activity, for example, attitude, access, personal and/or family preference. • Demonstrates understanding that we play a role in encouraging others.
CONFIDENCE AND SELF-ESTEEM		• Demonstrates self-reliance when faced with movement challenges in familiar and unfamiliar practice and performance environments. • Initiates and works co-operatively with others providing support and encouragement. • Self-assesses and acts as a peer assessor to provide constructive feedback to improve performance. • Celebrates, values and uses achievements as part of development and progress.
DETERMINATION AND RESILIENCE		• Identifies and discusses strategies around competition to cope appropriately with the outcomes. • Demonstrates understanding of the positive link between effort, perseverance, and personal achievement. • Recognises the variety of emotions that are associated with performing and the impact they have on behaviour and performance. • Develops the ability to manage emotions to enhance performance.
RESPONSIBILITY AND LEADERSHIP	**HWB 2-22a** **HWB 2-23a** (see above) **HWB 2-24a** By reflecting on my own and others' work and evaluating it against shared criteria, I can recognise improvement and achievement and use this to progress further.	• Demonstrates planning and organisational skills which are conducive to learning. • Identifies and adopts strategies to increase self-control for enjoyable individual performance and/or with others. • Adopts a variety of roles that lead to successful outcomes. • Demonstrates understanding of the leadership role.
RESPECT AND TOLERANCE		• Contributes to an inclusive ethos, showing mutual respect in practice and performance environments. • Listens to and responds to the ideas, thoughts and feelings of others, and is developing negotiation skills when dealing with movement challenges. • Enhances individual and group enjoyment of physical activity through fair play.
COMMUNICATION		• Takes account of the views of others. Responds appropriately, for example, by asking and answering questions, clarifying points and building on ideas. • Demonstrates understanding of a range of verbal and non-verbal communication skills and applies them appropriately in practice and performance environments, for example, shout and signal for the ball.

1

2

PHYSICAL FITNESS

E	STAMINA	HWB 0-22a I am developing my movement skills through practice and energetic play.	• Sustains energetic levels of play/activity. • Recognises different body parts required to sustain energetic activity. • Identifies different ways to be physically active. • Describes how the body changes when engaged in moderate to vigorous activity.
	SPEED		• Moves at different speeds – slowly, steadily and quickly. • Moves parts of the body at different speeds. • Starts and stops quickly. • Understands speed in simple terms.
	CORE STABILITY AND STRENGTH		• Is developing postural control when performing physical actions. • Moves in control and maintains shape. • Holds body weight/position of stillness for short periods of time.
	FLEXIBILITY		• Moves freely across a full range of movements.
1	STAMINA	HWB 1-22a I am developing skills and techniques and improving my level of performance and fitness.	• Participates in moderate to vigorous physical activity and sustains a level of activity that provides challenge. • Describes how the body feels during and after sustained activity. • Describes in simple terms the reasons why people participate in physical activity. • Sets targets for sustaining moderate to vigorous physical activity. • Demonstrates understanding of stamina in simple terms and how it affects health, and ability to perform.
	SPEED		• Moves at different speeds and is able to maintain balance whilst changing direction quickly. • Demonstrates short bursts of fast movement from stillness. • Moves parts of the body using different speeds and force. • Demonstrates understanding of speed in simple terms and how it affects ability to perform.
	CORE STABILITY AND STRENGTH		• Shows postural control when starting, stopping and changing direction. • Describes where 'core' is and demonstrates how it supports the body. • Holds body weight in a variety of positions.
	FLEXIBILITY		• Uses a full range of movement to perform actions effectively. • Demonstrates understanding of flexibility in simple terms and how it affects everyday life, and ability to perform.
2	STAMINA	HWB 2-22a I practise, consolidate and refine my skills to improve my performance. I am developing and sustaining my levels of fitness.[1]	• Demonstrates understanding of how to sustain moderate to vigorous physical activity that provides challenge. • Demonstrates understanding of heart rate and how to measure it. • Describes how personal preference and choice can influence participation in physical activity. • Sets personal goals for sustaining moderate to vigorous physical activity that lead to improvement. • Identifies types of physical activity where stamina is key to success.
	SPEED		• Moves at different speeds and changes direction quickly in balance and with control. • Accelerates quickly from a stationary position. • Experiments with the use of speed (with body parts and/or equipment), for example, fast arm when throwing a ball. • Sets personal goals to improve speed. • Identifies physical activities where speed is key to success.
	CORE STABILITY AND STRENGTH		• Shows postural control when performing physical actions with accuracy. • Explains and demonstrates how to make a balance more stable. • Experiments with the use of force (with body parts and/or equipment), for example, absorbing force with the ankles, knees and hips during landing. • Sets personal goals to improve core stability and strength. • Identifies physical activities where core stability and strength are key to success.
	FLEXIBILITY		• Performs a range of effective, dynamic movements specific to physical activities. • Demonstrates understanding of the impact of flexibility on everyday life and sets personal goals to improve. • Identifies physical activities where flexibility is key to success.

FOOD & HEALTH

The following Experiences & Outcomes / Benchmarks from 'Health & Wellbeing: Personal & Social Education' are also relevant here:

▸ [Activity,] Diet, Rest and Sleep (from 'Physical Activity and Sport' / 'Physical Activity and Health' on page 27)

FOOD AND HEALTH

Learners develop their understanding of a healthy diet, which is one composed of a variety and balance of foods and drinks. They acquire knowledge and skills to make healthy food choices and help to establish lifelong healthy eating habits. They develop an appreciation that eating can be an enjoyable activity and understand the role of food within social and cultural contexts. They explore how the dietary needs of individuals and groups vary through life stages, for example during pregnancy and puberty, and the role of breastfeeding during infancy.

Learners develop knowledge and understanding of safe and hygienic practices and their importance to health and wellbeing and apply these in practical activities and everyday routines including good oral health. They develop awareness that food practices and choices depend on many factors including availability, sustainability, season, cost, religious beliefs, culture, peer pressure, advertising and the media.

THE FOOD EXPERIENCE

TASTING, SELECTING AND EVALUATING THE SOCIAL CONTEXT RELIGIOUS AND CULTURAL INFLUENCES	HWB 0-29a / 1-29a / 2-29a I enjoy eating a diversity of foods in a range of social situations.	• Eats socially with others. • Recognises that we eat different foods at different times of the day and on different occasions. • Prepares and tastes a range of familiar and unfamiliar foods. • Recognises and respects that others' food choices may be different from their own.	E
		• Prepares, tastes and tries an increasing range of familiar and unfamiliar foods. • Explains likes and dislikes in relation to food. • Chooses appropriate foods to prepare for a given situation. • Describes appropriate table manners within different social situations.	1
		• Uses sensory descriptors to describe foods, for example, taste, texture, appearance, smell. • Identifies, prepares and selects foods for a range of situations, for example, social, cultural, religious events. • Devises guidelines for good table manners.	2

DEVELOPING HEALTHY CHOICES

LINKING FOOD AND HEALTH DECISION MAKING	HWB 0-30a Together we enjoy handling, tasting, talking and learning about different foods, discovering ways in which eating and drinking may help us to grow and keep healthy.	• Recognises that eating more of some types of foods and less of others is good for health. • Identifies, prepares and tastes a range of foods, for example, fruit, vegetables. • Identifies how much water should be consumed in a day.	E
	HWB 1-30a By investigating the range of foods available I can discuss how they contribute to a healthy diet. HWB 1-30b I experience a sense of enjoyment and achievement when preparing simple healthy foods and drinks.	• Recognises and names the main food groups, for example, The Eatwell Guide. • Sorts a selection of foods into the food groups. • Chooses foods from different food groups to create a balanced meal. • Assists in preparing healthy dishes for a variety of occasions, for example, an intergenerational visit. • Identifies at least one reason as to why it is important to drink enough water.	1
	HWB 2-30a By applying my knowledge and understanding of current healthy eating advice I can contribute to a healthy eating plan.	• Explains the proportions each food group should contribute to a healthy eating plan. • Identifies and classifies composite dishes according to the food groups, for example, lasagne, chicken stir fry. • Outlines at least three current healthy eating messages, for example, lowering salt and sugar intake. • Creates a healthy eating plan which reflects current dietary advice, prepares food which contributes to it and compares plan to own diet. • Identifies simple changes or improvements to own diet. • Explains the importance of keeping hydrated.	2

NUTRITIONAL NEEDS

VARIED DIET INDIVIDUAL NEEDS STAGES OF LIFE	HWB 0-32a I know that people need different kinds of food to keep them healthy.	• Uses the words lots, some and a little to prepare and describe the amount of food that should be eaten from each food group to stay healthy.	E
	HWB 1-32a I am beginning to understand that nutritional needs change at different stages of life, for example the role of breastfeeding in infant nutrition.	• Identifies at least two differences in individuals' dietary needs as they change through life, for example, infant, toddler, child, teenager, adult.	1
	HWB 2-32a I understand that people at different life stages have differing nutritional needs and that some people may eat or avoid certain foods.	• Recognises that all food and drink provides different levels of nutrients. • Lists the five nutrient groups. • Recognises that energy is provided by carbohydrates, fats and proteins and that vitamins and minerals are required to keep the body healthy. • Explains at least three nutritional requirements at different stages of life, for example energy, protein, calcium. • Suggests why people might avoid certain foods, for example, religion, culture, allergies, medical reasons.	2

KEEPING SAFE AND HYGIENIC
PRINCIPLES OF FOOD SAFETY AND HYGIENE • MINIMISING RISK • PREPARING FOOD DAFELY AND HYGIENICALLY

E	HWB 0-33a / 1-33a I am becoming aware of how cleanliness, hygiene and safety can affect health and wellbeing and I apply this knowledge in my everyday routines such as taking care of my teeth.	• Demonstrates how to perform daily hygiene routines, for example, hand washing, teeth brushing. • Gets ready to prepare food, for example, wash hands, tie hair back, wear an apron. • Demonstrates an understanding of basic food hygiene and safety through, for example, washing fruit and vegetables, storing perishables in the fridge. • Works safely when using simple kitchen equipment.
1	HWB 0-33a / 1-33a I am becoming aware of how cleanliness, hygiene and safety can affect health and wellbeing and I apply this knowledge in my everyday routines such as taking care of my teeth.	• Explains the importance of daily hygiene routines, for example, hand washing, teeth brushing and body cleanliness. • Works safely and hygienically before, during and after preparing foods, for example, adhering to appropriate allergy advice, getting ready to cook, storing ingredients appropriately, washing and drying equipment and surfaces. • Identifies where different types of food are stored. • Handles equipment safely, for example, when using hot or sharp kitchen tools.
2	HWB 2-33a Having learned about cleanliness, hygiene and safety, I can apply these principles to my everyday routines, understanding their importance to health and wellbeing.	• Makes food items safely and hygienically, adhering to allergies, cleaning, cross contamination, cooking, chilling. • Identifies ways to reduce the risk of food poisoning, for example, reheating food until piping hot, safe food storage, different coloured chopping boards. • Explains the difference between Use By and Best Before dates. • Creates a risk assessment for a practical food session.

THE JOURNEY OF FOOD
FROM FARM TO FORK • SUSTAINABILITY • INFLUENCES ON CONSUMER CHOICES • PREPARING FOOD APPROPRIATE TO LEARNING

E	HWB 0-35a I explore and discover where foods come from as I choose, prepare and taste different foods.	• Describes which foods come from plants and which come from animals when working with and tasting foods.
1	HWB 1-35a / 2-35a When preparing and cooking a variety of foods, I am becoming aware of the journeys which foods make from source to consumer, their seasonality, their local availability and their sustainability. HWB 1-37a I am discovering the different ways that advertising and the media can affect my choices.	• Describes the basic journey of food, for example, milk can come from a cow, bread comes from wheat / rye / oats. • Follows a recipe using fresh, local, seasonal produce, for example, making soup, hot or cold snack. • Identifies how to prevent food related waste, for example, composting peelings, reusing leftovers, reducing use of packaging. • Maps sources of food and drink in the local area. • Describes at least three ways that advertising and media can affect our food choices.
2	HWB 1-35a / 2-35a When preparing and cooking a variety of foods, I am becoming aware of the journeys which foods make from source to consumer, their seasonality, their local availability and their sustainability. HWB 2-34a Through exploration and discussion, I can understand that food practices and preferences are influenced by factors such as food sources, finance, culture and religion. HWB 2-36a By investigating food labelling systems, I can begin to understand how to use them to make healthy food choices. HWB 2-37a I can understand how advertising and the media are used to influence consumers.	• Describes the journey of food from source to plate for example, from the sea, farms or factories to markets, supermarkets or direct to consumer. • Creates a dish using fresh, local, seasonal ingredients and calculates food miles of key ingredients. • Explains the benefits of waste management, for example, the 3 'Rs' - reduce, reuse, recycle. • Compares the cost of identified ingredients to establish the most economical source. • Identifies factors that may influence food choice, for example, religious, cultural, geographical, ethical factors. • Uses different food labelling systems to select foods for a specified dietary requirement, for example, low in fat. • Identifies three methods of persuasion used by media/advertisers to influence consumers, for example, logos.

FOOD AND TEXTILE TECHNOLOGIES[1]

E	CREATIVITY
	DESIGN
	DEXTERITY
	PROBLEM SOLVING
	DEVELOPING APPROPRIATE ITEMS
		TCH 0-04a I enjoy exploring and working with foods in different contexts.
		
		TCH 0-04b I enjoy experimenting with a range of textiles.
		
		TCH 0-04c I can share their thoughts with others to help further develop ideas and solve problems.
			• Demonstrates simple food preparation techniques, for example, peeling, slicing, mixing, spreading.
			• Demonstrates simple techniques with textiles, for example, cutting, selecting materials, threading cards, gluing.
			• Within a food/textile context:
			  – Explores and identifies at least two ideas to solve a problem.
			  – Selects an appropriate solution.
			• Uses given resources to solve the problem / reach the solution.

1	CREATIVITY DESIGN DEXTERITY PROBLEM SOLVING DEVELOPING APPROPRIATE ITEMS	TCH 1-04a I can use a range of simple food preparation techniques when working with food. TCH 1-04b I can use a range of tools and equipment when working with textiles. TCH 1-04c I am developing and using problem solving strategies to meet challenges with a food or textile focus. TCH 1-04d I can adapt and improve ideas and can express my own thinking in different ways.	• Demonstrates a range of practical skills when preparing foods, for example, washing, using a peeler, juicing, grating, cutting, simple knife skills (claw grip/ bridge hold). • Uses a range of equipment when working with textiles, for example, scissors, rulers/tape measures, bodkin and wool. Within a food / textile context: • Investigates a simple problem / challenge. • Explores and identifies a range of ideas to solve the problem / challenge. • Selects and uses resources to reach the solution / solve the problem. • Assesses solution against given criteria.

[1] [Wordings of Benchmarks differ slightly from those in Technologies on page 125.]

CREATIVITY DESIGN	TCH 2-04a I am developing dexterity, creativity and confidence when preparing and cooking food.	• Demonstrates an increasing range of practical skills and cooking techniques, for example, weighing and measuring, kneading, chopping, baking, grilling.
DEXTERITY	TCH 2-04b I am developing dexterity, creativity and confidence when working with textiles.	• Demonstrates manual dexterity, for example, using a needle and thread, cutting more intricate shapes, manipulating fabrics and embellishments to create designs on fabric, attaching designs onto fabric.
PROBLEM SOLVING DEVELOPING APPROPRIATE ITEMS	TCH 2-04c I can extend and explore problem solving strategies to meet increasingly difficult challenges with a food or textile focus. TCH 2-04d I can discuss, debate and improve my ideas with increasing confidence and clear explanations.	Within a food / textile context: • Investigates a challenge / problem. • Identifies and demonstrates ways to solve the challenge / problem. • Plans and reaches the solution. • Assesses solution against own criteria. • Identifies at least one possible improvement.

2

APPENDIX - EXPLANATIONS

HWB: RoA
HWB

The following explanations of specific language are intended to help educators, parents, children and young people interpret the outcomes.

INTRODUCTORY STATEMENTS

Resilience
The development of resilience or coping skills is particularly important to young people as increasing numbers are struggling through school and life with social and emotional needs that greatly challenge schools and welfare agencies.

A resilient child can resist adversity, cope with uncertainty and recover more successfully from traumatic events or episodes.

MENTAL, EMOTIONAL, SOCIAL AND PHYSICAL WELLBEING

Mental wellbeing
Mental wellbeing refers to the health of the mind, the way we think, perceive, reflect on and make sense of the world.

Mental health
The World Health Organisation describes mental health as: "a state of wellbeing in which the individual realises his or her own abilities, can cope with the normal stresses of life, can work productively and fruitfully, and is able to make a contribution to his or her community."

Emotional wellbeing
Emotional wellbeing refers to recognising, understanding and effectively managing our feelings and emotions.

Social wellbeing
Social wellbeing refers to being and feeling secure in relationships with family, friends and community, having a sense of belonging and recognising and understanding our contribution in society.

Social wellbeing – HWB 0-12a, etc
This will be developed by raising the young person's awareness, understanding and experience of participation in consultation, citizenship and volunteering activities within the formal and informal curriculum.

Self-esteem/Self-worth
Self-esteem is a self rating of how well the self is doing. It means:
▸ the way we feel about ourselves
▸ the way we feel about our abilities
▸ the value we place on ourselves as human beings.

Physical wellbeing
Physical wellbeing refers to the knowledge, skills and attitudes that we need to understand how physical factors affect our health.

Physical wellbeing – HWB 0-18a, etc
This applies to all kinds of travel – whether on foot, bicycle, motor vehicle or public transport. To support the reduction of road accidents, it is the responsibility of all adults to teach and encourage good road safety practice and to reinforce this by modelling appropriate behaviour.

Particular attention should be paid at times of transition, especially during the transition from primary to secondary school, where there is a significant increase in road traffic accidents.

Emotional literacy
Being 'emotionally literate' means having the ability to identify, understand and express emotions in a healthy way.

PHYSICAL EDUCATION, PHYSICAL ACTIVITY AND SPORT

Physical education
Movement skills, competences and concepts
There are two progressive pathways within this line of development. The first concentrates on using your body to perform and link increasingly complex actions and is about developing physical competences in learners which allow them to participate in physical activities. This forms part of the social inclusion agenda.

The second concentrates on the development of high quality performance in a range of contexts, and improving fitness.

Physical experiences and contexts for learning within these lines of development include: gymnastics, dance, water-based activity, directly/indirectly competitive activities and individual/team activities.

Cooperation and competition
The term physical event is deliberately wide as it allows practitioners to utilise a variety of opportunities to deliver the outcome, including, school and local authority competitions, come and try sessions, participation days, festivals and other organised activities.

Physical activity and sport
This line of development addresses the role that schools play in widening activity participation and performance pathways in Scottish sport. Its placement encourages participation and performance at the age most suited to the individual. This should help establish a behaviour pattern in sport which evidence has shown is a strong predictor of participation into adult life.

Moderate activity is that of sufficient intensity to raise the heart and respiration rate. It is characterised by being slightly out of breath and having a raised body temperature.

Vigorous activity is of an intensity to significantly raise the heart and respiration rate. It is characterised by being breathless and perspiring.

RELATIONSHIPS, SEXUAL HEALTH AND PARENTHOOD

HWB 0-47b / HWB 1-47b
While it is important to acknowledge that people use different words for parts of the body associated with sexuality and sexual reproduction, it is essential to introduce and use the proper anatomical terms as early as possible, taking account of cultural and faith perspectives. This provides an appropriate language for learning about relationships and sexual health in establishments and is helpful to professionals and others with a health, care and welfare role.

LITERACY, ENGLISH & GÀIDHLIG

PRINCIPLES & PRACTICE

Statements for 'Literacy across learning: Responsibility of All Practitioners' (from the front of the original document) and for Literacy & English / Literacy & Gàidhlig as the responsibilty of teachers (in primary) and subject specialists (in primary and secondary) have been combined here.

Red shading in column 1 denotes ext from Literacy across learning on pages 20-23 of the original CfE document.

Lighter red shading in column 2 denotes text from the Principles & Practice for Literacy & English on pages 124-128 of that document.

Brown shading in column 3 denotes text appearing in the Principles & Practice for Literacy & English on pages 147-152 of that document.

Language and literacy are of personal, social and economic importance. Our ability to use language lies at the centre of the development and expression of our emotions, our thinking, our learning and our sense of personal identity. Language is itself a key aspect of our culture. Through language, children and young people can gain access to the literary heritage of humanity and develop their appreciation of the richness and breadth of Scotland's literary heritage. Children and young people encounter, enjoy and learn from the diversity of language used in their homes, their communities, by the media and by their peers.

Literacy is fundamental to all areas of learning, as it unlocks access to the wider curriculum. Being literate increases opportunities for the individual in all aspects of life, lays the foundations for lifelong learning and work, and contributes strongly to the development of all four capacities of Curriculum for Excellence.

Competence and confidence in literacy, including competence in grammar, spelling and the spoken word, are essential for progress in all areas of the curriculum. Because of this, all teachers have responsibility for promoting language and literacy development. Every teacher in each area of the curriculum needs to find opportunities to encourage young people to explain their thinking, debate their ideas and read and write at a level which will help them to develop their language skills further.

Building the Curriculum 1

The literacy experiences and outcomes promote the development of critical and creative thinking as well as competence in listening and talking, reading, writing and the personal, interpersonal and team-working skills which are so important in life and in the world of work. The framework provides, for learners, parents and teachers, broad descriptions of the range of learning opportunities which will contribute to the development of literacy, including critical literacy.

The Literacy and English / Literacy and Gàidhlig frameworks promotes the development of critical and creative thinking as well as competence in listening and talking, reading, writing and the personal, inter-personal and team-working skills which are so important in life and in the world of work. The framework provides, for learners, parents and teachers, broad descriptions of the range of learning opportunities which will contribute to the development of literacy, including critical literacy, creativity, and knowledge and appreciation of literature and culture.

Traditionally, all aspects of the language framework were developed by all practitioners in pre-school establishments and primary schools and by the English / Gàidhlig department in secondary schools. This will continue to be the case, but the framework recognises that all practitioners in secondary schools and in colleges and youth work settings have important responsibilities for and contributions to make towards the development of literacy.

WHAT IS MEANT BY LITERACY?

In defining literacy for the 21st century we must consider the changing forms of language which our children and young people will experience and use. Accordingly, our definition takes account of factors such as the speed with which information is shared and the ways it is shared. The breadth of our definition is intended to 'future proof' it. Within *Curriculum for Excellence*, therefore, literacy is defined as:

> the set of skills which allows an individual to engage fully in society and in learning, through the different forms of language, and the range of texts, which society values and finds useful.

The literacy experiences and outcomes promote the development of skills in using language, particularly those that are used regularly by everyone in their everyday lives. These include the ability to apply knowledge about language. They reflect the need for young people to be able to communicate effectively both face-to-face and in writing through an increasing range of media. They take account of national and international research and of other skills frameworks. They recognise the importance of listening and talking and of effective collaborative working in the development of thinking and in learning.

In particular, the experiences and outcomes address the important skills of critical literacy. Children and young people not only need to be able to read for information: they also need to be able to work out what trust they should place on the information and to identify when and how people are aiming to persuade or influence them.

HOW ARE THESE FRAMEWORKS STRUCTURED?

Each framework opens with a set of statements that describe the kinds of activity which all children and young people should experience throughout their learning, to nurture their skills and knowledge in literacy and language. Teachers will use them, alongside the more detailed experiences and outcomes, in planning for learning and teaching.

In Literacy and English / Literacy and Gàidhlig, the statements of experiences and outcomes themselves include both literacy and English / Gàidhlig statements. They emphasise that learning is an *active* process: for example, the outcomes stress *making* notes, rather than the passive activity implied by *taking* notes. Experiences represent important continuing aspects of learning such as exploring and enjoying text, and outcomes describe stages in the development of skills and understanding.

The three organisers are the same across Literacy, Literacy and English, Literacy and Gàidhlig, Gaelic (learners), and Modern Languages frameworks:

▶ **listening and talking**
▶ **reading**
▶ **writing.**

Within these organisers there are subdivisions.

▶ **Enjoyment and choice** experiences and outcomes highlight the importance of providing opportunities for young people to make increasingly sophisticated choices.
▶ The **tools** sections include important skills and knowledge: for example, in reading it includes such important matters as reading strategies and spelling.
▶ The sections on **finding and using information** include, in reading, critical literacy skills; while the understanding, analysing and evaluating statements encourage progression in understanding of texts, developing not only literal understanding but also the higher order skills.
▶ Finally, the **creating texts** experiences and outcomes describe the kind of opportunities which will help children and young people to develop their ability to communicate effectively, for example, by writing clear, well-structured explanations.

The experiences and outcomes have been written in an inclusive way which will allow teachers to interpret them for the needs of individual children and young people who use Braille, sign language and other forms of communication. This is exemplified in the words 'engaging with others' and 'interacting' within the listening and talking outcomes.

LITERACY ACROSS THE CURRICULUM / 'RESPONSIBLITY OF ALL'

The importance of the development of literacy skills across all areas of the curriculum is stressed in *Building the Curriculum 1*. All practitioners – from the early years, through primary and secondary education, in youth work settings and in colleges – are in a position to make important contributions to developing and reinforcing the literacy skills of children and young people, both through the learning activities which they plan and through their interaction with children and young people. Schools and their partners need to ensure a shared understanding of these responsibilities and that the approaches to learning and teaching will enable each child and young person to make good progress in developing their literacy skills.

It is expected that the literacy experiences and outcomes, and this accompanying paper, will be read by a range of practitioners, including those who work in school library resource centres, who make an enormous contribution to the development of the literacy skills of children and young people.

In order to highlight the shared nature of these responsibilities, the literacy experiences and outcomes also appear as a separate document, and implications for learning and teaching are explored further in the document which accompanies it.

WHAT THIS MEANS FOR TEACHING AND LEARNING

For teachers and other practitioners, it means asking the question, 'How am I meeting the literacy needs of the learners in front of me?' It means thinking about the kinds of literacy experiences provided for young people. It doesn't mean that every practitioner will teach everything that a secondary English teacher does. These experiences will sometimes be provided through collaborative working with other departments; but the greatest impact for learners will come from all practitioners, in all learning environments, including rich literacy experiences as part of their day-to-day learning and teaching programmes.

ASSESSMENT IN LITERACY (complements advice for literacy & English / literacy & Gàidhlig)

As literacy is the responsibility of all staff, and because of the importance of literacy across all aspects of a young person's learning, all staff should be clear about their responsibilities and their roles in the assessment of literacy. Assessment in literacy will focus on children and young people's progress in developing and applying essential skills in listening and talking, reading and writing. From the early years to the senior stages, and particularly at times of transition, it is vital to have a clear picture of the progress each child and young person is making across all aspects of literacy so that further learning can be planned and action can be taken if any ground has been lost.

Within the overall approach to assessing literacy, evidence of progress in developing and applying skills in day-to-day learning across the curriculum will complement evidence gathered from language lessons. Specific assessment tasks will also have an important part to play. Practitioners and learners need a common understanding of expectations in literacy across all curriculum areas, and discussion and sharing examples of work will help to achieve this.

Approaches to assessment should identify the extent to which children and young people can apply their literacy skills across their learning. For example:

▶ How well do they contribute to discussions and openly explain their thinking?
▶ Are they increasingly able to distil key ideas from texts?
▶ Can they apply their literacy skills successfully in different areas of their learning and their daily lives?

Children will demonstrate their progress in **reading** through their growing fluency and understanding, and their increasing confidence in reading to learn as well as learning to read.

Literacy experiences and outcomes emphasise the development of **critical literacy**. Progress here can be seen as children move from dealing with straightforward information towards analysing, evaluating and being aware of the trust that they should place on evidence.

Children and young people will demonstrate their progress in **writing** though the degree of independence they show, the organisation and quality of their ideas, their skills in spelling, punctuation and grammar, the match of their writing to audience and the effectiveness of their use of language.

Progress in **listening and talking** can be assessed through their interactions in social and learning contexts and through using individual talks, presentations and group discussions. This range of sources will provide evidence about their confidence, their increasing awareness of others in sustaining interactions, the clarity of their ideas and expression and their skills in listening to others and taking turns.

Learners' enthusiasm and motivation for using language will show in their growing use of different media and texts, their preferences in reading, their confidence in sharing experiences through talk and writing and in the ways they apply their skills in their learning and communicating. These aspects will be indicators of their long-term success in using literacy in learning in their lives as citizens and in preparing for the world of work.

BROAD FEATURES OF ASSESSMENT IN LITERACY & ENGLISH

Assessment in literacy and English will focus on the responses of children and young people to the language and to the ideas and information that they find in texts, and on the development and application of their skills in listening and talking, reading and writing.

Teachers will see evidence of their progress through children and young people's growing skills in communicating their thinking and using language appropriately for different purposes and audiences. Much of the evidence will be gathered as part of day-to-day learning. The use of specific assessment tasks is also important to provide evidence of progress, particularly at transitions.

Assessment of progress in literacy and English will focus on judgements about the success of children and young people in developing key literacy and English language skills and applying their skills in their learning and in their daily lives and in preparing for the world of work. For example:

▶ How well are they communicating with confidence to suit their purpose and audience and showing increasing awareness of others in interactions?
▶ How does their confidence in listening and talking help their personal development, social skills and ability to solve problems?
▶ To what extent are they exploring and enjoying fiction and non-fiction texts of increasing depth, complexity and variety and making increasingly sophisticated personal responses?
▶ How well do they engage with challenging issues raised in texts?

Long-term success in using literacy and English is closely linked to learners' motivation and capacity to engage with and complete tasks and assignments. For this reason, it is important to observe and discuss their enthusiasm for stories, poetry and prose, their interest in words, their preferences in reading, and their enthusiasm for sharing experiences through talk and writing. Their progress can be seen, for example, in their increasingly creative use of language and their developing appreciation of literature and culture.

BROAD FEATURES OF ASSESSMENT IN LITERACY & GÀIDHLIG

Assessment in literacy and Gàidhlig will focus firstly on the foundation of skills, initially in listening, progressively in talking and then in the development and application of skills in reading and writing. Teachers will see evidence of children and young people's progress in their growing skills in communicating and using language appropriately for different purposes and audiences and in their responses to the language, ideas and information that they find in Gàidhlig texts. Much of the evidence will be gathered as part of day-to-day learning; use of specific assessment tasks is also important in providing evidence, particularly at transitions.

Assessment of progress in literacy and Gàidhlig will focus on judgements about the success of children and young people in progressing in spoken and written language and applying their skills in their learning across the curriculum, in their daily lives, in preparing for the world of work and in cultural activities. For example:

▶ How well are they communicating with confidence to suit their purpose and audience and showing increasing awareness of others in interactions?

▶ How well are they extending their everyday and specialist vocabulary?

▶ How does their confidence in listening and talking help their personal development, social skills and ability to solve problems?

▶ To what extent are they exploring and enjoying Gàidhlig poetry and song, and stories of increasing complexity and variety and making personal responses?

▶ How well do they engage with challenging ethical issues raised in texts?

Children and young people's growing literacy and Gàidhlig skills bring access to learning, and communicating within and beyond school will shape their success as learners. Learners' motivation is closely linked to their long-term success in using literacy and Gàidhlig and to their capacity to engage with and complete extended tasks and assignments. For this reason, it is important to observe their enthusiasm for stories, poetry and prose, their interest in words, their preferences in reading, and their enthusiasm for sharing experiences through talk and writing. Their progress can be seen, for example, in their increasingly creative use of language and in their developing appreciation of Gàidhlig literature and culture.

WHERE TO BEGIN

You might begin by asking yourself to what extent you already provide literacy experiences for learners. As a first step, you might want to consider the ways in which you use listening, talking, reading and writing for learning day to day in your teaching programmes. For example, do you provide learners with opportunities to:

Listening and talking for learning
▶ engage with others in group and class discussions of appropriate complexity?
▶ learn collaboratively – for example, when problem-solving?
▶ explain their thinking to others?
▶ explore factors which influence them and persuade them in order to help them think about the reliability of information?

Reading for learning
▶ find, select, sort, summarise and link information from a variety of sources?
▶ consider the purpose and main concerns in texts, and understand the differences between fact and opinion?
▶ discuss similarities and differences between texts?

Writing for learning
▶ make notes, develop ideas and acknowledge sources in written work?
▶ develop and use effective vocabulary?
▶ create texts – for example, presentations – which allow learners to persuade/argue/explore ideas?

Where you answer 'yes' to these questions, you are contributing to the development of the literacy of the learners for whom you are responsible.

You will see that literacy is already reflected within the experiences and outcomes of the other curriculum area frameworks. It is important to use the literacy experiences and outcomes alongside those of the other curriculum areas when planning for learning.

EFFECTIVE LEARNING & TEACHING IN LITERACY & ENGLISH / LITERACY & GÀIDHLIG

Throughout their education, children and young people should experience an environment which is rich in language and which sets high expectations for literacy and the use of language. Children and young people need to spend time with stories, literature and other texts which will enrich their learning, develop their language skills and enable them to find enjoyment. Spoken language has particular importance in the early years. Teachers will balance play-based learning with more systematic development and learning of skills and techniques for reading, including phonics.

Throughout education, effective learning and teaching in literacy and English / literacy and Gàidhlig will involve a skilful mix of appropriate approaches including:

▶ the use of relevant, real-life and enjoyable contexts which build upon children and young people's own experiences

▶ effective direct and interactive teaching

▶ a balance of spontaneous play and planned activities

▶ harnessing the motivational benefits of following children and young people's interests through responsive planning

▶ collaborative working and independent thinking and learning

▶ making meaningful links for learners across different curriculum areas

▶ building on the principles of Assessment is for Learning

▶ frequent opportunities to communicate in a wide range of contexts, for relevant purposes and for real audiences within and beyond places of learning

▶ the development of problem-solving skills and approaches

▶ the appropriate and effective use of ICT.

The balance between these approaches will vary at different stages and across different sectors and areas of the curriculum. Continuing dialogue about learning and teaching approaches within and across sectors will help to ensure continuity and progression.

THE BROADNESS OF THE EXPERIENCE & OUTCOMES: HOW CAN WE BE SURE ABOUT PROGRESSION BETWEEN LEVELS?

The experiences and outcomes embody appropriate levels of proficiency at each level but do not place a ceiling on achievement. The range of experiences allows for different rates of progression and for additional depth or breadth of study through the use of different contexts for learning. Progression within and across levels will take place in a range of ways, including:

▶ continuing development and consolidation of the range of skills

▶ increasing independence in applying these skills, and the ability to use them across a widening range of contexts in learning and life

▶ gradually decreasing levels of support used by the learner (for example from teachers, classroom assistants, parents or peers), and reduced reliance upon techniques such as wordlists or writing frames

▶ the ability to mediate discussions without teacher intervention

▶ in reading, the increasing length and complexity of text (for example the text's ideas, structure and vocabulary)

▶ in talking and writing, the increasing length, complexity and accuracy of response

▶ increasing awareness of how to apply language rules effectively.

At all levels, teachers will plan to enable learners to develop their skills with increasing depth over a range of contexts. This will be especially important at early level for those young people who may require additional support.

CONNECTIONS BETWEEN THESE FRAMEWORKS AND OTHERS

Close attention has been paid to matching with Scottish Credit and Qualifications Framework (SCQF).
The level of achievement at the fourth level has been designed to approximate to that associated with SCQF level 4.
The framework has been developed to support essential skills within Skills for Scotland and within An Adult Literacy and Numeracy Framework for Scotland.

LINKS WITH OTHER AREAS OF THE CURRICULUM

In addition to the opportunities to develop literacy in all aspects of learning, there are strong connections between learning in English and learning in other areas of the curriculum. There are close links, for example, between the expressive arts and creative writing, and social studies and critical literacy. Interdisciplinary studies are likely to involve both research and a strong element of presentation and provide valuable opportunities to extend language skills. In numeracy, information handling outcomes link clearly to the critical literacy outcomes where learners are asked to assess the reliability of information.

Whatever the sector, whatever the subject area, young people will be:

▸ engaged in talking together to deepen their learning and thinking
▸ working together to prepare for reading unfamiliar texts
▸ reading a wide range of texts to gather and analyse information for a range of purposes
▸ writing clear explanations
▸ communicating information or opinions.

WHAT IS MEANT BY 'TEXTS'

The definition of 'texts' needs to be broad and future proof: therefore within *Curriculum for Excellence*,

> a text is the medium through which ideas, experiences, opinions and information can be communicated.

Reading and responding to literature and other texts play a central role in the development of learners' knowledge and understanding. Texts not only include those presented in traditional written or print form, but also orally, electronically or on film. Texts can be in continuous form, including traditional formal prose, or non-continuous, for example charts and graphs. The literacy and English / literacy and Gàidhlig framework reflects the increased use of multimodal texts, digital communication, social networking and the other forms of electronic communication encountered by children and young people in their daily lives. It recognises that the skills which children and young people need to learn to read these texts differ from the skills they need for reading continuous prose. Examples are given below.

Example of texts

novels, short stories, plays, poems
reference texts
the spoken word
charts, maps, graphs and timetables
advertisements, promotional leaflets
comics, newspapers and magazines
CVs, letters and emails
films, games and TV programmes
labels, signs and posters
recipes, manuals and instructions
reports and reviews
text messages, blogs and social networking sites
web pages, catalogues and directories

In planning for learning in any curriculum area it is important for practitioners to ensure that children and young people encounter a wide range of different types of text in different media. As they progress in their learning, children and young people will encounter texts of increasing complexity in terms of length, structure, vocabulary, ideas and concepts.

SCOTS AND SCOTTISH TEXTS

The languages, dialects and literature of Scotland provide a rich resource for children and young people to learn about Scotland's culture, identity and language. Through engaging with a wide range of texts they will develop an appreciation of Scotland's vibrant literary and linguistic heritage and its indigenous languages and dialects. This principle suffuses the experiences and outcomes and it is expected that practitioners will build upon the diversity of language represented within the communities of Scotland, valuing the languages which children and young people bring to school.

GÀIDHLIG IMMERSION

Children come to Gàidhlig education from a wide variety of backgrounds. These vary from a household within a strong Gàidhlig speaking community to an environment where no Gàidhlig is spoken. Whatever the circumstances, parents' desire to have Gàidhlig speaking bilingual children is often equally strong.

As learners acquiring Gàidhlig enter a Gàidhlig medium class, they hear and will, in time, speak, read and write Gàidhlig and be actively involved in working out the structure and rules of the language. They may take some time to develop sufficient confidence to use their newly acquired Gàidhlig. To increase their confidence and feeling of success, teachers will provide them with opportunities to interact with other Gàidhlig speakers in a range of situations.

Teachers will ensure that Gàidhlig is the language of learning and of communication, and that all areas of the curriculum are taught through the medium of Gàidhlig. As children and young people continue to enjoy their immersion in Gàidhlig through primary and secondary education, teachers will plan clear structures for learning to further develop Gàidhlig language skills. The learning environment will be a literacy-rich and visually stimulating place, which will encourage language development which focuses on the correct uses of language and subject-specific vocabulary. Adopting a range of appropriate teaching methodologies will make use of natural and real contexts to support children and young learners in developing their Gàidhlig language skills.

The experiences and outcomes play to the strengths of Gàidhlig teachers who are well placed to reflect on and further develop what the pupil has already achieved in home or community languages. The development of Gàidhlig grammatical structures, syntax and phonology are the responsibility of early years and primary practitioners and of Gàidhlig departments in the secondary. Teachers in all curriculum areas will reinforce accuracy in the use of the Gàidhlig language. A sensitive approach to the management of learning and teaching within groups which include children who are already fluent in Gàidhlig and those who are not will be particularly important.

Teachers will give careful consideration to planning activities to ensure that children and young people with additional support needs are fully supported in their learning.

Early years
At early stages practitioners will develop ways of teaching Gàidhlig that stress active learning. Practitioners will continue to use a range of teaching methodologies to support children's Gàidhlig to develop in natural and real contexts which are familiar to young learners. Exploring language using real-life and imaginary situations can challenge children's thinking and learning and provide an element of choice and ownership for their own learning.

Primary
In Gàidhlig medium classes learning and teaching is wholly through Gàidhlig during the immersion phase from P1 to P3. English language is then gradually introduced through the medium of Gàidhlig, with Gàidhlig remaining the predominant language of the classroom in all areas of the curriculum. It is important that teachers continue the immersion in Gàidhlig language through primary and secondary education, with teachers providing a clear structure for learning and further development of Gàidhlig language skills. An emphasis needs to be placed on listening and talking at all stages to allow learners to practise, use and enrich their Gàidhlig. Understanding by teachers of the stages of oral language acquisition will help to ensure a clear understanding of when and why Gàidhlig language and grammar is taught in a structured way.

Secondary
Where circumstances permit, Gàidhlig medium teaching should extend as far as possible across and beyond the curriculum. In order to provide opportunities to use Gàidhlig in practical situations, including the world of work, subject teachers involved in Gàidhlig medium teaching will seek out and develop links with the Gàidhlig business community and Gàidhlig-related organisations to build a sense of a vibrant and living language which has relevance to pupils' lives. Many teachers in the secondary sector may wish to access specialist training in the specific issues which affect Gaelic medium teaching in specialist subjects.

DOCUMENTS MENTIONED ABOVE

An Adult Literacy and Numeracy Framework for Scotland
http://www.lc.communitiesscotland.gov.uk/stellent/groups/public/documents/webpages/cs_008875.pdf

Skills for Scotland
http://www.scotland.gov.uk/Publications/2007/09/06091114/0

EXPERIENCES & OUTCOMES

LIT: RoA
ENG
GAI

The development of literacy skills plays an important role in all learning.

I develop and extend my literacy skills when I have opportunities to:

▸ communicate, collaborate and build relationships

▸ reflect on and explain my literacy and thinking skills, using feedback to help me improve and sensitively provide useful feedback for others

▸ engage with and create a wide range of texts[1] in different media, taking advantage of the opportunities offered by ICT

▸ develop my understanding of what is special, vibrant and valuable about my own and other cultures and their languages

▸ explore the richness and diversity of language[2], how it can affect me, and the wide range of ways in which I and others can be creative

▸ extend and enrich my vocabulary through listening, talking, watching and reading.

In developing my English / Gàidhlig language skills:

▸ I engage with a wide range of texts and am developing an appreciation of the richness and breadth of Scotland's literary and linguistic heritage

▸ I enjoy exploring and discussing word patterns and text structures.

| Responsibility of All | The statements in [*italics* on a yellow background] in both the Experiences and Outcomes and Benchmarks are the responsibility of all and, as such, evidence from across the curriculum should be considered when making judgements about achieving a level.* |

NOTES FROM THE LITERACY & GÀIDHLIG BENCHMARKS

Across the level, learners use words, phrases and communication learned from the use of Gaelic in a total immersion setting.	**E**
Across the level, learners use Gaelic language with increasing confidence and fluency in a total immersion and immersion setting.	**1**
Across the level, learners use Gaelic language with confidence, clarity, fluency and increased accuracy with grammar in an immersion setting.	**2**

Footnotes to Literacy / Literacy & English

1   Texts are defined in the principles and practice paper. They will include texts which are relevant to all areas of learning, and examples of writing by Scottish authors which relate to the history, heritage and culture of Scotland. They may also include writing in Scots, and Gaelic in translation.

2   The languages of Scotland will include the languages which children and young people bring to the classroom and other settings.

Footnotes to Literacy & Gàidhlig

1   Texts are defined in the principles and practice paper. They will include texts which are relevant to all areas of learning, and examples of writing by Scottish authors which relate to Gàidhlig and Scottish history, heritage and culture.

2   Staff will make full use of the range of language which children and young people bring to the classroom and other settings.

Footnotes regarding Responsibility of All

*   [This text is included as a footnote on every page of the Literacy & Gàidhlig version of *Benchmarks*. It does not appear in the Literacy & English version of *Benchmarks*; however, given that it also appears on all pages of the Benchmarks for Numeracy & Mathematics, this should be seen as an omission, rather than an intentional difference.]

LISTENING AND TALKING

ENJOYMENT AND CHOICE
within a motivating and challenging environment, developing an awareness of the relevance of texts in my life

E	*LIT 0-01a / 0-11a / 0-20a I enjoy exploring and playing with the patterns and sounds of language, and can use what I learn.*	• *Hears and says patterns in words.* • *Hears and says rhyming words and generates rhyme from a given word.* • *Hears and says the different single sounds made by letters.* • *Hears and says letter blends/sounds made by a combination of letters.* • *Participates actively in songs, rhymes and stories.*
	LIT 0-01b / 0-11b I enjoy exploring and choosing stories and other texts to watch, read or listen to, and can share my likes and dislikes. *LIT 0-01c I enjoy exploring events and characters in stories and other texts, sharing my thoughts in different ways.*	• *Chooses a story or other texts for enjoyment, making use of the cover, title, author and/or illustrator.* • *Engages with and enjoys watching, reading or listening to different texts, including stories, songs and rhymes, and can share likes and dislikes.* • *Engages with stories and texts in different ways, for example, retelling/re-enacting stories and/or using puppets/props.*

		1st Level:	**2nd Level:**
1 **2**	*LIT 1-01a / 2-01a I regularly select and listen to or watch texts which I enjoy and find interesting, and I can explain why I prefer certain sources.* *I regularly select subject, purpose, format and resources to create texts of my choice.*	• *Selects spoken texts regularly for enjoyment or to find information for a specific purpose and gives a reason for preferences.*	• *Selects spoken texts regularly for enjoyment or to find information for a specific purpose. Explains preferences.*

TOOLS FOR LISTENING AND TALKING
to help me when interacting or presenting within and beyond my place of learning

E	*LIT 0-02a / ENG 0-03a As I listen and talk in different situations, I am learning to take turns and am developing my awareness of when to talk and when to listen.*	• *Makes an attempt to take turns when listening and talking in a variety of contexts.* • *Makes an attempt to use appropriate body language when listening to others, for example, eye contact.* • *Listens and responds to others appropriately.* • *Asks questions and responds relevantly to questions from others.* • *Follows and gives simple instructions.* • *Shares ideas with a wider audience, for example, group or class.*
1	*LIT 1-02a When I engage with others, I know when and how to listen, when to talk, how much to say, when to ask questions and how to respond with respect.* *ENG 1-03a I am exploring how pace, gesture, expression, emphasis and choice of words are used to engage others, and I can use what I learn.*	• *Takes turns and contributes at the appropriate time when engaging with others in a variety of contexts.* • *Listens and responds appropriately to others in a respectful way, for example, by nodding or agreeing, asking and answering questions.* • *Applies a few techniques (verbal and non-verbal) when engaging with others, for example, vocabulary, eye contact, expression and/or body language.*
2	*LIT 2-02a When I engage with others, I can respond in ways appropriate to my role, show that I value others' contributions and use these to build on thinking.* *ENG 2-03a I can recognise how the features of spoken language can help in communication, and I can use what I learn.* *I can recognise different features of my own and others' spoken language.*	• *Contributes a number of relevant ideas, information and opinions when engaging with others.* • *Shows respect for the views of others and offers own viewpoint.* • *Builds on the contributions of others, for example, by asking or answering questions, clarifying points or supporting others' opinions or ideas.* • *Applies verbal and non-verbal techniques in oral presentations and interactions, for example, vocabulary, eye contact, body language, emphasis, pace and/or tone.* • *Recognises some techniques used to engage or influence the listener, for example, vocabulary, emphasis, tone and/or rhetorical questions.*

FINDING AND USING INFORMATION
when listening to, watching and talking about texts with increasingly complex ideas, structures and specialist vocabulary

E	*LIT 0-04a I listen or watch for useful or interesting information and I use this to make choices or learn new things.*	• *Understands and responds to spoken texts.* • *Identifies new or interesting information from spoken texts.*
1	*LIT 1-04a As I listen or watch, I can identify and discuss the purpose, key words and main ideas of the text, and use this information for a specific purpose.*	• *Identifies the purpose and main ideas of spoken texts and uses the information gathered for a specific purpose.*
	LIT 1-05a As I listen or watch, I am learning to make notes under given headings and use these to understand what I have listened to or watched and create new texts. *LIT 1-06a I can select ideas and relevant information, organise these in a logical sequence and use words which will be interesting and/or useful for others.*	• *Makes relevant notes under given headings and can use these for different purposes.* • *Uses notes to create and sequence new texts.*

LIT 2-04a *As I listen or watch, I can identify and discuss the purpose, main ideas and supporting detail contained within the text, and use this information for different purposes.*	• *Identifies the purpose of spoken texts with suitable explanation.* • *Identifies the main ideas of spoken texts, with supporting detail, and uses the information gathered for a specific purpose.*	**2**
LIT 2-05a *As I listen or watch, I can make notes, organise these under suitable headings and use these to understand ideas and information and create new texts, using my own words as appropriate.* **LIT 2-06a** *I can select ideas and relevant information, organise these in an appropriate way for my purpose and use suitable vocabulary for my audience.*	• *Makes relevant notes using own words, for the most part, and uses these to create new texts for a range of purposes.*	

UNDERSTANDING, ANALYSING AND EVALUATING
investigating and/or appreciating texts with increasingly complex ideas, structures and specialist vocabulary for different purposes

LIT 0-07a / LIT 0-16a / ENG 0-17a *To help me understand stories and other texts, I ask questions and link what I am learning with what I already know.*	• *Asks and answers questions about texts to show and support understanding.* • *Makes simple predictions about texts.*	**E**
LIT 1-07a *I can show my understanding of what I listen to or watch by responding to and asking different kinds of questions.* **LIT 1-08a** *To help me develop an informed view, I am learning to recognise the difference between fact and opinion.*	• *Asks and responds to different types of questions to show understanding of the main ideas of spoken texts.* • *Recognises simple differences between fact and opinion in spoken texts.*	**1**
LIT 2-07a *I can show my understanding of what I listen to or watch by responding to literal, inferential, evaluative and other types of questions, and by asking different kinds of questions of my own.* **LIT 2-08a** *To help me develop an informed view, I can distinguish fact from opinion, and I am learning to recognise when my sources try to influence me and how useful these are.*	• *Asks and responds to a range of questions, including literal, inferential and evaluative questions, to demonstrate understanding of spoken texts.* • *Identifies the difference between fact and opinion with suitable explanation.*	**2**

CREATING TEXTS
applying the elements others use to create different types of short and extended texts with increasingly complex ideas, structures and vocabulary

LIT 0-09a *Within real and imaginary situations, I share experiences and feelings, ideas and information in a way that communicates my message.* **LIT 0-09b / LIT 0-31a** *I enjoy exploring events and characters in stories and other texts and I use what I learn to invent my own, sharing these with others in imaginative ways.* **LIT 0-10a** *As I listen and take part in conversations and discussions, I discover new words and phrases which I use to help me express my ideas, thoughts and feelings.*	• *Talks clearly to others in different contexts, sharing feelings, ideas and thoughts.* • *Recounts experiences, stories and events in a logical sequence for different purposes.* • *Communicates and shares stories in different ways, for example, in imaginative play.* • *Uses new vocabulary and phrases in different contexts, for example, when expressing ideas and feelings or discussing a text.*	**E**
LIT 1-09a *When listening and talking with others for different purposes, I can exchange information, experiences, explanations, ideas and opinions, and clarify points by asking questions or by asking others to say more.* **LIT 1-10a** *I can communicate clearly when engaging with others within and beyond my place of learning, using selected resources[3] as required.*	• *Communicates clearly and audibly.* • *Contributes to group/class discussions, engaging with others for a range of purposes.* • *Selects and shares ideas/information using appropriate vocabulary in a logical order.* • *Selects and uses, with support, appropriate resources to engage with others, for example, objects, pictures and/or photographs.*	**1**
LIT 2-09a *When listening and talking with others for different purposes, I can:* ▸ *share information, experiences and opinions* ▸ *explain processes and ideas* ▸ *identify issues raised and summarise main points or findings* ▸ *clarify points by asking questions or by asking others to say more.* **LIT 2-10a** *I am developing confidence when engaging with others within and beyond my place of learning. I can communicate in a clear, expressive way and I am learning to select and organise resources independently.*	• *Communicates clearly, audibly and with expression in different contexts.* • *Plans and delivers an organised presentation/talk with relevant content and appropriate structure.* • *Uses suitable vocabulary for purpose and audience.* • *Selects and uses resources to support communication.*	**2**

---

[3]   This may include images, objects, audio, visual or digital resources.

READING

ENJOYMENT AND CHOICE
within a motivating and challenging environment, developing an awareness of the relevance of texts in my life

E	**LIT 0-01a / LIT 0-11a / LIT 0-20a** *I enjoy exploring and playing with the patterns and sounds of language and can use what I learn.* **LIT 0-01b / LIT 0-11b** *I enjoy exploring and choosing stories and other texts to watch, read or listen to, and can share my likes and dislikes.*	• *Chooses a story or other texts for enjoyment making use of the cover, title, author and/or illustrator.* • *Engages with and enjoys watching, reading or listening to different texts, including stories, songs and rhymes, and can share likes and dislikes.*
1	**LIT 1-11a / 2-11a** *I regularly select and read, listen to or watch texts which I enjoy and find interesting, and I can explain why I prefer certain texts and authors.*	• *Selects different texts regularly for enjoyment or for a specific purpose using, for example, cover, title, author, illustrator and/or blurb.* • *Explains preferences for particular texts and authors.*
2	**LIT 1-11a / 2-11a** *I regularly select and read, listen to or watch texts which I enjoy and find interesting, and I can explain why I prefer certain texts and authors.*	• *Selects texts regularly for enjoyment or to find information for a specific purpose.* • *Explains preferences for particular texts, authors or sources with supporting detail.*

TOOLS FOR READING
to help me use texts with increasingly complex or unfamiliar ideas, structures and vocabulary within and beyond my place of learning

E	**ENG 0-12a / LIT 0-13a / LIT 0-21a** *I explore sounds, letters and words, discovering how they work together, and I can use what I learn to help me as I read and write.*	• *Hears and says patterns in words.* • *Hears and says the different single sounds made by letters.* • *Hears and says blends/sounds made by a combination of letters.* • *Knows the difference between a letter, word and numeral.* • *Reads from left to right and top to bottom.* • *Uses knowledge of sounds, letters and patterns to read words.* • *Uses knowledge of sight vocabulary/tricky words to read familiar words in context.* • *Reads aloud familiar texts with attention to simple punctuation.* • *Uses context clues to support understanding of different texts.*
1	**ENG 1-12a** I can use my knowledge of sight vocabulary, phonics, context clues, punctuation and grammar to read with understanding and expression. **LIT 1-13a** *I am learning to select and use strategies and resources before I read, and as I read, to help make the meaning of texts clear.*	• *Reads aloud a familiar piece of text adding expression and can show understanding.* • *Reads an increasing number of common/high frequency words, key reading words, core topic words and words of personal significance.* • Uses a range of word recognition strategies independently. • Decodes unknown words by locating and pronouncing familiar letter patterns and blends. • Uses context clues to read and understand texts. • Uses punctuation and grammar to read with understanding and expression.
2	**ENG 2-12a / 3-12a / 4-12a** Through developing my knowledge of context clues, punctuation, grammar and layout, I can read unfamiliar texts with increasing fluency, understanding and expression. **LIT 2-13a** *I can select and use a range of strategies and resources before I read, and as I read, to make meaning clear and give reasons for my selection.* **LIT 4-13a** *Before and as I read, I can apply strategies and use resources independently to help me read a wide variety of texts and/or find the information I need.*	• *Reads with fluency, understanding and expression using appropriate pace and tone.* • Uses knowledge of context clues, punctuation, grammar and layout to read unfamiliar texts with understanding. • *Applies a range of reading skills and strategies to read and understand texts, for example, skimming, scanning, predicting, clarifying and/or summarising.*

FINDING AND USING INFORMATION

when reading and using fiction and non-fiction texts with increasingly complex ideas, structures and specialist vocabulary

LIT 0-14a I use signs, books or other texts to find useful or interesting information and I use this to plan, make choices or learn new things.	• Finds information in a text to learn new things. • Shows an awareness of a few features of fiction and non-fiction texts when using/choosing texts for particular purposes.	**E**
LIT 1-14a Using what I know about the features of different types of texts, I can find, select, sort and use information for a specific purpose.	• Identifies and finds key information in fiction and non-fiction texts using content page, index, headings, sub-headings and diagrams to help locate information.	**1**
LIT 1-15a I am learning to make notes under given headings and use them to understand information, explore ideas and problems and create new texts.	• Makes notes under given headings for different purposes.	
LIT 2-14a Using what I know about the features of different types of texts, I can find, select and sort information from a variety of sources and use this for different purposes.	• Skims texts to identify purpose and main ideas. • Scans texts to find key information. • Finds, selects and sorts relevant information from a range of sources.	**2**
LIT 2-15a I can make notes, organise them under suitable headings and use them to understand information, develop my thinking, explore problems and create new texts, using my own words as appropriate.	• Makes and organises notes using own words, for the most part. • Uses notes to create new texts that show understanding of the topic or issue.	

UNDERSTANDING, ANALYSING AND EVALUATING

investigating and/or appreciating fiction and non-fiction texts with increasingly complex ideas, structures and specialist vocabulary for different purposes

LIT 0-07a / LIT 0-16a / ENG 0-17a To help me understand stories and other texts, I ask questions and link what I am learning with what I already know.	• Engages with texts read to them. • Asks and answers questions about events and ideas in a text. • Answers questions to help predict what will happen next. • Contributes to discussions about events, characters and ideas relevant to the text.	**E**
LIT 0-19a I enjoy exploring events and characters in stories and other texts, sharing my thoughts in different ways.	• Shares thoughts and feelings about stories and other texts in different ways. • Retells familiar stories in different ways, for example, role play, puppets and/or drawings. • Relates information and ideas from a text to personal experiences.	
LIT 1-16a To show my understanding across different areas of learning, I can identify and consider the purpose and main ideas of a text.	• Identifies the main ideas of texts. • Makes appropriate suggestions about the purpose of a text.	**1**
ENG 1-17a To show my understanding, I can respond to different kinds of questions and other close reading tasks and I am learning to create some questions of my own.	• Answers literal, inferential and evaluative questions about texts. • Asks questions to help make sense of a text.	
LIT 1-18a To help me develop an informed view, I can recognise the difference between fact and opinion.	• Recognises the difference between fact and opinion.	
ENG 1-19a I can share my thoughts about structure, characters and/or setting, recognise the writer's message and relate it to my own experiences, and comment on the effective choice of words and other features.	• Offers own ideas about characters, writer's use of language, structure and/or setting. • Offers own ideas about the writer's message and, when appropriate, relates these to personal experiences.	
LIT 2-16a To show my understanding across different areas of learning, I can identify and consider the purpose and main ideas of a text and use supporting detail.	• Identifies the purpose of a text with suitable explanation. • Identifies the main ideas of a text with appropriate detail. • Makes relevant comments about features of language, for example, vocabulary, sentence structure and punctuation.	**2**
ENG 2-17a To show my understanding, I can respond to literal, inferential and evaluative questions and other close reading tasks and can create different kinds of questions of my own.	• Responds to a range of questions, including literal, inferential and evaluative questions, to demonstrate understanding of texts. • Creates different types of questions to show understanding of texts.	
LIT 2-18a To help me develop an informed view, I can identify and explain the difference between fact and opinion, recognise when I am being influenced, and have assessed how useful and believable my sources are.	• Distinguishes between fact and opinion with appropriate explanation. • Recognises techniques used to influence the reader, for example, word choice, emotive language, rhetorical questions and/or repetition. • Identifies which sources are most useful/reliable.	
ENG 2-19a I can: ▶ discuss structure, characterisation and/or setting ▶ recognise the relevance of the writer's theme and how this relates to my own and others' experiences ▶ discuss the writer's style and other features appropriate to genre.	• Makes relevant comments about structure, characterisation and/or setting with reference to the text. • Relates the writer's theme to own and/or others' experiences. • Makes relevant comments about aspects of the writer's style, use of language and other features appropriate to genre, with reference to the text.	

WRITING

ENJOYMENT AND CHOICE
within a motivating and challenging environment, developing an awareness of the relevance of texts in my life

E | *LIT 0-01a / 0-11a / 0-20a I enjoy exploring and playing with the patterns and sounds of language and can use what I learn.* | • *Writes for enjoyment, exploring patterns and sounds, in a range of play, imaginative and real contexts.*

1 | *LIT 1-20a / 2-20a I enjoy creating texts of my choice and I regularly select subject, purpose, format and resources to suit the needs of my audience.* | • *Creates texts selecting subject, purpose, format and resources for a range of purposes and audiences.*

2 | *LIT 1-20a / 2-20a I enjoy creating texts of my choice and I regularly select subject, purpose, format and resources to suit the needs of my audience.* | • *Creates texts regularly for a range of purposes and audiences selecting appropriate genre, form, structure and style.*

TOOLS FOR WRITING
using knowledge of technical aspects to help my writing communicate effectively within and beyond my place of learning

E | *ENG 0-12a / LIT 0-13a / LIT 0-21a I explore sounds, letters and words, discovering how they work together, and I can use what I learn to help me as I read or write.*

LIT 0-21b As I play and learn, I enjoy exploring interesting materials for writing and different ways of recording my experiences and feelings, ideas and information. |
• *Forms most lowercase letters legibly.*
• *Uses a pencil with increasing control and confidence.*
• *Knows the sounds of lowercase and some uppercase letters.*
• *Leaves a space between words when writing.*
• *Writes words from left to right.*
• *Makes an attempt to spell familiar words correctly.*
• *Makes an attempt to use a capital letter and a full stop in at least one sentence.*

1 | *LIT 1-21a I can spell the most commonly-used words, using my knowledge of letter patterns and spelling rules and use resources to help me spell tricky or unfamiliar words.* |
• *Spells most commonly used words correctly.*
• *Spells most vocabulary used across the curriculum correctly.*
• *Uses knowledge of phonics and spelling strategies when spelling familiar and unfamiliar words.*
• *Uses knowledge of the alphabet to locate words in a dictionary or other reference source to help spell tricky or unfamiliar words.*

LIT 1-22a I can write independently, use appropriate punctuation and order and link my sentences in a way that makes sense. |
• *Writes independently, punctuating most sentences accurately, for example, using a capital letter, full stop, question mark or exclamation mark.*
• *Links sentences using common conjunctions, for example, and, because, but or so.*
• *Starts sentences in a variety of ways to engage the reader.*

LIT 1-23a Throughout the writing process, I can check that my writing makes sense. |
• *Checks writing to ensure it makes sense.*

LIT 1-24a I can present my writing in a way that will make it legible and attractive for my reader, combining words, images and other features. |
• *Presents writing in a clear and legible way using images and other features as appropriate.*

2 | *LIT 2-21a I can spell most of the words I need to communicate, using spelling rules, specialist vocabulary, self-correction techniques and a range of resources.* |
• *Applies knowledge of spelling patterns, rules and strategies to spell most words correctly.*

LIT 2-22a In both short and extended texts, I can use appropriate punctuation, vary my sentence structures and divide my work into paragraphs in a way that makes sense to my reader. |
• *Uses a range of punctuation, for example, capital letters, full stops, commas, inverted commas (speech marks), exclamation marks, question marks and/or apostrophes. Punctuation is mainly accurate.*
• *Writes most sentences in a grammatically accurate way.*
• *Uses sentences of different lengths and types and varies sentence openings.*
• *Links sentences using a range of conjunctions.*
• *Uses paragraphs to separate thoughts and ideas.*
• *Writes in a fluent and legible way.*

LIT 2-23a Throughout the writing process, I can check that my writing makes sense and meets its purpose. |
• *Reviews and corrects writing to ensure it makes sense, is technically accurate and meets its purpose.*

LIT 2-24a I consider the impact that layout and presentation will have and can combine lettering, graphics and other features to engage my reader. |
• *Makes appropriate choices about layout and presentation, including in digital texts, to engage the reader, for example, headings, bullet points, fonts, graphics and/or captions.*

ORGANISING AND USING INFORMATION
considering texts to help create short and extended texts for different purposes

E | *LIT 0-26a Within real and imaginary situations, I share experiences and feelings, ideas and information in a way that communicates my message.* |
• *Writes to convey ideas, messages and information in different ways in play, imaginative and real contexts.*
• *Writes to reflect own experiences and feelings using appropriate vocabulary to convey meaning.*

LIT 1-25a *I am learning to use my notes and other types of writing to help me understand information and ideas, explore problems, generate and develop ideas or create new text.*	• *Plans and organises ideas and information using an appropriate format.* • *Makes notes to help plan writing and uses them to create new texts.*	**1**
LIT 1-26a *By considering the type of text I am creating,[4] I can select ideas and relevant information, organise these in a logical sequence and use words which will be interesting and/or useful for others.*	• *Includes relevant information in written texts.* • *Organises writing in a logical order and as appropriate to audience.* • *Uses relevant and/or interesting vocabulary as appropriate for the context.*	
LIT 2-25a *I can use my notes and other types of writing to help me understand information and ideas, explore problems, make decisions, generate and develop ideas or create new text.* *I recognise the need to acknowledge my sources and can do this appropriately.*	• *Uses notes and/or other sources to develop thinking and create new texts.* • *Acknowledges sources making clear where the information came from.*	**2**
LIT 2-26a *By considering the type of text I am creating, I can select ideas and relevant information, organise these in an appropriate way for my purpose and use suitable vocabulary for my audience.*	• *Organises information in a logical way.* • *Selects relevant ideas and information.* • *Uses appropriate vocabulary, including subject-specific vocabulary, to suit purpose and audience.*	

CREATING TEXTS
applying the elements which writers use to create different types of short and extended texts with increasingly complex ideas, structures and vocabulary

LIT 0-09b / 0-31a *I enjoy exploring events and characters in stories and other texts and I use what I learn to invent my own, sharing these with others in imaginative ways.*	• *Invents own stories and characters to share with others in play, imaginative and real contexts.* • *Shares feelings, experiences, information, messages or ideas in pictures, print or digital texts.*	**E**
LIT 1-28a / LIT 1-29a *I can convey information, describe events or processes, share my opinions or persuade my reader in different ways.*	• *Creates a variety of texts for different purposes.* *When writing to convey information, describe events or processes, share opinions or persuade readers in different ways:* • *Selects, organises and conveys information in different ways.* • *Uses vocabulary and language for specific purposes.* • *Shares own viewpoint and makes one or two attempts to persuade the reader as appropriate to the purpose.*	**1**
ENG 1-30a I can describe and share my experiences and how they made me feel. **ENG 1-31a** Having explored the elements which writers use in different genres, I can use what I learn to create my own stories, poems and plays with interesting structures, characters and/or settings.	When writing to describe and share experiences: • Writes about personal experiences in a logical order, using appropriate vocabulary to describe feelings, thoughts and events. When writing imaginatively and creatively: • Creates own texts, for example, stories, poems and plays, with recognisable features of genre. • Creates texts with evidence of structure. • Creates interesting characters through their feelings and actions and physical description.	
ENG 2-27a *I am learning to use language and style in a way which engages and/or influences my reader.*	• *Creates a range of short and extended texts regularly for different purposes.* • *Attempts to engage and/or influence the reader through vocabulary and/or use of language as appropriate to genre.*	**2**
LIT 2-28a *I can convey information, describe events, explain processes or combine ideas in different ways.*	*When writing to convey information, describe events, explain processes or combine ideas in different ways:* • *Uses appropriate style and format to convey information applying key features of the chosen genre.* • *Includes relevant ideas, knowledge and information.* • *Organises and presents information in a logical way.* • *Uses tone and vocabulary appropriate to purpose.*	
LIT 2-29a *I can persuade, argue, explore issues or express an opinion using relevant supporting detail and/or evidence.*	*When writing to persuade, evaluate, explore issues or express an opinion:* • *Presents relevant ideas and information, including supporting detail, to convey view point.* • *Organises ideas in a logical way.* • *Includes an introduction that makes the topic clear and a conclusion that rounds off the writing.* • *Attempts to use language to influence or persuade the reader, for example, word choice, punctuation, repetition, rhetorical questions and/or emotive language.*	
ENG 2-30a As I write for different purposes and readers, I can describe and share my experiences, expressing what they made me think about and how they made me feel. **ENG 2-31a** Having explored the elements which writers use in different genres, I can use what I learn to create stories, poems and plays with an interesting and appropriate structure, interesting characters and/or settings which come to life.	When writing to describe and share experiences: • Describes personal experiences, making context and events clear. • Describes thoughts and feelings about the experience. • Attempts to engage and/or influence the reader through vocabulary and/or use of language. When writing imaginatively and creatively: • Applies a few features of the chosen genre. • Creates interesting characters through, for example, their feelings and actions, physical description and/or dialogue. • Creates setting/context with some descriptive detail. • Attempts to use figurative language (imagery) to engage the reader, for example, simile, metaphor, alliteration and onomatopoeia. • Creates plots with clear structures, for example, suitable opening, turning point, climax and/or satisfactory ending.	

4 These will include the range of texts and media described in the principles and practice paper.

LISTENING AND TALKING

ENJOYMENT AND CHOICE
within a motivating and challenging environment, developing an awareness of the relevance of texts in my life

E	*LIT 0-01a / LIT 0-11a / LIT 0-20a I enjoy exploring and playing with the patterns and sounds of language, and can use what I learn.* *LIT 0-01b / LIT 0-11b I enjoy exploring and choosing stories and other texts to watch, read or listen to, and can share my likes and dislikes.*	• Participates in and recalls songs, rhymes and stories which support the learning of Gaelic language in a total immersion setting. • Listens to stories to help learn Gaelic, recognising and repeating familiar words and phrases, answering questions on the content with a decreasing reliance on English, using an appropriate range of strategies to support their acquiring fluency. • Recognises/uses/ repeats with accuracy words and phrases in Gaelic and demonstrates understanding through responses. • Identifies the different single sounds and the sounds made by a combination of letters of the Gaelic alphabet, for example mh, bh, th, str. • Identifies sounds learned within words. • Listens and responds to stories and other texts, sharing likes and dislikes using Gaelic words and phrases.
	LIT 0-01c I enjoy exploring events and characters in stories and other texts, sharing my thoughts in different ways.	• Engages with characters and events in stories, songs, role-play and texts in different ways, for example, using re-enacting and/or using puppets/prompts.

		1st Level:	2nd Level:
1 2	*LIT 1-01a / 2-01a I regularly select and listen to or watch texts which I enjoy and find interesting, and I can explain why I prefer certain sources.* *I regularly select subject, purpose, format and resources to create texts of my choice.*	• Selects and participates actively in songs, rhymes and stories which supports the learning of Gaelic language in a wider range of contexts. • Answers questions on a variety of texts to demonstrate understanding and preference. • Gives a reason for preferring particular texts, including those watched or listened to.	• Selects spoken texts regularly for enjoyment or to find information for a specific purpose. • Explains preferences for certain texts or sources.

TOOLS FOR LISTENING AND TALKING
to help me when interacting or presenting within and beyond my place of learning

E	*GAI 0-02a As I listen and take part in conversations, I discover new words and phrases. I use these to help talk to, play and work with others.* *LIT 0-02a / GAI 0-03a As I listen and talk in different situations, I am learning to take turns and am developing my awareness of when to talk and when to listen.*	• Listens to, demonstrates an understanding of and repeats new words and phrases from the use of Gaelic in a total immersion setting across a variety of contexts. The learner is becoming confident in their use of Gaelic in social situations and routines, such as when having snack. • Responds appropriately to questions, instructions and directions given in Gaelic relating to familiar situations in the playroom and classroom. • Uses songs, poems, rhymes and role-plays to show how they are developing a new language. • Talks about personal experiences and familiar situations using Gaelic words and phrases in a variety of contexts, including with adults and other children • Listens and responds to others, including following and giving simple instructions. • Makes an attempt to take turns when listening and talking in a variety of contexts. • Makes an attempt to use appropriate body language when listening to others, for example, eye contact. • Listens to the Gaelic that is being modelled by adults for accuracy and development, and repeats what is being said.
1	*GAI 1-02a As I listen and take part in conversations, I can use new words and phrases to help me to communicate.* *LIT 1-02a When I engage with others, I know when and how to listen, when to talk, how much to say, when to ask questions and how to respond with respect.* *GAI 1-03a I am exploring how pace, gesture, expression, emphasis and choice of words are used to engage others, and I can use what I learn.*	• Incorporates new Gaelic words and phrases into language appropriate for the audience with accuracy of pronunciation. • Shares appropriate ideas, opinions, information and experiences at an appropriate pace with clarity of expression and appropriate tone of voice. • Takes turns to speak, contributes at the appropriate time when engaging with others and is increasingly aware of the different roles within a group and is willing to take on these different roles. • Listens and responds appropriately to the views of others for example, by nodding or agreeing, asking and answering questions in a respectful way. • Applies a few techniques (verbal and non-verbal) when engaging with others for example, vocabulary, eye contact, facial expressions and/or body language.
2	*GAI 2-02a As I listen and take part in conversations, I can use new words, phrases and Gàidhlig idiom to help me to engage in a coherent manner using extended vocabulary and more complex language structures.* *LIT 2-02a When I engage with others, I can respond in ways appropriate to my role, show that I value others' contributions and use these to build on thinking.*	• Contributes a number of relevant ideas, information and opinions when engaging with others. • Shows respect for the views of others and offers own viewpoint. • Builds on the contributions of others for example, by asking or answering questions, clarifying points or supporting others' opinions or ideas. • Uses features of Gaelic language correctly and with increasing accuracy for example, grammatical structures and irregular verbs. • Incorporates a range of vocabulary, phrases and idiom into language appropriate for the audience and across curricular areas. • Applies features of spoken language in own oral presentations and interactions clearly for example, vocabularly, eye contact, body language, emphasis, pace and/or tone.
	GAI 2-03a I can recognise how the features of spoken language can help in communication, and I can use what I learn. I can recognise different features of my own and others' spoken language.	• Recognises and uses some techniques to engage or influence the listener, for example, word choice, emphasis, tone and/or rhetorical questions.

[3] This may include images, objects, audio, visual or digital resources.

FINDING AND USING INFORMATION
when listening to, watching and talking about texts with increasingly complex ideas, structures and specialist vocabulary

LIT 0-04a I listen or watch for useful or interesting information and I use this to make choices or learn new things.	• Conveys an understanding of something watched or listened to, and uses this information to make choices or learn new vocabulary within the context of a total immersion setting.	**E**
LIT 1-04a As I listen or watch, I can identify and discuss the purpose, key words and main ideas of the text, and use this information for a specific purpose. **LIT 1-05a** As I listen or watch, I am learning to make notes under given headings and use these to understand what I have listened to or watched and create new texts. **LIT 1-06a** I can select ideas and relevant information, organise these in a logical sequence and use words which will be interesting and/or useful for others.	• Identifies and discusses the purpose of texts, watched or listened to. • Asks and answers a range of questions to inform their understanding of a text. • Identifies and discusses the key ideas of spoken texts and uses the information gathered for a specific purpose such as recounting an experience or recalling an event. • Makes short notes under headings for texts listened to or watched, demonstrating understanding, and can use these for different purposes. • Uses own notes in a logical sequence to create new texts.	**1**
LIT 2-04a As I listen or watch, I can identify and discuss the purpose, main ideas and supporting detail contained within the text, and use this information for different purposes. **LIT 2-05a** As I listen or watch, I can make notes, organise these under suitable headings and use these to understand ideas and information and create new texts, using my own words as appropriate. **LIT 2-06a** I can select ideas and relevant information, organise these in an appropriate way for my purpose and use suitable vocabulary for my audience.	• Identifies the purpose of spoken texts with straightforward explanation. • Identifies and demonstrates understanding of the key ideas of a variety of spoken texts, with supporting detail, and uses the information gathered for a specific purpose. • Makes relevant notes, using a wide range of Gaelic vocabulary and chosen formats, and uses these to create new spoken texts for a range of purposes.	**2**

UNDERSTANDING, ANALYSING AND EVALUATING
investigating and/or appreciating texts with increasingly complex ideas, structures and specialist vocabulary for different purposes

LIT 0-07a / LIT 0-16a / GAI 0-17a To help me understand stories and other texts, I ask questions and link what I am learning with what I already know.	• Asks and answers different types of questions to show understanding of a range of texts using Gaelic. • Makes simple predictions about what happens next in texts. • Talks about own experiences as linked to the text and to aid understanding.	**E**
LIT 1-07a I can show my understanding of what I listen to or watch by responding to and asking different kinds of questions. **LIT 1-08a** To help me develop an informed view, I am learning to recognise the difference between fact and opinion.	• Asks and responds to different types of questions which shows understanding of the main ideas of texts listened to or watched. • Recognises simple differences between fact and opinion in spoken texts.	**1**
LIT 2-07a I can show my understanding of what I listen to or watch by responding to literal, inferential, evaluative and other types of questions, and by asking different kinds of questions of my own. **LIT 2-08a** To help me develop an informed view, I can distinguish fact from opinion, and I am learning to recognise when my sources try to influence me and how useful these are.	• Identifies and discusses the main features of texts, using technical language to show an understanding of a range of texts. • Asks and responds to literal, inferential and evaluative questions to inform their understanding. • Recognises the differences between fact and opinion giving appropriate explanation.	**2**

CREATING TEXTS
applying the elements others use to create different types of short and extended texts with increasingly complex ideas, structures and vocabulary

LIT 0-09a Within real and imaginary situations, I share experiences and feelings, ideas and information in a way that communicates my message. **LIT 0-09b / 0-31a** I enjoy exploring events and characters in stories and other texts and I use what I learn to invent my own, sharing these with others in imaginative ways. **LIT 0-10a** As I listen and take part in conversations and discussions, I discover new words and phrases which I use to help me express my ideas, thoughts and feelings.	• Shares experiences, feelings, ideas and thoughts with others, talking clearly and logically, using words, phrases and simple sentences • Uses a range of Gaelic vocabulary and phrases which is added to through different contexts. • Invents and shares own stories in different ways, for example, using puppets, as part of imaginary play, using Gaelic words and phrases. • Retells a story in a logical sequence using Gaelic words and phrases as well as mime and role-play to aid learners' developing language. • Relates information and ideas from a text to personal experiences using Gaelic words and phrases.	**E**
LIT 1-09a When listening and talking with others for different purposes, I can exchange information, experiences, explanations, ideas and opinions, and clarify points by asking questions or by asking others to say more. **LIT 1-10a** I can communicate clearly when engaging with others within and beyond my place of learning, using selected resources[3] as required.	• Engages with others for a range of purposes, communicating clearly and audibly. • Contributes to group/class discussions in a meaningful way, asking and answering questions. • Creates spoken texts, embedding appropriately new vocabulary and phrases on topics related to different areas of the curriculum. • Selects and shares ideas/information using appropriate vocabulary in a logical order and is mindful of audience.	**1**
LIT 2-09a When listening and talking with others for different purposes, I can: ▸ share information, experiences and opinions ▸ explain processes and ideas ▸ identify issues raised and summarise main points or findings ▸ clarify points by asking questions or by asking others to say more. **LIT 2-10a** I am developing confidence when engaging with others within and beyond my place of learning. I can communicate in a clear, expressive way and I am learning to select and organise resources independently.	• Communicates confidently and fluently, with some expression in different contexts. • Plans and delivers organised presentations/talks on topics related to those being studied as part of the curriculum, with appropriate content and logical sequence and structure. • Uses an appropriate range of vocabulary for purpose and audience. • Applies verbal and non-verbal skills to communicate clearly, for example, eye contact, body language, pace and tone. • Selects and uses resources as appropriate to support communication including digital technology.	**2**

READING

ENJOYMENT AND CHOICE
within a motivating and challenging environment, developing an awareness of the relevance of texts in my life

E	*LIT 0-01a / LIT 0-11a / LIT 0-20a I enjoy exploring and playing with the patterns and sounds of language and can use what I learn.*	• Recalls songs, rhymes and poems, as part of learning and exploring a new language through total immersion.
	LIT 0-01b / LIT 0-11b I enjoy exploring and choosing stories and other texts to watch, read or listen to, and can share my likes and dislikes.	• Chooses a story, book or text to share with others by making use of the illustrations as visual cues to understand what is happening. • Chooses and discusses a variety of texts and can share likes and dislikes • Listens to stories being read aloud, using pictures and repetitive parts of the story to help anticipate and predict what is going to happen.
1	*LIT 1-11a / 2-11a I regularly select and read, listen to or watch texts which I enjoy and find interesting, and I can explain why I prefer certain texts and authors.*	• Selects books and other texts using, for example, cover, title, author, illustrator and/or blurb. • Selects regularly texts for different purposes including for enjoyment and to support the development of language. • Explains preferences for particular texts and authors.
2	*LIT 1-11a / 2-11a I regularly select and read, listen to or watch texts which I enjoy and find interesting, and I can explain why I prefer certain texts and authors.*	• Selects texts regularly for a range of purposes including for enjoyment or to find information for a specific purpose. • Explains preferences for particular texts, authors or sources with supporting detail which offers a personal response.

TOOLS FOR READING
to help me use texts with increasingly complex or unfamiliar ideas, structures and vocabulary within and beyond my place of learning

E	*GAI 0-12a / LIT 0-13a / LIT 0-21a I explore sounds, letters and words, discovering how they work together, and I can use what I learn to help me as I read and write.*	• Understands that print is read from left to right and top to bottom and knows the difference between a letter, word and space. • Hears and says sounds, letters, and uses blending and patterns in Gaelic language to read new words and recognises these words when part of text. • Recognises some common words and reads aloud simple texts, including the labelling in the learning environment and demonstrates understanding. • Reads aloud familiar short texts, for example, labels and snack menu with attention to simple punctuation. • Uses context clues and illustrations to support understanding of words and different texts.
1	*GAI 1-12a I can use my knowledge of sight vocabulary, phonics, context clues, punctuation and grammar to read with understanding and expression.* *LIT 1-13a I am learning to select and use strategies and resources before I read, and as I read, to help make the meaning of texts clear.*	• Reads aloud a familiar piece of text adding appropriate expression and demonstrating understanding. • Reads with increased fluency an increasing number of common/high frequency words, key reading words, core topic words, words being learnt through immersion and words of personal significance. • Independently uses a range of word recognition strategies to read and develop fluency. • Decodes unknown words by locating familiar letter patterns and blends. • Uses context clues to read and understand texts. • Uses punctuation and grammar to help read with understanding and expression. • Uses resources such as age-appropriate glossaries, word lists, dictionary and thesaurus to support understanding of texts.
2	*GAI 2-12a / 3-12a / 4-12a Through developing my knowledge of context clues, punctuation, grammar and layout, I can read unfamiliar texts with increasing fluency, understanding and expression.* *LIT 2-13a I can select and use a range of strategies and resources before I read, and as I read, to make meaning clear and give reasons for my selection.*	• Reads fluently and with expression, using appropriate pace and tone, demonstrating understanding of the text. • Uses knowledge of context clues, grammar, punctuation and layout along with reading strategies, to read unfamiliar texts with understanding. • Applies a range of reading skills and strategies to read and understand texts for example, skimming, scanning, predicting, clarifying and/or summarising. • Makes appropriate predictions about texts with supporting evidence. • Uses strategies and resources to read and understand and clarify unfamiliar vocabulary, for example use a dictionary.

FINDING AND USING INFORMATION
when reading and using fiction and non-fiction texts with increasingly complex ideas, structures and specialist vocabulary

LIT 0-14a I use signs, books or other texts to find useful or interesting information and I use this to plan, make choices or learn new things.	• *Finds simple information in a text to learn new things* • *Makes choices based on what has been read or watched to learn new things.* • *Recognises some words in the environment by their shape or feature.* • *Shows an awareness of a few features of fiction and non-fiction texts when using and choosing texts for a particular purpose.*	**E**
LIT 1-14a Using what I know about the features of different types of texts, I can find, select, sort and use information for a specific purpose. *LIT 1-15a I am learning to make notes under given headings and use them to understand information, explore ideas and problems and create new texts.*	• *Identifies the key features of fiction and non-fiction books.* • *Finds key information from fiction and non-fiction texts using content page, index, headings, sub-headings, and diagrams to help locate information.* • *Makes notes to show understanding, under given headings, for different purposes.*	**1**
LIT 2-14a Using what I know about the features of different types of texts, I can find, select and sort information from a variety of sources and use this for different purposes. *LIT 2-15a I can make notes, organise them under suitable headings and use them to understand information, develop my thinking, explore problems and create new texts, using my own words as appropriate.*	• *Skims texts to identify purpose and main ideas.* • *Scans texts to find key information.* • *Finds, sorts and selects relevant information from a range of sources including digital texts.* • *Makes and organises notes using own words, for the most part.* • *Uses notes to create new texts that demonstrate an understanding of the topic or issue.*	**2**

UNDERSTANDING, ANALYSING AND EVALUATING
investigating and/or appreciating fiction and non-fiction texts with increasingly complex ideas, structures and specialist vocabulary for different purposes

LIT 0-07a / LIT 0-16a / GAI 0-17a To help me understand stories and other texts, I ask questions and link what I am learning with what I already know. *LIT 0-19a I enjoy exploring events and characters in stories and other texts, sharing my thoughts in different ways.*	• *Engages with texts read to them.* • *Retells familiar stories in different ways for example, role-play, puppets, and drawings.* • *Asks and answers questions about events and ideas in a text.* • *Answers questions to help predict what will happen next.* • *Discusses characters and events relevant to the text.* • *Shares thoughts and feelings about stories and other texts in different ways.* • *Relates information and ideas from a text to personal experiences.*	**E**
LIT 1-16a To show my understanding across different areas of learning, I can identify and consider the purpose and main ideas of a text. *GAI 1-17a To show my understanding, I can respond to different kinds of questions and other close reading tasks and I am learning to create some questions of my own.* *LIT 1-18a To help me develop an informed view, I can recognise the difference between fact and opinion.* *GAI 1-19a I can share my thoughts about structure, characters and/or setting, recognise the writer's message and relate it to my own experiences, and comment on the effective choice of words and other features.*	• *Identifies and can discuss the main ideas of a variety of texts.* • *Makes appropriate suggestions about the purpose of the text.* • *Answers literal, inferential and evaluative questions about texts.* • *Asks questions to help make sense of a text.* • *Identifies the key features of fiction and non-fiction texts.* • *Recognises the difference between fact and opinion.* • *Offers own ideas about aspects of characters, writer's use of language, structure and/or setting.* • *Offers own ideas about writer's message and theme and when appropriate relates it to personal experiences.*	**1**
LIT 2-16a To show my understanding across different areas of learning, I can identify and consider the purpose and main ideas of a text and use supporting detail. *GAI 2-17a To show my understanding, I can respond to literal, inferential and evaluative questions and other close reading tasks and can create different kinds of questions of my own.* *LIT 2-18a To help me develop an informed view, I can identify and explain the difference between fact and opinion, recognise when I am being influenced, and have assessed how useful and believable my sources are.* *GAI 2-19a I can:* ▸ discuss structure, characterisation and/or setting ▸ recognise the relevance of the writer's theme and how this relates to my own and others' experiences ▸ discuss the writer's style and other features appropriate to genre.	• *Identifies the purpose of texts with appropriate explanation.* • *Identifies the key ideas of a text with appropriate detail.* • *Makes relevant comments about simple features of language for example, word choice, sentence structure and punctuation.* • *Responds appropriately to a range of questions including, literal, inferential and evaluative questions to demonstrate understanding of texts.* • *Creates different types of questions to show understanding of texts.* • *Distinguishes between fact and opinion with appropriate explanation.* • *Recognises techniques used to influence the reader for example, word choice, emotive language, rhetorical questions and repetition.* • *Recognises and can explain which sources are most useful/ accurate.* • *Makes relevant comments, to show an understanding of techniques, for example, use of language, theme, style, structure, characterisation and/or setting, making predictions with supporting evidence from the text.* • *Relates the writer's theme to own and/or others' experiences.*	**2**

WRITING

ENJOYMENT AND CHOICE
within a motivating and challenging environment, developing an awareness of the relevance of texts in my life

E	*LIT 0-01a / LIT 0-11a / LIT 0-20a I enjoy exploring and playing with the patterns and sounds of language and can use what I learn.*	• Explores writing through a range of imaginary and real-life contexts, for example, through play, shopping lists, labels, signs. • Uses a range of stimuli to develop ideas for writing, for example, talk, songs, pictures, objects, own experiences and role-play. • Shares feelings, experiences, information, messages or ideas in pictures and print.
1	*LIT 1-20a / 2-20a I enjoy creating texts of my choice and I regularly select subject, purpose, format and resources to suit the needs of my audience.*	• Creates texts for a range of purposes and audiences. • Makes choices about words and language structures, format and resources.
2	*LIT 1-20a / 2-20a I enjoy creating texts of my choice and I regularly select subject, purpose, format and resources to suit the needs of my audience.*	• Writes regularly for a range of purposes and audiences selecting appropriate genre, form, structure and style.

TOOLS FOR WRITING
using knowledge of technical aspects to help my writing communicate effectively within and beyond my place of learning

E	*GAI 0-12a / LIT 0-13a / LIT 0-21a I explore sounds, letters and words, discovering how they work together, and I can use what I learn to help me as I read or write.* *LIT 0-21b As I play and learn, I enjoy exploring interesting materials for writing and different ways of recording my experiences and feelings, ideas and information.*	• Forms most lowercase and upper case letters correctly and legibly. • Uses a pencil with increasing control and confidence • Recites the alphabet sounds in order, recognising the names and sounds for lowercase and some uppercase letters. • Leaves a space between words when writing. • Understands that words are written from left to right. • Uses letters, sounds and phonemes to help spell and construct words, with common words spelt correctly. • Uses wall-charts, books, picture dictionaries or asks someone to support spelling and writing. • Recognises within a text simple punctuation such as full stop and question marks. • Uses a capital letter and a full stop correctly.
1	*LIT 1-21a I can spell the most commonly-used words, using my knowledge of letter patterns and spelling rules and use resources to help me spell tricky or unfamiliar words.*	• Spells most commonly used words correctly. • Spells vocabulary being used across the curriculum with accuracy, for example, topic work, reading book. • Uses knowledge of phonic and spelling strategies when spelling familiar and unfamiliar words. • Uses knowledge of the alphabet to locate words in a dictionary, or other reference sources, to help spell tricky or unfamiliar words.
	LIT 1-22a I can write independently, use appropriate punctuation and order and link my sentences in a way that makes sense.	• Writes independently, punctuating most sentences accurately using a capital letter, full stop, question mark, commas and/or exclamation marks as appropriate. • Links sentences using common conjunctions for example, and, because, but, when. • Starts sentences in a variety of ways, to engage the reader, making appropriate use of tenses. • Uses adjectives, ambitious words, appropriate and differing lengths of sentences.
	LIT 1-23a Throughout the writing process, I can check that my writing makes sense.	• Proof-reads work, recognises spelling errors and applies strategies to ensure writing makes sense.
	LIT 1-24a I can present my writing in a way that will make it legible and attractive for my reader, combining words, images and other features.	• Presents writing in a clear and legible way using joined up writing, images, digital technology and other features as appropriate, as well as presenting writing through.
2	*LIT 2-21a I can spell most of the words I need to communicate, using spelling rules, specialist vocabulary, self-correction techniques and a range of resources.*	• Applies knowledge of spelling patterns, rules and strategies to spell most words correctly. • Uses resources, including dictionaries and digital technology, to support spelling.
	LIT 2-22a In both short and extended texts, I can use appropriate punctuation, vary my sentence structures and divide my work into paragraphs in a way that makes sense to my reader.	• Uses a range of punctuation for example, capital letters, full stops, commas, inverted commas (speech marks), exclamation marks, question marks and apostrophes. Punctuation is mainly accurate. • Writes most sentences in a grammatically accurate way, for example, merges verbal nouns with separate pronouns in a sentence. • Uses sentences of different lengths and types and varies sentence beginnings. • Links sentences using a range of conjunctions. • Uses paragraphs confidently to link separate thoughts and ideas. • Writes in a fluent and legible way.
	LIT 2-23a Throughout the writing process, I can check that my writing makes sense and meets its purpose.	• Reviews and corrects writing to ensure it makes sense, is technically accurate, including using accents appropriately. and meets its purpose.
	LIT 2-24a I consider the impact that layout and presentation will have and can combine lettering, graphics and other features to engage my reader.	• Makes appropriate choices about layout and presentation, to engage the reader including in digital texts, for example, headings, bullet points, font, graphics and captions.

---

4   These will include the range of texts and media described in the principles and practice paper.

ORGANISING AND USING INFORMATION considering texts to help create short and extended texts for different purposes

LIT 0-26a Within real and imaginary situations, I share experiences and feelings, ideas and information in a way that communicates my message.	• *Talks about and attempts to write about a range of experiences and feelings using such strategies as ordering pictures, magnetic letters, voice-assisted technology and writing.*	**E**
LIT 1-25a I am learning to use my notes and other types of writing to help me understand information and ideas, explore problems, generate and develop ideas or create new text.	• *Plans and organises ideas and information using an appropriate format.* • *Makes notes to help plan writing and uses them to create new text.*	**1**
LIT 1-26a By considering the type of text I am creating,[4] I can select ideas and relevant information, organise these in a logical sequence and use words which will be interesting and/or useful for others.	• *Includes relevant information in writing to make meaning clear.* • *Organises writing appropriate to audience and in a logical sequence, using relevant and/or interesting Gaelic vocabulary.*	
LIT 2-25a I can use my notes and other types of writing to help me understand information and ideas, explore problems, make decisions, generate and develop ideas or create new text. *I recognise the need to acknowledge my sources and can do this appropriately.*	• *Uses notes and a variety of texts across the curriculum to develop thinking and create new texts.* • *Selects relevant ideas and information.* • *Acknowledges sources appropriately making clear where the information came from.*	**2**
LIT 2-26a By considering the type of text I am creating, I can select ideas and relevant information, organise these in an appropriate way for my purpose and use suitable vocabulary for my audience.	• *Organises information in a logical way.* • *Uses appropriate vocabulary, including subject-specific vocabulary, to suit purpose and audience*	

CREATING TEXTS
applying the elements which writers use to create different types of short and extended texts with increasingly complex ideas, structures and vocabulary

LIT 0-09b / LIT 0-31a I enjoy exploring events and characters in stories and other texts and I use what I learn to invent my own, sharing these with others in imaginative ways.	• *Uses common Gaelic words to create simple sentences.* • *Creates own stories and characters, using a range of visual and oral strategies, for example drawing, print or digital texts.*	**E**
LIT 1-28a / LIT 1-29a I can convey information, describe events or processes, share my opinions or persuade my reader in different ways.	• *Creates a variety of texts for different purposes.* *When writing to convey information, describe events or processes, share opinions or persuade readers in different ways:* • *Selects, organises and conveys information in different ways.* • *Uses vocabulary learned from a range of contexts and texts across the curriculum appropriately in writing.* • *Shares own viewpoint and makes use of vocabulary and language to attempt to persuade the reader as appropriate to the purpose.*	**1**
GAI 1-30a I can describe and share my experiences and how they made me feel. GAI 1-31a Having explored the elements which writers use in different genres, I can use what I learn to create my own stories, poems and plays with interesting structures, characters and/or settings.	When writing to describe and share experiences: • Writes about personal experiences in a correct sequence, using appropriate Gaelic vocabulary to describe feelings, thoughts and events. When writing imaginatively and creatively: • Creates own texts for example, simple stories, poems and plays with recognisable features of genre. • Creates texts with evidence of structure. • Creates interesting characters through their feelings and actions and physical description.	
GAI 2-27a I am learning to use language and style in a way which engages and/or influences my reader.	• *Creates a range of short and extended texts regularly for different purposes.* • Attempts to engage and/or influence the reader through word choice and/or use of language.	
LIT 2-28a I can convey information, describe events, explain processes or combine ideas in different ways.	*When writing to convey information, describe events, explain processes or combine ideas in different ways:* • *Uses appropriate style and format to convey information applying key features of the chosen genre.* • *Includes relevant ideas, knowledge and information.* • *Organises and presents information in a logical way.* • *Uses tone and vocabulary appropriate to purpose.*	
LIT 2-29a I can persuade, argue, explore issues or express an opinion using relevant supporting detail and/or evidence.	*When writing to persuade, evaluate, explore issues or express an opinion:* • *Presents relevant ideas and information, including supporting detail, to convey view point.* • *Organises information in a logical way.* • *Uses linking words or phrases as appropriate.* • *Includes an introduction that makes the topic clear and a conclusion that rounds off the writing.* • *Attempts to use language to influence or persuade the reader for example, word choice, punctuation, repetition, rhetorical questions and/or emotive language.*	**2**
GAI 2-30a As I write for different purposes and readers, I can describe and share my experiences, expressing what they made me think about and how they made me feel.	When writing to describe and share experiences: • Describes personal experiences, making context and events clear. • Uses suitable vocabulary to describe thoughts and feelings. • Attempts to engage and/or influence the reader through vocabulary and/or use of language.	
GAI 2-31a Having explored the elements which writers use in different genres, I can use what I learn to create stories, poems and plays with an interesting and appropriate structure, interesting characters and/or settings which come to life.	When writing imaginatively and creatively: • Applies key features of chosen genre appropriately • Creates interesting character/s through for example, their feelings and actions, physical description, and/or dialogue. • Creates setting/context with some descriptive detail. • Attempts to use figurative language (imagery) to engage the reader, for example, simile, metaphor, alliteration and onomatopoeia • Creates plots with clear structures for example, suitable opening, turning point, climax and/or satisfactory ending.	

MODERN LANGUAGES
PRINCIPLES & PRACTICE

WHAT CAN LEARNING IN MODERN LANGUAGES ENABLE CHILDREN AND YOUNG PEOPLE TO ACHIEVE?

Learning other languages enables children and young people to make connections with different people and their cultures and to play a fuller part as global citizens.

Learning through the languages area of the curriculum enables children and young people to:

▶ develop their ability to communicate their thoughts and feelings and respond to those of other people

▶ develop the high level of skills in listening, talking, reading and writing which are essential for learning, work and life

▶ use different media effectively for learning and communication

▶ develop a secure understanding of how language works, and use language well to communicate ideas and information in English and other languages

▶ exercise their intellectual curiosity by questioning and developing their understanding, and use creative and critical thinking to synthesise ideas and arguments

▶ enhance their enjoyment and their understanding of their own and other cultures through literature and other forms of language

▶ develop competence in different languages so that they can understand and communicate including, for some, in work settings.

Building the Curriculum 1

It is important for the nation's prosperity that young people are attracted to learning a modern language and that they become confident users of a modern language, well equipped with the skills needed in the new Europe and in the global marketplace. This framework of experiences and outcomes is intended to help to address this national need.

Through their planning of a wide and rich range of learning activities in modern languages to develop literacy and language skills teachers will support children and young people to become:

▶ **successful learners,** who can reflect on how they have acquired and learned their first language and how this can assist them in further language learning

▶ **confident individuals,** who, through experiencing success and support, can interact with others in real-life situations, talk about topics of personal interest and deliver presentations in their new language

▶ **effective contributors,** who can work in individual, paired and group situations, and establish and maintain contact with other speakers of the target language

▶ **responsible citizens,** who have a growing awareness of life in another society and of the issues facing citizens in the countries where their new language is spoken.

The ability to use language lies at the centre of thinking and learning. The interconnected nature of language learning lies at the heart of the modern languages experiences and outcomes.

By the time they begin their study of a modern language, learners will have acquired their home language(s) and will have begun to study English in a school context. Both primary and secondary teachers are in an ideal position to help children and young people to reflect on what they have already achieved in English and in other home or community languages (for example, how to listen, speak, read, write and how to understand phonics), and how this will help them to learn a new language. However, the learning of a new language also provides the opportunity to help learners to reflect on their first language and actively seek comparisons between the features of their first and second languages. In this way, teachers of modern languages have a unique contribution to make in helping learners not only to reflect on the skills required to learn a new language, but also to revisit, improve and understand more securely aspects of literacy in their first language.

The study of a modern language has a unique contribution to make to the development of cultural awareness as it provides children and young people with a means of communicating directly with people from different cultures, enhancing their understanding and enjoyment of other cultures and of their own. They gain insights into other ways of thinking and other views of the world and therefore develop a much richer understanding of active citizenship.

One of the key aims of modern languages teaching is to develop young people's 'communicative competence' so that they are able to use and enjoy the language effectively in real situations and for a range of relevant purposes in work and leisure throughout their life.

STRUCTURE OF FRAMEWORK

The introductory statements for modern languages highlight three key aims of learning modern languages which make a unique contribution to the aims of Curriculum for Excellence: the interconnected nature of languages, active citizenship and communicative competence.

The experiences and outcomes for modern languages are described at second, third and fourth levels. Schools and centres which implement an earlier start should work towards the outcomes described at second level, providing children with stimulating opportunities for early achievement of some or all of the second level outcomes and, in the longer term, opportunities for depth and breadth of learning.

In order to make clear the links between learning in English, Gaelic, Gàidhlig and modern languages, the experiences and outcomes in all of these areas are organised within the same structure. The organisers are:

▸ **listening and talking**
▸ **reading**
▸ **writing.**

Experiences and outcomes within each organiser are subdivided to group together similar skills. Teachers will use these lines of development to support and track progression in each skill across the three levels.

The level of achievement at the fourth level has been designed to approximate to that associated with SCQF level 4.

USEFUL APPROACHES TO LEARNING & TEACHING

How does the framework promote effective teaching and learning where children start their learning of a modern language before P6?

Although Primary 6 is currently the most common point at which pupils begin to learn a modern language, many children begin earlier, including in pre-school. The experiences and outcomes take account of differing starting points.

At early and at first levels, children will be developing generic skills in their first language. These include taking part in conversations, developing listening, reading and writing skills and knowledge about language. All of these are relevant to learning other languages. Within modern languages at these stages teachers will build on children's natural curiosity for sounds and words, and their strong desire to communicate. Activities will include playing games, singing songs, carrying out simple instructions, and playing with simple poetry and rhyme. In this way they can begin to be enthusiastic, confident language learners from the outset.

Whenever they start their learning of another language, children need to experience success by taking part in practical activities that they can enjoy. Language learning is greatly enhanced where it is linked to or embedded in the wider curriculum so that children and young people can enjoy exploring and using language in meaningful contexts. Very importantly, teachers can make great use of opportunities to link language learning with progress in English and with other languages used by people in the school community, enabling children to explore and experiment with sound patterns and make links and comparisons between languages.

What does the framework mean more generally for teachers?

Learning in the modern languages provides opportunities to create relevant, coherent, enjoyable and successful learning experiences which include the following four elements:

▸ awareness of the skills required to be an effective learner of languages

▸ awareness of social, cultural and geographical aspects of the countries where a particular language is spoken

▸ knowledge about language structures that allows the learner to check the accuracy of her/his language use and to create new language

▸ the ability to communicate in relevant and realistic contexts.

As children and young people develop their modern language skills, teachers will plan to achieve an appropriate balance between the development of language learning skills and the development of competence in the new language. This may involve changing the balance of these four elements: the first two of these elements being more predominant in the earlier stages of language learning and the final two being more predominant in later language learning.

The open-ended nature of the experiences and outcomes allows for creativity and flexibility and allows primary teachers to focus on teaching methodologies for skills development and for a deeper understanding without having to plan for too much content/topic coverage.

The statements of experiences and outcomes provide support to primary teachers as they plan to:

▸ establish a solid basis for the lifelong learning of modern languages

▸ ensure that young people experience success and retain initial enthusiasm

▸ achieve balance between coverage of language content and development of effective language learning skills

▸ discuss similarities and differences of how pupils have acquired and learned their first or home language and how this impacts on the learning of a second language

▸ encourage young people to investigate and report back on aspects of culture and geography.

As teachers use these statements of experiences and outcomes to support their planning, by the end of Primary 7, the majority of children will have learned the skills necessary to:

▸ give a short presentation about themselves
▸ take part in simple conversations and transactions
▸ understand classroom instructions and personal information
▸ enjoy listening to a story, song or poem
▸ read aloud a simple text
▸ read and understand a short text
▸ write a few sentences about themselves and others.

The framework supports secondary teachers in liaising closely with primary teachers to build not only on what has been achieved but also on the learning experiences with which children and young people will be increasingly familiar.

By embedding the principles of Assessment is for Learning within their classrooms, teachers will encourage young people to reflect on, to take increasing ownership of and to assume more responsibility for their own learning; they will make use of self-assessment to identify their strengths and development needs from the evidence of their efforts and act on feedback given from peers as well as teachers in order to plan their next steps.

The statements of experiences and outcomes provide support to secondary teachers as they plan to:

▶ create meaningful relevant contexts for learning including the appropriate use of ICT

▶ develop interdisciplinary projects where appropriate to build on collaborative learning

▶ make clear the links between the learning and teaching of modern languages and other areas of the young people's learning, including enterprise, international education and citizenship

▶ establish an acceptable level of competence approximating to SCQF Level 4 and achievable by most pupils by end of S3.

How can effective use of information and communications technology (ICT) help to improve learning and teaching?
Curriculum for Excellence offers an opportunity to further develop learning and teaching experiences that are relevant and enjoyable. This includes making effective use of information and communication technology to enhance teaching and learning, and to provide real-life contexts that motivate children and young people and help them to see a purpose to their language learning. Online research by teachers and learners alike will help them to develop their knowledge, understanding and appreciation of the culture surrounding the language which they are learning, and the use of ICT can bring them directly into contact with people from around the world.

Will the framework help to address the need for our young people to be equipped with high levels of language learning skills? Are we 'raising the bar' in terms of what we expect from our learners?
We are certainly raising the bar to the extent that, without placing a 'ceiling' on higher levels of achievement, we expect the majority of young people to achieve by the end of S3 a level of performance in each language skill which approximates to the level of performance associated with SCQF level 4. The achievement of fourth level outcomes represents a substantial and useful level of competence closely linked to Basic User level on the Common European Framework of Reference for Languages (CEFR).

PROGRESSION

The experiences and outcomes for modern languages are described at second, third and fourth levels. The outcomes embody an appropriate level of proficiency at each level but do not place a ceiling on achievement. The range of experiences within the framework allows for different rates of progression.

Within the modern languages framework young people will demonstrate their progression as they move through levels in terms of:

▶ increasing independence and reduced level of support, including peer or teacher support, and support through

wordlists and dictionaries

▶ increasing length and complexity of text and task in listening and reading

▶ increasing length, complexity and accuracy of response in talking and writing

▶ new areas of language content and language use (personal, transactional, language related to the world of work and to the culture of the countries in which the language is spoken)

▶ increasing awareness of language rules, including knowledge about language

▶ increasing confidence in taking the initiative (including asking for help) and sustaining communication.

BROAD FEATURES OF ASSESSMENT

Assessment in modern languages will focus on children and young people's progress in developing and applying their skills in listening, talking, reading and writing.

Teachers can gather evidence of progress as part of day-to-day learning during individual and collaborative activities, for example engaging in relevant conversation or correspondence with peers and adults about people, places and daily life where the language is spoken, and through talks, writing, and presentations, using ICT as appropriate. Specific assessment tasks will also be valuable in assessing progress. From the time when children and young people begin their learning of a modern language through to the senior stages, they will demonstrate progress in their skills in communication and language learning, in their knowledge about language structure, and in their awareness of social, cultural and geographical aspects.

Approaches to assessment should identify the extent to which children and young people can apply these skills in their learning and their daily lives and in preparing for the world of work. For example:

▶ How well do they contribute to discussions?

▶ Are they increasingly able to extract key information from texts?

Assessment of progress in modern languages involves making judgements about the success of children and young people in extending and using their vocabulary, increasing their comprehension of the written and spoken word, developing their understanding of language structures and rules and applying these accurately in familiar and new real-life situations, including in social contexts or in giving instructions or directions. For example, they:

▶ communicate with increasing confidence, accuracy and fluency

▶ demonstrate through responses their enthusiasm and motivation for modern language learning and their developing cultural and international awareness.

Assessment should promote enthusiasm, motivation and willingness to try out the language in other areas of the curriculum and beyond school. These will be indicators of children and young people's long-term success as modern language learners and global citizens.

ALLOTING TIME TO MODERN LANGUAGES

There are no specific input requirements in terms of time allocations. The emphasis in modern languages is on ensuring that each learner achieves an acceptable level of proficiency in the language. This level of proficiency is linked to Basic User Level of the CEFR. The national expectation is that almost all young people study modern languages to the third level as part of their general education for our young people. This may be achieved in different ways:

> *Curriculum for Excellence* allows for both professional autonomy and responsibility when planning and delivering the curriculum ... The framework provides flexibility to organise, schedule and deliver the experiences and outcomes in ways that meet the needs of all learners, but also provides reassurance about consistency where necessary.
>
> Such flexibility will result in a more varied pattern of curriculum structures to reflect local needs and circumstances.
>
> *Building the Curriculum 3*

CONNECTIONS WITH OTHER AREAS OF THE CURRICULUM

The study of any modern language plays a central role in the development of literacy skills. It can also contribute to the development of numeracy skills through, for example, learning and exploring the use of the number system in a new language. Learning a modern language provides opportunities for interdisciplinary work by providing a global dimension to a variety of curriculum areas and, particularly, to the areas of active citizenship and cultural awareness. Making connections between different areas of learning and developing relevant course content will be important in attracting our young people to learning a modern language.

CONNECTIONS WITH OTHER FRAMEWORKS FOR LANGUAGE LEARNING

The framework provides an opportunity for children and young people's achievement to be recognised at second, third and fourth levels. The level of achievement at fourth level is broadly equivalent to that associated with Scottish Credit and Qualifications Framework (SCQF) Level 4.

Curriculum for Excellence levels have been linked to those being developed as part of the CEFR so that the level of competence achieved by learners will have a European-wide equivalence. The CEFR comprehensively describes what language learners have to learn to do in order to use a language for communication and defines levels of proficiency which allow learners' progress to be measured at each stage of learning on a lifelong basis.

EXPERIENCES & OUTCOMES

Learning a new language encourages children and young people to broaden their horizons as they explore the language and its associated culture.

Through my learning of a new language:

▸ I gain a deeper understanding of my first language and appreciate the richness and interconnected nature of languages
▸ I enhance my understanding and enjoyment of other cultures and of my own and gain insights into other ways of thinking and other views of the world
▸ I develop skills that I can use and enjoy in work and leisure throughout my life.

The study of language plays an important role in all language learning and the development of literacy skills.

I develop and extend my literacy skills when I have opportunities to:

▸ communicate, collaborate and build relationships
▸ reflect on and explain my literacy and thinking skills, using feedback to help me improve and sensitively provide useful feedback for others
▸ engage with and create a wide range of texts in different media, taking advantage of the opportunities offered by ICT
▸ develop my understanding of what is special, vibrant and valuable about my own and other cultures and their languages
▸ explore the richness and diversity of language, how it can affect me and the wide range of ways in which I and others can be creative
▸ extend and enrich my vocabulary through listening, talking, watching and reading.

[NOTE ON FIRST LEVEL EXPERIENCES & OUTCOMES]

The original (2009) Es & Os did not include Experiences and Outcomes for First Level, and the content for other levels differed. The revised framework was included in the original version of the Benchmarks (March 2017). The original Es & Os are included as an appendix to *Curriculum for Excellence: Complete Edition* (see back cover).

LISTENING AND TALKING

LISTENING FOR INFORMATION

1	**MLAN 1-01a** I explore the patterns and sounds of language through songs and rhymes and show understanding verbally or non-verbally	• Participates actively in songs, rhymes and poems in the target language. • Identifies some rhyming words. • Recalls selected 'missing' words/phrases in songs, rhymes or poems which have been well-practised and with the support of, for example, pictures and/or puppets.
	MLAN 1-01b I am learning to take an active part in daily routines, responding to simple instructions which are accompanied by gesture and expression.	• Demonstrates understanding of simple classroom instructions through, for example, physical movement, pointing, gesture, symbols, or responding in the target language.
	MLAN 1-01c I can listen to and show understanding of language from familiar voices and sources.	• Demonstrates understanding of familiar words and simple phrases conveying mostly personal information.
2	**MLAN 2-01a** I explore the patterns and sounds of language through songs and rhymes and show understanding and enjoyment by listening, joining in and responding.	• Participates actively in songs, rhymes and poems in the target language. • Demonstrates understanding of songs and rhymes through, for example, retelling, appropriate gestures and mimes. • Identifies rhyming words. • Predicts 'missing' words from familiar songs, rhymes or poems. • Recalls and can repeat parts of well-known songs or rhymes, sometimes with the support of, for example, pictures or gestures.
	MLAN 2-01b I take an active part in daily routines, responding to instructions which are accompanied by gesture and expression.	• Demonstrates understanding of a range of classroom instructions through, for example, physical movement, carrying out some tasks or responding in the target language.
	MLAN 2-01c I can listen to and show understanding of familiar instructions and language from familiar voices and sources.	• Demonstrates understanding of familiar words and phrases in increasingly full sentences/phrases which convey information about familiar contexts, for example, self, home, family, school.

LISTENING AND TALKING WITH OTHERS

1	**MLAN 1-02a** I am beginning to identify key information from a short predictable conversation and react with words and/or gesture.	• Responds appropriately to simple questions about themselves using simple sentences, words and gestures, for example, nodding and/or pointing.
	MLAN 1-02b I am beginning to share information about myself using familiar vocabulary and basic language structures.	• Shares simple, personal information about themselves on familiar topics, for example, when expressing likes or dislikes, • Uses a few simple adjectives such as those related to size or colour and attempts to use some connectors, for example and, with.
	MLAN 1-03 With support I am becoming an active listener and can understand, ask and answer simple questions to share information.	• Listens and responds at the appropriate time to others by answering and asking simple questions in the target language. • Uses some polite social terms to begin and end interactions.
	MLAN 1-05a I enjoy listening to stories, songs, rhymes and poems in the language I am learning by joining in and responding to show my understanding.	• Gives a personal response to stories, songs, rhymes and poems in the target language. • Can translate simple/key words and phrases from the target language into their own language. • Demonstrates understanding of songs, rhymes, poems and games in the target language through appropriate actions, gestures and mime.
	MLAN 1-05b I can participate in a range of collaborative activities.	• Collaborates with others in a range of activities, for example, short role plays, animated/recorded dialogues, games and performances.
2	**MLAN 2-02a** I explore how gesture, expression and emphasis are used to help understanding. I can listen and respond to familiar voices in short, predictable conversations using straightforward language and non-verbal techniques as appropriate such as gesture and eye contact.	• Responds appropriately to questions about him/herself using sentences, phrases, words and gestures such as nodding and/or pointing. • Applies non-verbal techniques when engaging with others, for example, eye contact, facial expressions and/or body language.
	MLAN 2-03a When listening and talking with others, I am developing an awareness of when to listen and when to talk. I am learning new words which I use to share information about myself and others.	• Shares personal information on familiar topics such as expressing likes or dislikes with increasing confidence and accuracy. Speaks increasingly in fuller sentences/phrases, using basic connectors such as 'and, but, with, because'. • Uses a number of familiar adjectives such as those related to describing self and others. • Listens and responds at the appropriate time to others by answering and asking simple questions, applying previously rehearsed language. • Uses polite social terms to begin and end interactions. • Talks, for example, about him/herself and others, with an increasing range of vocabulary.

MLAN 2-03b I can take part effectively in prepared conversations by sharing information about myself and others or interests of my choice, using familiar vocabulary and basic language structures.	• Listens, takes turns and contributes appropriately when engaging with others in increasingly sustained conversations and role-plays, albeit using simple and familiar language structures. • Responds appropriately to the views of others, by asking and answering questions in the target language about familiar topics, for example about likes/dislikes in terms of food and drink, sport, school subjects, local community. • Is able to begin and end conversations appropriately.
MLAN 2-04a I can ask for help confidently using learned phrases and familiar language.	• In the target language, requests that others, for example, 'repeat' or 'slow down'.
MLAN 2-05a I explore simple songs and rhymes and I enjoy learning with others as we talk and listen together.	• Demonstrates understanding of songs and rhymes in the target language through appropriate repetition of key words or sections, actions, gestures and mime. • Uses contextual clues to infer the meaning of any new vocabulary.
MLAN 2-05b I can participate in familiar collaborative activities including games, paired speaking and short role plays.	• Collaborates with others to play a variety of games in the target language such as playground games, board and card games in digital and traditional formats. • Participates in paired speaking activities and role-plays with support, for example, from pictures or symbols. • Works collaboratively on speaking tasks in the target language, conveying personal information and information about others. Sustains conversations long enough to demonstrate understanding and use of basic structures and familiar vocabulary in different contexts.

ORGANISING AND USING INFORMATION

MLAN 1-06 Through a variety of media, I am developing an awareness of social, cultural and geographical aspects of locations in a country where the language I am learning is spoken.	• Identifies the location of the country and some main geographical features, for example, the capital city, important landmarks, the national flag(s). • Demonstrates understanding of basic cultural references to the country/countries where the target language is spoken. This may include, for example, references to food or national celebrations. • Identifies some similarities and differences between Scotland and the country/countries where the target language is spoken, for example, the school day, the climate or different currencies.
MLAN 2-06a I can deliver a brief presentation on a familiar topic using familiar language and phrases.	• Presents to group or class, in the target language, a brief presentation on a theme which interests him/her using, for example, pictures, power point, podcast or video recording as support. Sustains presentations long enough to demonstrate accuracy in pronunciation and expression appropriate to the level.
MLAN 2-06b I have worked with others, using a variety of media including ICT where appropriate, and can contribute successfully to a presentation in English, supported by use of the language I am learning, on an aspect of life in a country where the language I am learning is spoken.	• Works collaboratively to demonstrate understanding of cultural aspects of the country/countries where the target language is spoken via a presentation on a theme of his/her choice. • Can identify some similarities and differences between Scotland and the country/countries where the target language is spoken, such as differences in school systems, foods, how festivals are celebrated.

USING KNOWLEDGE ABOUT LANGUAGE

MLAN 1-07a I am beginning to explore similarities and differences between sound patterns in different languages through play, rhymes, songs and discussion.	• Identifies sounds, letters and patterns to read words contained in familiar rhymes, songs and/or short texts. • Uses words which are similar in English to support understanding of unfamiliar words. • Recognises familiar words in different contexts in, for example, well-known short stories, games and rhymes.
MLAN 1-07b I can use my knowledge about language and pronunciation to ensure that others can understand me when I say familiar words and phrases.	• Pronounces familiar words clearly to support communication, for example, when talking about themselves, giving details such as name, age, family, pets, favourite colours/foods/animals.
MLAN 2-07a I explore comparisons and connections between sound patterns in different languages through play, discussion and experimentation.	• Applies knowledge of sounds/phonics in the target language to support pronunciation and understanding of words, sounds, letters and patterns to read familiar words in texts and attempts unfamiliar words and phrases with increasing confidence and accuracy. • Uses words that are similar in different languages and contextual clues to support understanding of unfamiliar words. • Recognises familiar words in different contexts, for example, in short stories, games and rhymes.
MLAN 2-07b I can use my knowledge about language and pronunciation to ensure that others can understand me when I read aloud or say familiar words, phrases and short texts.	• Pronounces familiar words clearly to support communication. • Applies phonics knowledge and pronunciation rules of the target language to pronounce unfamiliar words with increasing confidence and accuracy. Adds expression to show understanding when reading familiar texts.

Design: © Harold Raitt / SeeHearTeach.scot (2019)   Content: © Crown copyright (2017)

READING

FINDING AND USING INFORMATION

1

MLAN 1-08a I can recognise labels and environmental print. I am beginning to organise images and text. With support, I can sequence images and text to demonstrate my understanding.

- Reconstructs a known text /story in a logical sequence, using for example, simple words, pictures, labels, puppets or props to show understanding of written text in the target language.
- Matches images with appropriate word/ text in the target language.

MLAN 1-08b I can work on my own or with others to demonstrate my understanding of words and phrases containing familiar language.

- Shows understanding of an increasing number of phrases, core topic words and words of personal significance, alone or in text.

2

MLAN 2-08a I work on my own and with others to understand text using appropriate resources, demonstrating my understanding by matching written words to pictures and by reconstructing the text in a logical sequence, for example.

- Matches images to appropriate text in the target language.
- Uses context clues to read and understand the meaning of texts in the target language containing unfamiliar words.
- Sequences pictures/labels to order key events in a text written in the target language.
- Summarises the text in English.

MLAN 2-08b I can read and demonstrate understanding of of words, signs, phrases and simple texts containing mainly familiar language.

- Shows understanding of an increasing number of common/high frequency words, such as core topic words, and phrases, seen either individually or within a text. For example, this might include language used when describing others or free time activities. It may also include vocabulary connected to interdisciplinary themes where opportunities to understand or use the target language are integral to the tasks involved.

READING TO APPRECIATE OTHER CULTURES

1

MLAN 1-09a I am beginning to recognise similarities and differences between Scotland and a country where the language I am learning is spoken, using varied simple texts, visual prompts and media.

- Identifies some key cultural differences between Scotland and the country/countries where the language is spoken through visual texts with simple vocabulary, for example, video clips or texts supported by pictures.

2

MLAN 2-09a I work on my own and with others to read and discuss simple texts in the language I am learning. I can share simple facts about features of life in some of the countries where the language I am learning is spoken.

- Demonstrates understanding of a range of simple texts appropriate to the level, including photographs, maps, artefacts and artworks in the target language by, for example, explaining to others the gist of the text in English, noting down facts from the text in English, or answering some questions in English about the texts they have read. Identifies cultural differences and similarities between Scotland and the target language country/countries.

READING FOR INTEREST AND ENJOYMENT

1

MLAN 1-10a I have experienced a variety of simple texts, which may have been adapted for young learners.

- Demonstrates understanding of simple texts in the target language through, for example, retelling some details in English, selecting and sequencing appropriate images, matching activities or talking about the bits they liked best.

2

MLAN 2-10a I can choose and can read, on my own and with others, a variety of straightforward texts of different types, including non-fiction, short imaginative accounts, prose and poetry, which may have been adapted.

- Demonstrates understanding of texts in both familiar and unfamiliar contexts which are written mainly in the present tense and come from a range of genre.
- Expresses opinions in English about texts they have read in the target language.

USING KNOWLEDGE ABOUT LANGUAGE

1

MLAN 1-11a I am beginning to use illustrated word-banks, picture prompts, picture dictionaries and displays to support my understanding of simple texts.

- Uses a variety of familiar resources to support their understanding of simple texts.

2

MLAN 2-11a I can understand how a bilingual dictionary works and use it with support.

- Uses a bilingual dictionary to support understanding of unfamiliar vocabulary in the target language and to cross-check words or phrases they have written in the target language. Can explain the similarities and differences between using a monolingual and bilingual dictionary.

MLAN 2-11b I can make comparisons and explore connections between spelling patterns in English and the language I am learning.

- Identifies words in the target language which are similar in different languages to support understanding of unfamiliar words.
- Applies knowledge of alphabetical order to locate words in a dictionary or other reference source to help spell tricky or unfamiliar words.
- Applies understanding of the different sounds made by letters and letter blends in the target language.

MLAN 2-11c I experiment with new language, working out the meaning of words and phrases using vocabulary I have learned so far.

- Decodes unfamiliar vocabulary and structures using knowledge of spelling patterns in the target language and through recognition of similar words in English.

MLAN 2-11d I can recognise and comment on other features of my own language which help to make sense of words in the language I am learning.

- Identifies parts of speech such as nouns, adjectives, adverbs, verbs after discussion in English.
- Applies this knowledge of grammatical structures as appropriate when reading in the target language to support comprehension.

WRITING

ORGANISING AND USING INFORMATION

MLAN 1-13 With support, I am beginning to experiment with writing in the language I am learning.	• Creates simple new texts based around the familiar words and phrases practised during talking, listening and reading activities, using support materials, for example, word banks, picture dictionaries, and/or writing frames. • Shows some awareness of punctuation and accents and attempts to use them when writing in the target language. • Writes simple phrases to convey personal information, labels in the target language for objects in the classroom and around the school.	**1**

MLAN 2-12a / **3-12a** / **4-12a** I use the support of others and access appropriate reference materials of my choice to help me plan my writing in ways that engage my reader, using ICT when appropriate.
 	
MLAN 2-13a I have opportunities to express myself in writing, exploring and experimenting with words and phrases using resources, to ensure my writing makes sense.
 	
MLAN 2-13b I can use familiar language to describe myself and to exchange straightforward information.
 	
MLAN 2-14a¹ I use my knowledge about language and success criteria to help me, and I can check that I have written familiar words and phrases accurately.
	• Works with others to plan and check written work.
	• Uses support such as a bilingual dictionary, word banks, cloze activities or writing frames to produce written text in the target language.
	• Uses ICT when appropriate to check words and to produce written text in different formats
	• With support from reference materials, produces written work in the target language which is mostly accurate in terms of basic grammar such as use of verbs, adjectives and word order.
	• Writes for a variety of purposes and audiences.
	• Produces written work in the target language which is mostly accurate in terms of:
	  – Punctuation
	  – Spelling
	  – Accents.
		2

USING KNOWLEDGE ABOUT LANGUAGE

No Experiences and Outcomes at First Level

MLAN 2-14a I use my knowledge about language and success criteria to help me, and I can check that I have written familiar words and phrases accurately.	[The benchmarks for MLAN 2-14a are found under the 'Organising and Using Information' organiser.]	**2**

---

¹ [This is the order in *Benchmarks*. In *Es & Os*, and contextually, MLAN 2-14a belongs, with 3-14a/4-14a, under 'Using Knowledge About Language'.]

APPENDIX - EXPLANATIONS

The first level outcomes are fewer in number and reflect the early stages of language development, where the emphasis is on oral and aural skills. The information below is a guide to some of the expectations of each skill at first and second level.

LISTENING FOR INFORMATION

The expectation in this skill at first level in the L2[1] (first additional language) is that children will be able to understand and take part in daily routines and respond verbally and non-verbally to simple instructions, which are embedded through frequent repetition and support from the class teacher. They will be able to explore the language they are learning through songs, stories and rhymes (e.g. MLAN 1-01a; MLAN 1-01b).

The expectation at second level is that children will be able to understand an increasing range of everyday expressions relating to personal details and classroom instructions (familiar language) and enjoy listening to a story, song or poem to engage their interest (e.g. MLAN 2-01a). They may need to listen several times to get the information they require depending on how fast and how clearly the speaker talks.[2]

This ensures opportunities to build on literacy skills already being developed in English. (For advice on the role of Gaelic Medium Education please refer to *The Role of Gaelic Education 3-18 in 'Language Learning in Scotland: A 1+2 Approach'*[3]).

LISTENING AND TALKING WITH OTHERS

At first level, the expectation is that children will be able to take part in simple conversations to share information using familiar language and basic structures (e.g. MLAN 1-02a; MLAN 1-02b).

From second level onwards, learners will take part in conversations (e.g. MLAN 2-02a/MLAN 2-03b), in collaborative / transactional situations (e.g. MLAN 2-05b) and in presentations (e.g. MLAN 2-06a/MLAN 2-06b), while being able to ask for help and support as necessary (e.g. MLAN 2-04a) and while ensuring pronunciation is sufficiently accurate to be understood by a sympathetic native speaker (e.g. MLAN 2-07b).

The expectation at second level is that learners will be able to give a short presentation about themselves, take part in simple conversations and transactions, and read aloud a simple text. Their pronunciation will not always be completely accurate but their meaning will be clear.

READING

At first level, children will be able to demonstrate understanding of simple texts and environmental print. They should begin to develop strategies to link the written and spoken word. With support, learners will be begin to use illustrated word-banks and other similar resources (e.g. MLAN 1-11a)

From second level, learners will read text in order to use and find information (e.g. MLAN 2-08b), to appreciate other cultures (e.g. MLAN 2-09a) and for interest and enjoyment (e.g. MLAN 2-10a), while developing a range of reading strategies including the use of dictionary (e.g. MLAN 2-11a), knowledge of English and, possibly, other languages with which they are familiar (e.g. MLAN 2-11b/MLAN 2-11d) and knowledge of the target language (e.g. MLAN 2-11c).

At second level, children will be able to understand the main points from a short written text presented in traditional print form or electronically, and draw upon a range of support including glossaries, word lists, peer and teacher support.

WRITING

At first level the expectation is that children will begin to experiment with writing in L2[1] in any appropriate form and will be able to build on the writing skills they use in English. This will be by primary 4 for most but earlier for some. (For advice on the role of Gaelic Medium Education, please refer to *The Role of Gaelic Education 3-18 in 'Language Learning in Scotland: A 1+2 Approach'*[3])

The expectation at second level is that learners will be able to write a few sentences about themselves and others using expressions which they have already learned and, with support, including writing frames, peer and teacher input, demonstrate an awareness of the writing system of the L2[1].

Across all levels, learners will write in order to describe themselves and exchange straightforward information (e.g. MLAN 1-13a. MLAN 2-13b). From second level onwards, learners will be developing an increasing awareness of the accuracy required in writing information previously used in speaking (e.g. MLAN 2-14a).

TERMINOLOGY WHICH IS OPEN TO DIFFERENT INTERPRETATIONS

MLAN 2-10a A text, spoken or written, may be seen as the medium through which ideas, experiences, opinions and information can be communicated. Text is made more demanding and more complex by the content, the length, the density of sentence structure and the range of vocabulary and structures.

---

[1] Note these experiences and outcomes may also be used to benchmark progress in L3 – the second additional language.
[2] [The original (2009) Es & Os also stated 'They should be aware of how people address each other both formally and informally' at this point.]
[3] [At the time of going to press, broken links at education.gov.scot meant this document did not seem to be available directly from Education Scotland. Other similarly titled documents were easier to find. The document in question is (the editor believes) an undated, 11- page document, which is included as an appendix to *Curriculum for Excellence: Complete Edition* (see back cover).]

GAELIC (LEARNERS)

PRINCIPLES & PRACTICE

WHAT CAN LEARNING GAELIC ENABLE CHILDREN AND YOUNG PEOPLE TO ACHIEVE?

Learning Gaelic as an additional language contributes to learners' wider education and life experiences.

Language lies at the centre of our thinking and learning. The interconnected nature of language learning lies at the heart of the Gaelic (learners) experiences and outcomes in *Curriculum for Excellence*:

> When they begin to learn another language, children and young people need to make connections with the skills and knowledge they have already developed in their own language. To help this, teachers can make use of the diversity of languages which children and young people may bring to school.
>
> *Building the Curriculum 1*

By the time they begin their study of Gaelic, children will have acquired their home language(s) and will have begun to study English in a school context. Both primary and secondary teachers will support children and young people to reflect on what they have already achieved in English and in other home or community languages and will help them understand how this helps them to learn Gaelic. Learners will also recognise the links between Gaelic and English through, for example, place names.

The study of Gaelic supports learners to gain a deeper understanding of Gaelic language, culture and heritage. Children and young people will enjoy Gaelic as a living language with a rich culture and heritage. Teachers will use the framework of experiences and outcomes to heighten the awareness children and young people have of what is special, vibrant and valuable about Gaelic culture and heritage.

As children and young people use Gaelic in real and relevant contexts, they will see a purpose to their language learning and develop skills that they can use and enjoy in work and leisure throughout their lives.

FRAMEWORK STRUCTURE

The experiences and outcomes for Gaelic (learners) are described from early to fourth levels. These represent an appropriate level of proficiency at each level but do not place a ceiling on achievement. The range of experiences within the framework supports different rates of progression.

Learners' knowledge of Gaelic will range across the spectrum from some who are able to use Gaelic appropriately in limited contexts to those with no Gaelic. Some children will begin to learn Gaelic from the early years of primary while others may start in late primary or early secondary. The framework

provides suitable routes for all learners. This framework can be used in association with the literacy and Gàidhlig framework as appropriate.

The experiences and outcomes in Gaelic use the same organisers as in literacy and Gàidhlig, literacy and English and modern languages. The three organisers are:

▶ **listening and talking**
▶ **reading**
▶ **writing.**

The balance between reading, writing and talking and listening will be different at different stages. Teachers will plan teaching and learning in an integrated way: for example, learners may be engaged in talking to prepare for reading an unfamiliar text, in reading to gather information for a presentation, or talking to prepare for writing.

Experiences and outcomes within each organiser are subdivided to group together similar skills. Teachers will use these lines of development to support and track progression in each skill across the levels. The level of achievement at the fourth level has been designed to approximate to that associated with SCQF level 4.

SUPPORT FOR EFFECTIVE TEACHING AND LEARNING

The structure supports teachers and learners to become aware of:

▶ the links between the study of Gaelic and the four capacities of Curriculum for Excellence
▶ the need to promote a positive attitude to language learning so that pupils retain their initial enthusiasm
▶ the need to develop effective language learning skills for learning languages throughout life
▶ the use of ICT as an effective learning and teaching tool to establish links with Gaelic speakers.

Teachers will use the framework of experiences and outcomes to create relevant, enjoyable, coherent and successful learning experiences which will encourage children and young people to develop:

▶ awareness of the skills required to be an effective learner of languages
▶ awareness of social and cultural aspects of Gaelic culture, heritage and tradition
▶ knowledge about Gaelic language structure and idiom that allows the learner to check the accuracy of her/his language use and to create new language
▶ the ability to communicate in relevant and realistic contexts.

The four elements should be present in the learning experience at all stages but teachers will vary the balance among them to meet the needs of learners at different stages.

WHICH LEARNING AND TEACHING APPROACHES SHOULD BE ADOPTED?

Teachers will draw on a wide and varied range of approaches, including:

▶ active learning and planned, purposeful play

▶ the development of problem-solving skills

▶ the use of appropriate contexts and experiences familiar to children and young people

▶ embedding ICT in all learning and teaching

▶ building on the principles of Assessment is for Learning

▶ both collaborative and independent thinking and learning

▶ developing children and young people's understanding of how they have acquired and learned their first language and how this relates to their study of Gaelic.

Teachers will support learners of Gaelic in developing sufficient confidence to use their newly acquired Gaelic. They will provide opportunities for children and young people to hear, speak, read and write in Gaelic in a variety of contexts whilst accessing a range of texts. To increase learners' confidence and feeling of success, teachers will give them opportunities to practise their newly acquired language with fluent Gaelic speakers as well as with other Gaelic learners.

As teachers use the statements of experiences and outcomes to plan learning, their teaching approaches will:

▶ establish a solid foundation by the end of primary school for the lifelong learning of languages which encourages young people to learn, should they choose, additional languages later

▶ promote enjoyment through games, stories, poems, songs and stimulating tasks, and an awareness of the life and culture of countries where Gaelic is spoken

▶ ensure a smooth transition from P7 into S1 with secondary experience building on prior learning and on learning and teaching approaches.

SUPPORT FOR PROGRESSION

At the early and first levels teachers will build on children's natural curiosity for exploring and enjoying sounds and words and their strong desire to communicate. The experiences and outcomes at these levels are designed with this in mind.

Because the development of skills in listening and talking provides the foundation for the development of reading and writing skills, the experiences and outcomes have been written at early level in an integrated way and are repeated across listening and talking, reading and writing.

In the early years of primary school, children further develop generic skills in their first language which continue to be relevant when learning another language. These include engaging in conversation, developing reading skills, listening skills and knowledge about language. Teachers will ensure that learners take part in enjoyable practical activities, for example playing games or singing songs, and use their growing language skills in the everyday interactions of the classroom. The emphasis at this stage will be on experimenting with and enjoying the new language and building confidence through positive feedback.

Within the Gaelic framework pupils will show their progression as they move through levels in terms of:

▶ increasing independence and reduced level of support, including peer or teacher support, and support through wordlists, dictionaries and writing frames

▶ increasing length and complexity of text and task in listening and reading

▶ increasing length, complexity and accuracy of response in talking and writing

▶ new areas of language content and language use

▶ increasing awareness of language rules, including knowledge about language

▶ increasing confidence in taking the initiative and sustaining communication.

At all levels, the breadth of the experiences and outcomes ensures that learners develop their skills with increasing depth over a range of contexts. Teachers will plan to meet the needs of individuals, recognising that the learning curve for a new language may require additional support at different times.

BROAD FEATURES OF ASSESSMENT

Assessment will focus on children and young people's skills in listening and talking, reading and writing. Teachers will gather evidence of progress as part of children and young people's day-to-day learning as they observe the responses of children and young people engaging in conversation or correspondence with peers and adults, planning and carrying out enquiries about people, daily life and places where Gaelic is spoken, and through talk, writing, and presentations, using ICT as appropriate. Specific assessment tasks will also be helpful periodically to provide evidence of progress.

Approaches to assessment should identify the extent to which children and young people can apply their skills in their learning and their daily lives and in preparing for the world of work. For example:

▶ How capable are they in communicating with increasing confidence, accuracy and fluency?

▶ To what extent are they exploring and enjoying Gaelic poetry and song, and stories of increasing complexity and variety?

▶ Are they extending their vocabulary, developing their understanding of language structures and rules and applying these accurately in familiar and new real-life situations?

Teachers will also observe the progress made by learners in the ways in which they apply their skills in their learning across the curriculum and in cultural activities.

Assessment should link with other areas of the curriculum, within and outside the classroom, offering children and young people opportunities to demonstrate their growing knowledge and skills in Gaelic in a wide range of contexts. Their responses will also show their enthusiasm and motivation for Gaelic learning and their developing cultural awareness. Assessing and promoting these aspects and their willingness to try out Gaelic in other areas of the curriculum and beyond school will be indicators of their long-term success as Gaelic learners.

CONNECTIONS ACROSS THE CURRICULUM

The study of Gaelic plays a central role in the development of literacy skills. It can contribute to the development of numeracy skills through, for example, learning and exploring the use of number systems. It provides valuable opportunities for interdisciplinary work by providing a strong cultural dimension to a variety of curriculum areas such as social studies or expressive arts. Making connections between different areas of learning and developing relevant learning activities will be important in attracting our young people to learning Gaelic and sustaining their interest.

WHAT IS MEANT BY 'TEXTS'

The definition of 'texts' needs to be broad and future proof: therefore within *Curriculum for Excellence*,

> a text is the medium through which ideas, experiences, opinions and information can be communicated.

Reading and responding to literature and other texts play a central role in the development of learners' knowledge and understanding. Texts not only include those presented in traditional written or print form, but also orally, electronically or on film. Texts can be in continuous form, including traditional formal prose, or non-continuous, for example charts and graphs. The literacy and Gàidhlig framework reflects the increased use of multimodal texts, digital communication, social networking and the other forms of electronic communication encountered by children and young people in their daily lives. It recognises that the skills which children and young people need to learn to read these texts differ from the skills they need for reading continuous prose. Examples are given below.

Example of texts

novels, short stories, plays, poems
reference texts
the spoken word
charts, maps, graphs and timetables
advertisements, promotional leaflets
comics, newspapers and magazines
CVs, letters and emails
films, games and TV programmes
labels, signs and posters
recipes, manuals and instructions
reports and reviews
text messages, blogs and social networking sites
web pages, catalogues and directories

In planning for learning in any curriculum area it is important for practitioners to ensure that children and young people encounter a wide range of different types of text in different media. As they progress in their learning, children and young people will encounter texts of increasing complexity in terms of length, structure, vocabulary, ideas and concepts.

EXPERIENCES & OUTCOMES

Learning a new language encourages children and young people to broaden their horizons as they explore the language and its associated culture.

Through my learning of a new language:

▸ I gain a deeper understanding of my first language and appreciate the richness and interconnected nature of languages
▸ I enhance my understanding and enjoyment of other cultures within and outwith Scotland, including Gaelic, and gain insights into other ways of thinking and other views of the world
▸ I develop skills that I can use and enjoy in work and leisure throughout my life.

The study of language plays an important role in all language learning and the development of literacy skills.

I develop and extend my literacy skills when I have opportunities to:

▸ communicate, collaborate and build relationships
▸ reflect on and explain my literacy and thinking skills, using feedback to help me improve and sensitively provide useful feedback for others
▸ engage with and create a wide range of texts in different media, taking advantage of the opportunities offered by ICT
▸ develop my understanding of what is special, vibrant and valuable about my own and other cultures and their languages
▸ explore the richness and diversity of language, how it can affect me and the wide range of ways in which I and others can be creative
▸ extend and enrich my vocabulary through listening, talking, watching and reading.

LISTENING AND TALKING

LISTENING FOR INFORMATION

E	**LGL 0-01a / LGL 0-05a / LGL 0-07a /LGL 0-08a** Through listening to and joining in with story-telling, games, rhymes and songs, I have explored and experimented with sound patterns, words and phrases in Gaelic.	• Participates actively in rhymes, songs, games and storytelling. • Repeats and uses words and simple phrases, for example, *tha mi ag iarraidh deoch, seo leabhar*. • Responds appropriately to basic classroom instructions, particularly those connected to routines. • Uses and demonstrates understanding of Gaelic in basic daily routines.
1	**LGL 1-01a** I can take part in play activities and games linked to simple poems, familiar stories and short role plays, and pronounce familiar Gaelic words and phrases.	• Participates actively in Gaelic songs, rhymes, storytelling and games. • Uses familiar phrases and words in play and game activities. • Recognises words and phrases in simple poems and short role-plays to demonstrate an understanding of Gaelic Language. • Responds appropriately to classroom instructions given in Gaelic. • Recalls favourite songs, poems and rhymes.
2	**LGL 2-01a** I can listen to and show understanding of familiar instructions and language from familiar voices and sources.	• Participates in a range of language activities, for example, teacher exposition, language learning games, stories, short role-plays and presentations which extend vocabulary and phrases. • Demonstrates an understanding of language used in language activities such as games, stories and songs through, for example, appropriate responses, repetition and/or retelling. • Demonstrates an understanding of a variety of listening texts in which they identify individual words and gist, and respond appropriately to questions. • Demonstrates understanding of classroom instructions through appropriate responses.

LISTENING AND TALKING WITH OTHERS

E	**LGL 0-02a** I have explored and experimented with the patterns and sounds of the language and can use what I have learned. **LGL 0-04a** Through daily experiences and play I can listen or watch for interesting or useful information. **LGL 0-01a / LGL 0-05a / LGL 0-07a / LGL 0-08a** Through listening to and joining in with story-telling, games, rhymes and songs, I have explored and experimented with sound patterns, words and phrases in Gaelic.	• Memorises songs, rhymes, poems and enjoys performing these. Repeats words and phrases from songs, rhymes, poems and the use of everyday Gaelic. • Uses words and phrases learned from everyday use of Gaelic, story books, songs and programmes as set phrases as part of language learning. • Recognises and uses accurately changes made in pronunciations within familiar contexts such as songs, for example, *glè mhath* and not *math*. • Responds to simple questions to give personal information about themselves for example, *Is mise ... agus tha mi ceithir*. • Answers simple questions on self, using familiar vocabulary and phrases. • Follows simple instructions and prompts in a range of contexts related to play and routines. • Repeats vocabulary learned from a range of personal topics.
1	**LGL 1-02a** I can respond verbally and non-verbally to a range of requests from teachers and others. **LGL 1-03a** I can use familiar words and phrases to give simple information. **LGL 1-04a** I can ask for help using simple or familiar learned phrases or words. **LGL 1-05a** When joining in with story-telling, games, rhymes, songs and poems in Gaelic, I can use familiar words and simple phrases.	• Listens and responds appropriately to a range of requests from the teacher and others using simple sentences, words and gestures. • Recognises and uses the present tense. • Responds appropriately to simple questions on familiar topics, such as personal information, using simple sentences, words and gestures, for example, *Tha mi ochd. Tha mi a' fuireach ann an Inbhir Nis.* • Shares simple, personal information about themselves on familiar topics, for example, when expressing likes or dislikes using learned words and simple phrases. • Uses simple or familiar learned phrases and words such as to ask for something or help, for example, *Tha mi ag iarraidh uisge.* • Uses a few simple adjectives such as those related to size or colour and some simple connectives, for example and. • Recognises and explains the meaning of individual words learned from poems, songs and stories. • Memorises and uses simple phrases when taking part in conversation. • Uses a few polite social terms to begin and end interactions.
2	**LGL 2-02a** I can listen and respond to familiar voices in short, predictable conversations using straightforward language and/or non-verbal techniques such as gesture and eye contact. **LGL 2-03a** I can take part effectively in prepared conversations by sharing information about myself, others or interests of my choice, using familiar vocabulary and basic language structures.	• Listens and responds appropriately to a range of requests from the teacher and others. • Participates in conversations, responding using straightforward language. • Applies non-verbal techniques when engaging with others, for example, eye contact, facial expressions and/or body language. • Responds appropriately to questions about themselves using learned phrases, sentences and words. • Shares personal information about themselves on familiar topics, for example, when expressing likes or dislikes with confidence. • Applies and uses grammatical rules for example, lenition of initial consonants, the use of the vocative case.

LGL 2-04a I can ask for help confidently, using learned phrases and familiar language. LGL 2-05a I can participate in familiar collaborative activities in Gaelic including games, paired speaking and short role plays.	• Uses the present tense with accuracy and some common past tenses for example, *Chaidh, Bha, Cha robh, Fhuair, Chunnaic.* • Uses the correct forms of pronouns to respond to questions about others for example, *Tha bràthair agam. Tha e deich.* • Uses familiar learned phrases and words connected to themes of interest for example, pets and foods and in using Gaelic as the target language of the classroom and the school. • Uses vocabulary correctly to give more detail for example, colours - *Tha cù dubh agus geal agam.* • Uses learned phrases and familiar language to ask for help and to use Gaelic as the language of the classroom, for example the vocative case in taking the register. • Participates and uses learned phrases in a range of activities with others, for example, games, paired speaking and role-play activities. • Listens and responds appropriately to others by answering and asking simple questions, applying previously rehearsed and memorised language. • Uses a variety of polite social terms to begin and end interactions. • Listens, takes turns and contributes at the appropriate time when engaging with others in increasingly sustained conversations and role-plays. • Responds appropriately to the views of others, by asking and answering questions about familiar contexts for example self, family, friends, school, weather.

ORGANISING AND USING INFORMATION

LGL 0-06a I can listen, watch and use play to explore aspects of Gaelic culture.	• Responds to and takes part in Gaelic cultural activities such as St Andrews Day celebrations, local and national Mod events, or local and play situations connected to Gaelic culture. • Uses information from a spoken text or play activity to explore aspects of Gaelic culture.	E
LGL 1-06a I can listen and respond in different ways to the experiences of others when exploring aspects of Gaelic culture.	• Uses learned words and phrases appropriately to demonstrate understanding when exploring aspects of Gaelic culture. • Responds appropriately, to their own and others' cultural experiences, using words and phrases learned, for example, taking part in local and national Mod events, St Andrews Day celebrations, localised cultural events and in drama and role-play.	1
LGL 2-06a I can deliver a brief presentation on a familiar topic using familiar language and phrases. LGL 2-06b I have worked with others, using ICT and other media where appropriate, and can contribute successfully to a presentation in English, supported by Gaelic vocabulary, on an aspect of Gaelic culture and tradition.	• Presents to a group or class, a theme which interests them or other familiar topic, using for example, pictures, digital technology, flashcards or cue cards as support. • Sustains a brief presentation to demonstrate accuracy with pronunciation and expression. • Uses learned words and phrases appropriately to demonstrate understanding when exploring aspects of Gaelic culture. • Works collaboratively, using digital technology and a range of media, to demonstrate understanding of aspects of Gaelic culture through for example, answering questions using Gaelic, contributing to presentations.	2

USING KNOWLEDGE ABOUT LANGUAGE

LGL 0-01a / LGL 0-05a / LGL 0-07a / LGL 0-08a Through listening to and joining in with story-telling, games, rhymes and songs, I have explored and experimented with sound patterns, words and phrases.	• Responds to simple questions and prompts about self while using familiar vocabulary.	E
LGL 1-07a When reading on my own or with others, I can read familiar words and simple phrases and sentences.	• Identifies and reads, familiar words, simple sentences and phrases learned from a variety of topics both independently and with others.	1
LGL 2-07a I can use my knowledge about language and pronunciation to ensure that others can understand me when I read aloud or say familiar words, phrases and short texts.	• Uses knowledge of sounds, letters and sound patterns to support pronunciation and understanding of words contained in familiar texts. • Pronounces familiar words clearly to support communication. • Responds to questions and prompts using learned vocabulary and phrases. • Recognises familiar words in different contexts in, for example, short stories, games and rhymes. • Applies pronunciation rules to unfamiliar words. • Uses appropriate intonation.	2

READING

FINDING AND USING INFORMATION

E

LGL 0-01a / LGL 0-05a / LGL 0-07a / LGL 0-08a
Through listening to and joining in with story-telling, games, rhymes and songs, I have explored and enjoyed using sound patterns, words and phrases in Gaelic.

- Uses some Gaelic words, for example, asking how someone is, greetings, colours and instructions, as part of play and in daily routines.
- Demonstrates understanding through using illustrations, mime and explanations.

1

LGL 1-08a I have worked on my own and with others and I can demonstrate my understanding of words, signs and phrases containing familiar language.

- Reads familiar words, simple phrases, sentences and short texts independently or with others.
- Responds appropriately to questions asked about simple texts.
- Demonstrates understanding of words and phrases through appropriate responses.
- Matches images with appropriate text.
- Talks about a short text in a familiar context using familiar words and phrases.
- Uses illustrated word banks, picture prompts, picture dictionaries and displays to support understanding of simple texts.

2

LGL 2-08a I have worked on my own and with others to understand texts using appropriate resources. I can read and demonstrate my understanding of sentences and simple texts containing familiar language.

- Reads familiar words, phrases, sentences and short texts about personal and daily situations.
- Responds appropriately to questions asked about texts.
- Demonstrates understanding of words and phrases through appropriate responses.
- Responds to a short text in a familiar context using familiar words and phrases.

READING FOR CULTURAL APPRECIATION

No Experiences and Outcomes at Early Level

1

LGL 1-09a I have worked with others to read and discuss simple Gaelic texts. I can share simple facts about the life of Gaelic communities in Scotland.

- Collaborates with others to read simple Gaelic texts using features of the text to help with understanding the meaning of words.
- Answers questions appropriately on simple texts which demonstrates understanding.
- Finds and shares information in Gaelic from a text relating to aspects of Gaelic culture different in communities.

2

LGL 2-09a I have worked on my own and with others to read and discuss Gaelic texts. I can share simple facts about life in some of the countries where Gaelic and related languages are spoken.

- Reads Gaelic texts using features of the text to support the understanding of less familiar words.
- Answers questions appropriately on texts which demonstrates understanding.
- Finds and shares information from a text relating to aspects of Gaelic culture in countries where Gaelic and related languages are spoken.

READING FOR INTEREST AND ENJOYMENT

No Experiences and Outcomes at Early Level

1

LGL 1-10a I enjoy engaging with simple texts on my own and with others.

- Chooses a story, book or text to share with others.
- Participates in storytelling sessions, using pictures and repetitive parts of the story to anticipate and predict what is going to happen.

2

LGL 2-10a I have selected and can read, on my own and with others, a variety of straightforward texts of different types, which may have been adapted.

- Selects a range of texts to share with others.
- Reads independently and with others a range of texts for different purposes.

USING KNOWLEDGE ABOUT LANGUAGE

E

LGL 0-11a / LGL 0-12a / LGL 0-13a I have explored and experimented with Gaelic words and phrases.

- Recognises and repeats Gaelic sounds in texts.
- Identifies simple Gaelic sound patterns in words.
- Recognises key words in phrases.
- Demonstrates understanding through mime and illustrations, for example.

1

LGL 1-11a I have explored sounds, letters and words, discovering how they work together, and can use what I have learned to help me read.

- Uses knowledge of sounds, letters, blending and patterns in Gaelic language to read new words.
- Recognises some common words and reads aloud simple texts, demonstrating understanding.
- Uses a variety of familiar resources to support understanding of simple texts.
- Applies reading strategies to work out the meaning of words from contexts or illustrations.

2

LGL 2-11a I can understand how a bilingual dictionary works and use it with support.

LGL 2-11b I can make comparisons and explore connections between spelling patterns in English and Gaelic.

LGL 2-11c I can recognise and comment on other features of my own language, which help me to make sense of words in Gaelic.

- Knows how to use a bilingual word list, glossary, digital technology or dictionary to look up the meaning of vocabulary.
- Recognises common words and words from different topics and reads aloud texts, demonstrating understanding.
- Reads and understands texts that incorporate vocabulary and structures learned in both familiar and unfamiliar contexts.
- Reads and demonstrates understanding of texts written in the present tense to which expression is added.
- Reads and demonstrates understanding of sentences which include basic adjectives, adverbs and use of numerals.
- Uses knowledge of sounds, letters and patterns, grammar and structures, in Gaelic, to read and understand words contained in familiar texts.
- Applies reading strategies such as skimming to work out the meaning of words from contexts.

WRITING

ORGANISING AND USING INFORMATION

LGL 0-11a / 0-12a / 0-13a I have explored and experimented with Gaelic words and phrases.	• Selects words from resources such as word banks and word walls to construct simple sentences. • Explores and experiments with letters as part of mark making or play.	E
LGL 1-12a I can write familiar words and simple phrases in Gaelic.	• Writes familiar words and simple phrases, for example, greetings on a card or invitation, labelling a picture or a diagram. • Writes simple phrases to convey personal information. • Demonstrates awareness of accents and uses them appropriately when writing.	1
LGL 2-12a I can use familiar language to describe my circumstances and exchange straightforward information. I can make reference to aspects of Gaelic culture and tradition.	• Creates short written texts which convey some information, for example, about themselves and others, the promotion of events such as *Mòd* or *Fèis*, brief social media message or a fact file. • Writes using connected sentences, using simple conjunctions, for example, *agus, o chionn, neo ach*, which reads coherently. Writing is mainly in the present tense with simple adjectives and verbs and use of accents. • Writes to express likes and dislikes. • Writes for communication to be clear on first reading with errors not impeding overall understanding.	2

USING KNOWLEDGE ABOUT LANGUAGE

LGL 0-11a / 0-12a / 0-13a I have explored and experimented with Gaelic words and phrases.	• Selects words from resources such as word banks and word walls to construct simple sentences. • Explores and experiments with letters as part of mark making or play.	E
LGL 1-13a I can use a variety of sources to help me check the accuracy of my Gaelic spelling and punctuation.	• Uses word banks, digital technology, vocabulary lists, classroom displays and support from others to check spelling and accuracy of unfamiliar vocabulary. • Collaborates with peers or the teacher to proof-read and edit writing according to success criteria and targets for improvement.	1
LGL 2-13a I have used my knowledge about language and success criteria to help me, and I can check that I have written familiar words and phrases accurately.	• Demonstrates increasingly accurate use of accents, verbs and adjectives. • Spells most commonly used words correctly, using reference materials for example, word banks, digital technology, vocabulary lists, dictionaries and classroom displays to check the accuracy of spelling and unfamiliar vocabulary of their own and others' written work. • Punctuates most sentences accurately, using punctuation norms. • Works with a peer or the teacher to proof-read and edit writing according to success criteria and targets for improvement.	2

APPENDIX - EXPLANATIONS

Early level – inclusion of sound patterns at early and first level

At early level learners would engage predominantly in oral activities which may include exploring patterns within stories, poems, rhymes and songs. At early level learners will have an awareness of environmental print written in Gaelic. They will actively engage with different types of texts, including visual and auditory sources, which are repetitive, predictable and meaningful to the learner.

Gaelic culture

Gaelic heritage and cultural awareness can be developed by practitioners and learners through opportunities to explore customs and traditions. This may include exploring and experimenting with songs, folklore, place names, the arts, festivals, food and traditions. Learners could make comparisons with their own lives in meaningful contexts.

Lack of texts

The choice of texts will take account of young people's interests, and their cultural identity and background. This will include harnessing their interest in popular culture and the types of texts that they regularly use and create with ease in their lives beyond school. Practitioners will be conscious of the increasing range of Gaelic texts available through Gàidhlig Air-Loidhne (Gàidhlig Online, www. LTScotland.org.uk/gaidhlig), Glow and recent Stòrlann publications.

Reading at early and first levels

At early level learners would engage predominantly in oral activities which may include exploring patterns within stories, poems, rhymes and songs. At first level learners will read words they already know how to pronounce. They would be encouraged to actively think and reflect when interacting with texts. At early and first level learners would have an awareness of environmental print written in Gaelic. Learners will actively engage with different types of texts, including visual and auditory sources, which are repetitive, predictable and meaningful to the learner.

NUMERACY & MATHEMATICS

PRINCIPLES & PRACTICE FOR NUMERACY: RESPONSIBILITY OF ALL

see also Principles & Practice for Mathematics on page 76

> All teachers have responsibility for promoting the development of numeracy. With an increased emphasis upon numeracy for all young people, teachers will need to plan to revisit and consolidate numeracy skills throughout schooling.
>
> *Building the Curriculum 1*

All schools, working with their partners, need to have strategies to ensure that all children and young people develop high levels of numeracy skills through their learning across the curriculum. These strategies will be built upon a shared understanding amongst staff of how children and young people progress in numeracy and of good learning and teaching in numeracy. Collaborative working with colleagues within their own early years setting, school, youth work setting or college and across sectors will support staff in identifying opportunities to develop and reinforce numeracy skills within their own teaching activities.

WHAT IT MEANS TO BE NUMERATE

Being numerate helps us to function responsibly in everyday life and contribute effectively to society. It increases our opportunities within the world of work and establishes foundations which can be built upon through lifelong learning. Numeracy is not only a subset of mathematics; it is also a life skill which permeates and supports all areas of learning, allowing young people access to the wider curriculum.

We are numerate if we have developed:

> *the confidence and competence in using number which will allow individuals to solve problems, analyse information and make informed decisions based on calculations.*

A numerate person will have acquired and developed fundamental skills and be able to carry out number processes but, beyond this, being numerate also allows us to access and interpret information, identify possibilities, weigh up different options and decide on which option is most appropriate.

Numeracy is a skill for life, learning and work. Having well-developed numeracy skills allows young people to be more confident in social settings and enhances enjoyment in a large number of leisure activities. For these and many other reasons, all teachers have important parts to play in enhancing the numeracy skills of all children and young people.

Numerate people rely on the accumulation of knowledge, concepts and skills they have developed, and continually revisit and add to these. All practitioners, as they make use of the statements of experiences and outcomes to plan learning, will ensure that the numeracy skills developed from early levels and beyond are revisited and refreshed throughout schooling and into lifelong learning.

STRUCTURE OF NUMERACY OUTCOMES AND EXPERIENCES

The numeracy experiences and outcomes have been structured using eight organisers:

- Estimation and rounding
- Number and number processes
- Fractions, decimal fractions and percentages
- Money
- Time
- Measurement
- Data and analysis
- Ideas of chance and uncertainty.

All of these areas of numeracy will be familiar and all teachers will recognise how they impact on their own lives. Reflecting on this will help teachers to identify where opportunities may exist to develop numeracy for children and young people.

MATHEMATICS IS NOT MY SPECIALISM. HOW WILL I CONTRIBUTE TO THE DEVELOPMENT OF NUMERACY SKILLS?

For individual teachers in secondary schools and other practitioners, it means asking the question, 'How am I meeting the numeracy needs of the learners in front of me?' This does not mean that you will teach everything that a mathematics teacher develops but that you think of the numeracy experiences you can provide for young people. The greatest impact for learners will come where all practitioners, in all learning environments, include rich numeracy experiences as part of their day-to-day learning and teaching programmes.

You might begin by asking to what extent you already provide numeracy experiences for learners. As a first step, you may want to consider where numeracy plays a part in the aspects you contribute to the curriculum. Does your programme involve estimating, measuring, using and managing time, carrying out money calculations? Does it involve reading information from charts and tables or explaining consequences of actions? If it does, and you highlight this and build upon it in the learning activities, you are making a valuable contribution to developing numeracy in all learners.

FEATURES OF EFFECTIVE LEARNING AND TEACHING

The experiences and outcomes promote and support effective learning and teaching methodologies which will stimulate the interest of children and young people and promote creativity and ingenuity.

A rich and supportive learning environment will support a skilful mix of a variety of approaches, including:

▸ active learning and planned, purposeful play
▸ development of problem-solving capabilities
▸ developing mental agility
▸ frequently asking children to explain their thinking
▸ use of relevant contexts and experiences, familiar to children and young people
▸ using technology in appropriate and effective ways
▸ building on the principles of Assessment is for Learning, including understanding the purpose and relevance of the activities
▸ both collaborative and independent learning
▸ making frequent links across the curriculum, so that concepts and skills are developed further by being applied in different, relevant contexts
▸ promoting an interest and enthusiasm for numeracy.

Teachers will plan to establish and consolidate children's fundamental numeracy skills using imaginative, interactive approaches, so that young people develop a sound understanding of number. Through such approaches they will grow in confidence in recall and use of number bonds and multiplication facts, in their understanding of place-value, and in the application of mental strategies. Teachers will reinforce these skills continually throughout the education of each child and young person.

PROMOTING PROGRESSION, WHICH NUMERICAL SKILLS TO DEVELOP AND HOW TO KNOW THEY ARE AT AN APPROPRIATE LEVEL

Children and young people will most effectively develop their numeracy through cumulative growth in their understanding of key concepts and the application of their skills in new contexts. There are fundamental points of learning along these 'pathways of progression': these allow teachers to identify the progression within a child or young person's understanding and what his or her next steps in development will be. It is essential for teachers to work together to extend their shared understanding of progression.

The statements of experiences and outcomes do not have ceilings, so that all children and young people can be challenged at an appropriate level. Collaboration with colleagues in relation to pathways of progression will encourage a shared understanding of expectations of standards as well as effective learning and teaching within numeracy.

Shared planning for the contexts in which children and young people learn and apply numeracy skills is also crucial. Children and young people need opportunities to bring together different combinations of numeracy skills from the various lines of progression. High quality learning depends upon achieving a suitable balance between developing key facts and integrating and applying them in relevant and imaginative contexts.

HIGHER EXPECTATIONS

Our expectations for numeracy are indeed higher than previously. This is because of the increasing recognition that we must raise levels of performance in numeracy and sustain them throughout lifelong learning. Many other countries are raising the numeracy performance of their children, young people and wider population. Scotland needs to perform at the highest level, so raising the bar in numeracy is important for each individual and also for the prosperity of the nation.

To support this, experiences and outcomes without ceilings should ensure young people are challenged at an appropriate level and are given the opportunity to progress at a suitably aspirational pace. The level of achievement at the fourth level has been designed to approximate to that associated with SCQF level 4.

This paper and the experiences and outcomes in numeracy provide a clear statement of the expectations that will support all practitioners in contributing confidently to the important responsibility which we all share for developing the numeracy skills of our children and young people.

BROAD FEATURES OF ASSESSMENT
(This section complements the advice for mathematics and numeracy on page 77)

As numeracy is the responsibility of all staff, and because of the importance of numeracy across all aspects of a young person's learning, all staff should be clear about their responsibilities and their roles in the assessment of numeracy. Assessment will focus on how well children and young people can work with numbers and data and how well they can use them in their learning and lives, including preparation for future work. From the early years to the senior stages, and particularly at times of transition, it is vital to have a clear picture of the progress each child and young person is making across all aspects of numeracy so that further learning can be planned and action can be taken if any ground has been lost.

Teachers can gather evidence of progress as part of day-to-day learning both in mathematics classes and across the curriculum. The use of specific assessment tasks will be important in assessing progress at key points of learning. Children and young people's progress will be seen in their skills in using number to solve problems, in analysing information and in making informed decisions based on calculations. Approaches to assessment should identify the extent to which children and young people can apply these skills in their learning in and beyond the classroom, in their daily lives and in preparing for the world of work.

As children and young people gradually build up the concepts and skills contained in the experiences and outcomes, they will demonstrate their competence and confidence in applying them in a number of ways. For example:

▸ Can they explain their thinking to show their understanding of number processes and concepts?

▸ Are they developing securely the full range of the skills and attributes set out within the experiences and outcomes? As they apply these to problems, can they draw on skills and concepts learned previously?

▸ As they tackle problems in unfamiliar contexts, can they confidently identify which skills and concepts are relevant to the problem? Can they then apply their skills accurately when working independently and with others, and can they then evaluate their solutions?

▸ Are they developing their understanding of personal finance?

▸ Can they evaluate data to make informed decisions?

▸ Are they developing the capacity to engage with and complete tasks and assignments?

Assessment of numeracy across learning, within and outside the classroom, offers children and young people opportunities to practise and extend their skills, for example within enterprise activities, social studies, technologies and science.

PRINCIPLES & PRACTICE FOR MATHEMATICS

see also Principles & Practice for Numeracy: Responsibility of All on page 74

WHAT CAN LEARNING IN MATHEMATICS ENABLE CHILDREN AND YOUNG PEOPLE TO ACHIEVE?

Mathematics is important in our everyday life, allowing us to make sense of the world around us and to manage our lives. Using mathematics enables us to model real-life situations and make connections and informed predictions. It equips us with the skills we need to interpret and analyse information, simplify and solve problems, assess risk and make informed decisions.

Mathematics plays an important role in areas such as science or technologies, and is vital to research and development in fields such as engineering, computing science, medicine and finance. Learning mathematics gives children and young people access to the wider curriculum and the opportunity to pursue further studies and interests.

Because mathematics is rich and stimulating, it engages and fascinates learners of all ages, interests and abilities. Learning mathematics develops logical reasoning, analysis, problem-solving skills, creativity and the ability to think in abstract ways. It uses a universal language of numbers and symbols which allows us to communicate ideas in a concise, unambiguous and rigorous way.

> To face the challenges of the 21st century, each young person needs to have confidence in using mathematical skills, and Scotland needs both specialist mathematicians and a highly numerate population.
>
> *Building the Curriculum 1*

Mathematics equips us with many of the skills required for life, learning and work. Understanding the part that mathematics plays in almost all aspects of life is crucial. This reinforces the need for mathematics to play an integral part in lifelong learning and be appreciated for the richness it brings.

FRAMEWORK STRUCTURE

Within the mathematics framework, some statements of experiences and outcomes are also identified as statements of experiences and outcomes in numeracy. These form an important part of the mathematics education of all children and young people as they include many of the numerical and analytical skills required by each of us to function effectively and successfully in everyday life. All teachers with a responsibility for the development of mathematics will be familiar with the role of numeracy within mathematics and with the means by which numeracy is developed across the range of learning experiences. The numeracy subset of the mathematics experiences and outcomes is also published separately; further information can be found in the numeracy principles and practice paper.

The mathematics experiences and outcomes are structured within three main organisers, each of which contains a number of subdivisions:

Number, money and measure
▸ Estimation and rounding
▸ Number and number processes
▸ Multiples, factors and primes
▸ Powers and roots
▸ Fractions, decimal fractions and percentages
▸ Money
▸ Time
▸ Measurement
▸ Mathematics – its impact on the world, past, present and future
▸ Patterns and relationships
▸ Expressions and equations.

Shape, position and movement
▸ Properties of 2D shapes and 3D objects
▸ Angle, symmetry and transformation.

Information handling
▸ Data and analysis
▸ Ideas of chance and uncertainty.

The mathematics framework as a whole includes a strong emphasis on the important part mathematics has played, and will continue to play, in the advancement of society, and the relevance it has for daily life.

A key feature of the mathematics framework is the development of algebraic thinking from an early stage. Research shows that the earlier algebraic thinking is introduced, the deeper the mathematical understanding will be and the greater the confidence in using mathematics.

Teachers will use the statements of experiences and

outcomes in information handling to emphasise the interpretation of statistical information in the world around us and to emphasise the knowledge and skills required to take account of chance and uncertainty when making decisions.

The level of achievement at the fourth level has been designed to approximate to that associated with SCQF level 4.

FEATURES OF EFFECTIVE LEARNING AND TEACHING

From the early stages onwards, children and young people should experience success in mathematics and develop the confidence to take risks, ask questions and explore alternative solutions without fear of being wrong. They will enjoy exploring and applying mathematical concepts to understand and solve problems, explaining their thinking and presenting their solutions to others in a variety of ways. At all stages, an emphasis on collaborative learning will encourage children to reason logically and creatively through discussion of mathematical ideas and concepts.

Through their use of effective questioning and discussion, teachers will use misconceptions and wrong answers as opportunities to improve and deepen children's understanding of mathematical concepts.

The experiences and outcomes encourage learning and teaching approaches that challenge and stimulate children and young people and promote their enjoyment of mathematics. To achieve this, teachers will use a skilful mix of approaches, including:

▸ planned active learning which provides opportunities to observe, explore, investigate, experiment, play, discuss and reflect

▸ modelling and scaffolding the development of mathematical thinking skills

▸ learning collaboratively and independently

▸ opportunities for discussion, communication and explanation of thinking

▸ developing mental agility

▸ using relevant contexts and experiences, familiar to young people

▸ making links across the curriculum to show how mathematical concepts are applied in a wide range of contexts, such as those provided by science and social studies

▸ using technology in appropriate and effective ways

▸ building on the principles of Assessment is for Learning, ensuring that young people understand the purpose and relevance of what they are learning

▸ developing problem-solving capabilities and critical thinking skills.

Mathematics is at its most powerful when the knowledge and understanding that have been developed are used to solve problems. Problem-solving will be at the heart of all our learning and teaching. We should regularly encourage children and young people to explore different options: 'what would happen if…?' is the fundamental question for teachers and learners to ask as mathematical thinking develops.

PROGRESS WITHIN & BETWEEN LEVELS

As children and young people develop concepts within mathematics, these will need continual reinforcement and revisiting in order to maintain progression. Teachers can plan this development and progression through providing children and young people with more challenging contexts in which to use their skills. When the experience or outcome spans two levels within a line of development, this will be all the more important.

One case in point would be the third level outcome on displaying information. The expectation is that young people will continue to use and refine the skills developed at second level to display charts, graphs and diagrams. The contexts should ensure progression and there are clear opportunities to use other curriculum areas when extending young people's understanding.

BROAD FEATURES OF ASSESSMENT

(This section should be read alongside the advice for numeracy on page 75)

Assessment in mathematics will focus on children and young people's abilities to work increasingly skilfully with numbers, data and mathematical concepts and processes and use them in a range of contexts. Teachers can gather evidence of progress as part of day-to-day learning about number, money and measurement, shape, position and movement and information handling. The use of specific assessment tasks will be important in assessing progress at key points of learning including transitions.

From the early years through to the senior stages, children and young people will demonstrate progress in their skills in interpreting and analysing information, simplifying and solving problems, assessing risk and making informed choices. They will also show evidence of progress through their skills in collaborating and working independently as they observe, explore, experiment with and investigate mathematical problems.

Approaches to assessment should identify the extent to which children and young people can apply their skills in their learning, in their daily lives and in preparing for the world of work. Progress will be seen as children and young people demonstrate their competence and confidence in applying mathematical concepts and skills. For example:

▸ Do they relish the challenge of number puzzles, patterns and relationships? Can they explain increasingly more abstract ideas of algebraic thinking?

▸ Can they successfully carry out mathematical processes and use their developing range of skills and attributes as set out in the experiences and outcomes? As they apply these to problems, can they draw on skills and concepts learned previously?

▸ As they tackle problems in unfamiliar contexts, can they confidently identify which skills and concepts are relevant to the problem? Can they then apply their skills accurately and then evaluate their solutions?

▸ Can they explain their thinking and demonstrate their understanding of 2D shapes and 3D objects?

▸ Can they evaluate data to make informed decisions?

▸ Are they developing the capacity to engage with and complete tasks and assignments?

Assessment should also link with other areas of the curriculum, within and outside the classroom, offering children and young people opportunities to develop and demonstrate their understanding of mathematics through social studies, technologies and science, and cultural and enterprise activities.

CONNECTIONS WITHIN AND BEYOND MATHEMATICS

Within mathematics there are rich opportunities for links among different concepts: a ready example is provided by investigations into area and perimeter which can involve estimation, patterns and relationships and a variety of numbers. When children and young people investigate number processes, there will be regular opportunities to develop mental strategies and mental agility. Teachers will make use of opportunities to develop algebraic thinking and introduce symbols, such as those opportunities afforded at early stages when reinforcing number bonds or later when investigating the sum of the angles in a triangle.

There are many opportunities to develop mathematical concepts in all other areas of the curriculum. Patterns and symmetry are fundamental to art and music; time, money and measure regularly occur in modern languages, home economics, design technology and various aspects of health and wellbeing; graphs and charts are regularly used in science and social studies; scale and proportion can be developed within social studies; formulae are used in areas including health and wellbeing, technologies and sciences; while shape, position and movement can be developed in all areas of the curriculum.

EXPERIENCES & OUTCOMES FOR NUMERACY: RESPONSIBILITY OF ALL

My learning in numeracy enables me to:

▸ develop essential numeracy skills which will allow me to participate fully in society
▸ understand that successful independent living requires financial awareness, effective money management, using schedules and other related skills
▸ interpret numerical information appropriately and use it to draw conclusions, assess risk, make reasoned evaluations and informed decisions
▸ apply skills and understanding creatively and logically to solve problems, within a variety of contexts
▸ appreciate how the imaginative and effective use of technologies can enhance the development of skills and concepts.

EXPERIENCES & OUTCOMES FOR MATHEMATICS

My learning in mathematics enables me to:

▸ develop a secure understanding of the concepts, principles and processes of mathematics and apply these in different contexts, including the world of work
▸ engage with more abstract mathematical concepts and develop important new kinds of thinking
▸ understand the application of mathematics, its impact on our society past and present, and its potential for the future
▸ develop essential numeracy skills which will allow me to participate fully in society
▸ establish firm foundations for further specialist learning
▸ understand that successful independent living requires financial awareness, effective money management, using schedules and other related skills
▸ interpret numerical information appropriately and use it to draw conclusions, assess risk, and make reasoned evaluations and informed decisions
▸ apply skills and understanding creatively and logically to solve problems, within a variety of contexts
▸ appreciate how the imaginative and effective use of technologies can enhance the development of skills and concepts.

Responsibility of All

The statements in [*italics* on a yellow background] in both the Experiences and Outcomes and Benchmarks are the responsibility of all and, as such, evidence from across the curriculum should be considered when making judgements about achieving a level.

NUMERACY & MATHEMATICAL SKILLS

Numeracy and mathematical skills are embedded in the Experiences and Outcomes and cannot be taught in isolation. These skills can be developed through careful planning of learning activities, questions and a range of assessments. These should encourage learners to think about the concepts, going beyond the recall of knowledge and encouraging them to explain their thinking. As learners progress through Curriculum for Excellence levels, they should demonstrate increasing sophistication and independence in their ability to demonstrate, link, transfer and apply the following skills in a range of increasingly more challenging contexts:

- ▶ interpret questions
- ▶ select and communicate processes and solutions
- ▶ justify choice of strategy used
- ▶ link mathematical concepts
- ▶ use mathematical vocabulary and notation
- ▶ use mental agility
- ▶ reason algebraically
- ▶ determine the reasonableness of a solution.

The table below provides a brief outline of the key features of each skill.

	▼ KEY FEATURES	▼ ADDITIONAL GUIDANCE
INTERPRET QUESTIONS	▶ selects the relevant information ▶ interprets data ▶ highlights key words or phrases ▶ makes notes ▶ draws diagrams ▶ chooses appropriate operations.	Learners need to: ▶ interpret questions successfully in order to work out solutions ▶ select relevant information and be able to identify redundant or missing information in a question ▶ interpret data and understand information presented to work out the solution ▶ be supported to develop their skills of interpreting questions by highlighting key words or phrases, making notes or drawing diagrams ▶ make important decisions about which operations to choose when solving a word problem.
SELECT AND COMMUNICATE PROCESSES AND SOLUTIONS	▶ explains choice of process ▶ shares thinking ▶ verbalises or demonstrates thought processes.	Learners need to: ▶ be able to explain why they have chosen a particular process as it demonstrates their understanding of the task, question or assessment ▶ have frequent opportunities to discuss their thinking with their peers and teachers ▶ select from a range of processes and increasingly choose processes which are most efficient ▶ discuss their solutions to verbalise their thought process, either through explaining their thinking or demonstrating it pictorially ▶ become more confident in their abilities to select from a growing repertoire of strategies, articulate their chosen approaches with increasing clarity and make greater use of specialised vocabulary.
JUSTIFY CHOICE OF STRATEGY USED	▶ shows and talks though their thinking ▶ explains their strategy ▶ justifies choice of strategy compared to other approaches.	Learners need to: ▶ show and talk through their thinking to better understand and explain their own strategies ▶ regularly work in pairs and groups to learn with and from each other to refine their strategies ▶ justify their choice of strategy, identifying the most efficient strategies for different types of task.
LINK MATHEMATICAL CONCEPTS	▶ understands and applies links between mathematical concepts ▶ transfers learning in one area to another ▶ uses connections to solve problems.	Learners need to: ▶ be able to link mathematical concepts through inverse operations and equivalences ▶ transfer and apply their knowledge and skills within numeracy and mathematics and across the curriculum to solve a range of problems.
USE MATHEMATICAL VOCABULARY AND NOTATION	▶ uses correct mathematical vocabulary	Learners need to: ▶ apply the correct mathematical vocabulary, notation and appropriate units in a range of contexts.
MENTAL AGILITY	▶ knowledge of number facts ▶ manipulates numbers.	Learners need to: ▶ develop fluency in mental processes through a sound knowledge of key number facts ▶ use strategies to manipulate an appropriate range of numbers and apply these to solve open-ended problems.
REASON ALGEBRAICALLY	▶ finds the unknown quantity ▶ understands and uses the commutative, associative and distributive laws.	Learners need to: ▶ understand that numbers can be replaced by pictures or symbols and use this to solve problems ▶ apply commutative, associative and distributive laws to work with expressions and equations.
DETERMINE THE REASON-ABLENESS OF A SOLUTION	▶ routinely uses estimation and rounding skills ▶ selects the most appropriate degree of accuracy.	Learners need to: ▶ use estimation and rounding to estimate and check the reasonableness of a solution ▶ consider the context of the question when determining the reasonableness of the solution ▶ select the appropriate degree of accuracy for the given task.

NUMBER, MONEY AND MEASURE

ESTIMATION AND ROUNDING

E	*MNU 0-01a I am developing a sense of size and amount by observing, exploring, using and communicating with others about things in the world around me.*	• Recognises the number of objects in a group, without counting (subitising) and uses this information to estimate the number of objects in other groups. • Checks estimates by counting. • Demonstrates skills of estimation in the contexts of number and measure using relevant vocabulary, including less than, longer than, more than and the same.
1	*MNU 1-01a I can share ideas with others to develop ways of estimating the answer to a calculation or problem, work out the actual answer, then check my solution by comparing it with the estimate.*	• Uses strategies to estimate an answer to a calculation or problem, for example, doubling and rounding. • Rounds whole numbers to the nearest 10 and 100 and uses this routinely to estimate and check the reasonableness of a solution.
2	*MNU 2-01a I can use my knowledge of rounding to routinely estimate the answer to a problem, then after calculating, decide if my answer is reasonable, sharing my solution with others.*	• Rounds whole numbers to the nearest 1000, 10 000 and 100 000. • Rounds decimal fractions to the nearest whole number, to one decimal place and two decimal places. • Applies knowledge of rounding to give an estimate to a calculation appropriate to the context.

NUMBER AND NUMBER PROCESSES

E	*MNU 0-02a I have explored numbers, understanding that they represent quantities and I can use them to count, create sequences and describe order.* *MNU 0-03a I use practical materials and can 'count on and back' to help me to understand addition and subtraction, recording my ideas and solutions in different ways.*	• Explains that zero means there is none of a particular quantity and is represented by the numeral 0. • Recalls the number sequence forwards within the range 0 - 30, from any given number. • Recalls the number sequence backwards from 20. • Identifies and recognises numbers from 0 to 20. • Orders all numbers forwards and backwards within the range 0 - 20. • Identifies the number before, the number after and missing numbers in a sequence within 20. • Uses one-to-one correspondence to count a given number of objects to 20. • Identifies 'how many?' in regular dot patterns, for example, arrays, five frames, ten frames, dice and irregular dot patterns, without having to count (subitising).	• Groups items recognising that the appearance of the group has no effect on the overall total (conservation of number). • Uses ordinal numbers in real life contexts, for example, 'I am third in the line'. • Uses the language of before, after and in-between. • Counts on and back in ones to add and subtract. • Doubles numbers to a total of 10 mentally. • When counting objects, understands that the number name of the last object counted is the name given to the total number of objects in the group. • Partitions quantities to 10 into two or more parts and recognises that this does not affect the total. • Adds and subtracts mentally to 10. • Uses appropriately the mathematical symbols +, – and =. • Solves simple missing number problems.
1	*MNU 1-02a I have investigated how whole numbers are constructed, can understand the importance of zero within the system and can use my knowledge to explain the link between a digit, its place and its value.* *MNU 1-03a I can use addition, subtraction, multiplication and division when solving problems, making best use of the mental strategies and written skills I have developed.*	• Reads, writes, orders and recites whole numbers to 1000, starting from any number in the sequence. • Demonstrates understanding of zero as a placeholder in whole numbers to 1000. • Uses correct mathematical vocabulary when discussing the four operations including, subtract, add, sum of, total, multiply, product, divide and shared equally. • Identifies the value of each digit in a whole number with three digits, for example, 867 = 800 + 60 + 7. • Counts forwards and backwards in 2s, 5s, 10s and 100s. • Demonstrates understanding of the commutative law, for example, 6 + 3 = 3 + 6 or 2 × 4 = 4 × 2. • Applies strategies to determine multiplication facts, for example, repeated addition, grouping, arrays and multiplication facts. • Solves addition and subtraction problems with three digit whole numbers. • Adds and subtracts multiples of 10 or 100 to or from any whole number to 1000. • Applies strategies to determine division facts, for example, repeated subtraction, equal groups, sharing equally, arrays and multiplication facts. • Uses multiplication and division facts to solve problems within the number range 0 to 1000. • Multiplies and divides whole numbers by 10 and 100 (whole number answers only). • Applies knowledge of inverse operations (addition and subtraction; multiplication and division). • Solves two step problems.	
2	*MNU 2-02a I have extended the range of whole numbers I can work with and having explored how decimal fractions are constructed, can explain the link between a digit, its place and its value.* *MNU 2-03a Having determined which calculations are needed, I can solve problems involving whole numbers using a range of methods, sharing my approaches and solutions with others.* *MNU 2-03b I have explored the contexts in which problems involving decimal fractions occur and can solve related problems using a variety of methods.*	• Reads, writes and orders whole numbers to 1 000 000, starting from any number in the sequence. • Explains the link between a digit, its place and its value for whole numbers to 1 000 000. • Reads, writes and orders sets of decimal fractions to three decimal places. • Explains the link between a digit, its place and its value for numbers to three decimal places. • Partitions a wide range of whole numbers and decimal fractions to three decimal places, for example, 3·6 = 3 ones and 6 tenths = 36 tenths. • Adds and subtracts multiples of 10, 100 and 1000 to and from whole numbers and decimal fractions to two decimal places. • Adds and subtracts whole numbers and decimal fractions to two decimal places, within the number range 0 to 1 000 000. • Uses multiplication and division facts to the 10th multiplication table. • Multiplies and divides whole numbers by multiples of 10, 100 and 1000. • Multiplies and divides decimal fractions to two decimal places by 10, 100 and 1000. • Multiplies whole numbers by two digit numbers. • Multiplies decimal fractions to two decimal places by a single digit. • Divides whole numbers and decimal fractions to two decimal places, by a single digit, including answers expressed as decimal fractions, for example, 43 ÷ 5 = 8·6.	

MTH 2-03c Having explored the need for rules for the order of operations in number calculations, I can apply them correctly when solving simple problems.	• Applies the correct order of operations in number calculations when solving multi-step problems.	**2**
MNU 2-04a I can show my understanding of how the number line extends to include numbers less than zero and have investigated how these numbers occur and are used.	• Identifies familiar contexts in which negative numbers are used. • Orders numbers less than zero and locates them on a number line.	

MULTIPLES, FACTORS AND PRIMES

No Experiences and Outcomes at Early or First Level

MTH 2-05a Having explored the patterns and relationships in multiplication and division, I can investigate and identify the multiples and factors of numbers.	• Identifies multiples and factors of whole numbers and applies knowledge and understanding of these when solving relevant problems in number, money and measurement.	**2**

FRACTIONS, DECIMALS AND PERCENTAGES

MNU 0-07a I can share out a group of items by making smaller groups and can split a whole object into smaller parts.	• Splits a whole into smaller parts and explains that equal parts are the same size. • Uses appropriate vocabulary to describe halves. • Shares out a group of items equally into smaller groups.	**E**
MNU 1-07a Having explored fractions by taking part in practical activities, I can show my understanding of: ▸ how a single item can be shared equally ▸ the notation and vocabulary associated with fractions ▸ where simple fractions lie on the number line. **MNU 1-07b** Through exploring how groups of items can be shared equally, I can find a fraction of an amount by applying my knowledge of division.	• Explains what a fraction is using concrete materials, pictorial representations and appropriate mathematical vocabulary. • Demonstrates understanding that the greater the number of equal parts, the smaller the size of each share. • Uses the correct notation for common fractions to tenths, for example, $\frac{1}{2}$, $\frac{2}{4}$ and $\frac{5}{8}$. • Compares the size of fractions and places simple fractions in order on a number line.	**1**
MTH 1-07c Through taking part in practical activities including use of pictorial representations, I can demonstrate my understanding of simple fractions which are equivalent.	• Uses pictorial representations and other models to demonstrate understanding of simple equivalent fractions, for example, $\frac{1}{2} = \frac{2}{4} = \frac{3}{6}$. • Explains the role of the numerator and denominator. • Uses known multiplication and division facts and other strategies to find unit fractions of whole numbers, for example, $\frac{1}{2}$ or $\frac{1}{4}$.	
MNU 2-07a I have investigated the everyday contexts in which simple fractions, percentages or decimal fractions are used and can carry out the necessary calculations to solve related problems. **MNU 2-07b** I can show the equivalent forms of simple fractions, decimal fractions and percentages and can choose my preferred form when solving a problem, explaining my choice of method. **MTH 2-07c** I have investigated how a set of equivalent fractions can be created, understanding the meaning of simplest form, and can apply my knowledge to compare and order the most commonly used fractions.	• Uses knowledge of equivalent forms of common fractions, decimal fractions and percentages, for example, $\frac{3}{4} = 0{\cdot}75 = 75\%$, to solve problems. • Calculates simple percentages of a quantity, and uses this knowledge to solve problems in everyday contexts, for example, calculates the sale price of an item with a discount of 15%. • Calculates simple fractions of a quantity and uses this knowledge to solve problems, for example, find $\frac{3}{5}$ of 60. • Creates equivalent fractions and uses this knowledge to put a set of most commonly used fractions in order. • Expresses fractions in their simplest form.	**2**

MONEY

MNU 0-09a I am developing my awareness of how money is used and can recognise and use a range of coins.	• Identifies all coins to £2. • Applies addition and subtraction skills and uses 1p, 2p, 5p and 10p coins to pay the exact value for items to 10p.	**E**
MNU 1-09a I can use money to pay for items and can work out how much change I should receive. **MNU 1-09b** I have investigated how different combinations of coins and notes can be used to pay for goods or be given in change.	• Identifies and uses all coins and notes to £20 and explores different ways of making the same total. • Records amounts accurately in different ways using the correct notation, for example, 149p = £1·49 and 7p = £0·07. • Uses a variety of coin and note combinations, to pay for items and give change within £10. • Applies mental agility number skills to calculate the total spent in a shopping situation and is able to calculate change. • Demonstrates awareness of how goods can be paid for using cards and digital technology.	**1**
MNU 2-09a I can manage money, compare costs from different retailers, and determine what I can afford to buy. **MNU 2-09b** I understand the costs, benefits and risks of using bank cards to purchase goods or obtain cash and realise that budgeting is important. **MNU 2-09c** I can use the terms profit and loss in buying and selling activities and can make simple calculations for this.	• Carries out money calculations involving the four operations. • Compares costs and determines affordability within a given budget. • Demonstrates understanding of the benefits and risks of using bank cards and digital technologies. • Calculates profit and loss accurately, for example, when working with a budget for an enterprise activity.	**2**

TIME

E	**MNU 0-10a** I am aware of how routines and events in my world link with times and seasons, and have explored ways to record and display these using clocks, calendars and other methods.	• Links daily routines and personal events to time sequences. • Names the days of the week in sequence, knows the months of the year and talks about features of the four seasons in relevant contexts. • Recognises, talks about and where appropriate, engages with everyday devices used to measure or display time, including clocks, calendars, sand timers and visual timetables. • Reads analogue and digital o'clock times (12 hour only) and represents this on a digital display or clock face. • Uses appropriate language when discussing time, including before, after, o'clock, hour hand and minute hand.
1	**MNU 1-10a**[1] I can tell the time using 12 hour clocks, realising there is a link with 24 hour notation, explain how it impacts on my daily routine and ensure that I am organised and ready for events throughout my day.	• Tells the time using half past, quarter past and quarter to using analogue and digital 12 hour clocks. • Records 12 hour times using am and pm and is able to identify 24 hour notation, for example, on a mobile phone or computer.
	MNU 1-10b I can use a calendar to plan and be organised for key events for myself and my class throughout the year.	• Records the date in a variety of ways, using words and numbers. • Uses and interprets a variety of calendars and 12 hour timetables to plan key events. • Knows the number of seconds in a minute, minutes in an hour, hours in a day, days in each month, weeks and days in a year. • Orders the months of the year and relates these to the appropriate seasons.
	MNU 1-10c I have begun to develop a sense of how long tasks take by measuring the time taken to complete a range of activities using a variety of timers.	• Selects and uses appropriate timers for specific purposes.
2	**MNU 2-10a** I can use and interpret electronic and paper-based timetables and schedules to plan events and activities, and make time calculations as part of my planning.	• Reads and records time in both 12 hour and 24 hour notation and converts between the two. • Knows the relationships between commonly used units of time and carries out simple conversion calculations, for example, changes $1\frac{3}{4}$ hours into minutes. • Uses and interprets a range of electronic and paper-based timetables and calendars to plan events or activities and solve real life problems. • Calculates durations of activities and events including situations bridging across several hours and parts of hours using both 12 hour clock and 24 hour notation.
	MNU 2-10b I can carry out practical tasks and investigations involving timed events and can explain which unit of time would be most appropriate to use.	• Chooses the most appropriate timing device in practical situations and records using relevant units, including hundredths of a second. • Selects the most appropriate unit of time for a given task and justifies choice.
	MNU 2-10c Using simple time periods, I can give a good estimate of how long a journey should take, based on my knowledge of the link between time, speed and distance.	• Estimates the duration of a journey based on knowledge of the link between speed, distance and time.

MEASUREMENT

E	**MNU 0-11a** I have experimented with everyday items as units of measure to investigate and compare sizes and amounts in my environment, sharing my findings with others.	• Shares relevant experiences in which measurements of lengths, heights, mass and capacities are used, for example, in baking. • Describes common objects using appropriate measurement language, including tall, heavy and empty. • Compares and describes lengths, heights, mass and capacities using everyday language, including longer, shorter, taller, heavier, lighter, more and less. • Estimates, then measures, the length, height, mass and capacity of familiar objects using a range of appropriate non-standard units.
1	**MNU 1-11a** I can estimate how long or heavy an object is, or what amount it holds, using everyday things as a guide, then measure or weigh it using appropriate instruments and units.	• Uses knowledge of everyday objects to provide reasonable estimates of length, height, mass and capacity. • Makes accurate use of a range of instruments including rulers, metre sticks, digital scales and measuring jugs when measuring lengths, heights, mass and capacities using the most appropriate instrument for the task. • Records measurements of length, height, mass and capacity to the nearest standard unit, for example, millimetres (mm), centimetres (cm), grams (g), kilograms (kg), millilitres (ml), litres (l). • Compares measures with estimates. • Uses knowledge of relationships between units of measure to make simple conversions, for example, 1m 58cm = 158cm. • Reads a variety of scales on measuring devices including those with simple fractions, for example, $\frac{1}{2}$ litre.
	MNU 1-11b I can estimate the area of a shape by counting squares or other methods.	• Uses square grids to estimate then measure the areas of a variety of simple 2D shapes to the nearest half square. • Creates shapes with a given area to the nearest half square using square tiles or grids. • Recognises that different shapes can have the same area (conservation of area).

[1] **From the Appendix to the Es & Os: Explanation for MNU 1-10a**
Developing a child's understanding of 12 hour time in depth takes place through first level. Young learners will become familiar with 24 hour notation in their surroundings through TV listings, computers, cookers, DVD players and videos. They will naturally make links with 24 hour notation and the routines in their day. The next stage of development, the formal manipulation of 24 hour time, is included in MNU 2-10a – understanding and using timetables.

***MNU 2-11a** I can use my knowledge of the sizes of familiar objects or places to assist me when making an estimate of measure.* ***MNU 2-11b** I can use the common units of measure, convert between related units of the metric system and carry out calculations when solving problems.*	• *Uses the comparative size of familiar objects to make reasonable estimations of length, mass, area and capacity.* • *Estimates to the nearest appropriate unit, then measures accurately: length, height and distance in millimetres (mm), centimetres (cm), metres (m) and kilometres (km); mass in grams (g) and kilograms (kg); and capacity in millilitres (ml) and litres (l).* • *Calculates the perimeter of simple straight sided 2D shapes in millimetres (mm), centimetres (cm) and metres (m).* • *Calculates the area of squares, rectangles and right-angled triangles in square millimetres (mm^2), square centimetres (cm^2) and square metres (m^2).* • *Calculates the volume of cubes and cuboids in cubic centimetres (cm^3) and cubic metres (m^3).* • *Converts between common units of measurement using decimal notation, for example, 550 cm = 5·5 m; 3·009 kg = 3009 g.* • *Chooses the most appropriate measuring device for a given task and carries out the required calculation, recording results in the correct unit.* • *Reads a variety of scales accurately.* • *Shows awareness of imperial units used in everyday life, for example, miles or stones.*
***MNU 2-11c** I can explain how different methods can be used to find the perimeter and area of a simple 2D shape or volume of a simple 3D object.*	• *Draws squares and rectangles accurately with a given perimeter or area.* • *Demonstrates understanding of the conservation of measurement, for example, draw three different rectangles each with an area of 24cm^2.*

MATHEMATICS – ITS IMPACT ON THE WORLD, PAST PRESENT AND FUTURE

No Experiences and Outcomes at Early Level

MTH 1-12a I have discussed the important part that numbers play in the world and explored a variety of systems that have been used by civilisations throughout history to record numbers.	• Investigates and shares understanding of the importance of numbers in learning, life and work. • Investigates and shares understanding of a variety of number systems used throughout history.
MTH 2-12a I have worked with others to explore, and present our findings on, how mathematics impacts on the world and the important part it has played in advances and inventions.	• Researches and presents examples of the impact mathematics has in the world of life and work. • Contributes to discussions and activities on the role of mathematics in the creation of important inventions, now and in the past.

PATTERNS AND RELATIONSHIPS

MTH 0-13a I have spotted and explored patterns in my own and the wider environment and can copy and continue these and create my own patterns.	• Copies, continues and creates simple patterns involving objects, shapes and numbers. • Explores, recognises and continues simple number patterns. • Finds missing numbers on a number line within the range 0 – 20.
MTH 1-13a I can continue and devise more involved repeating patterns or designs, using a variety of media. **MTH 1-13b** Through exploring number patterns, I can recognise and continue simple number sequences and can explain the rule I have applied.	• Counts forwards and backwards in 2s, 5s and 10s from any whole number up to 1000. • Describes patterns in number, for example, in the multiplication tables and hundred square. • Continues and creates repeating patterns involving shapes, pictures and symbols. • Describes, continues and creates number patterns using addition, subtraction, doubling, halving, counting in jumps (skip counting) and known multiples.
MTH 2-13a Having explored more complex number sequences, including well-known named number patterns, I can explain the rule used to generate the sequence, and apply it to extend the pattern.	• Explains and uses a rule to extend well known number sequences including square numbers, triangular numbers and Fibonacci sequence. • Applies knowledge of multiples, square numbers and triangular numbers to generate number patterns.

EXPRESSIONS AND EQUATIONS

No Experiences and Outcomes at Early Level

MTH 1-15a I can compare, describe and show number relationships, using appropriate vocabulary and the symbols for equals, not equal to, less than and greater than.	• Understands and accurately uses the terms 'equal to', 'not equal to', 'less than', 'greater than', and the related symbols (=, ≠, <, >) when comparing quantities.
MTH 1-15b When a picture or symbol is used to replace a number in a number statement, I can find its value using my knowledge of number facts and explain my thinking to others.	• Applies understanding of the equals sign as a balance, and knowledge of number facts, to solve simple algebraic problems where a picture or symbol is used to represent a number, for example, ◆ + 17 = 30 and ◆ × 6 = 30.
MTH 2-15a I can apply my knowledge of number facts to solve problems where an unknown value is represented by a symbol or letter.	• Solves simple algebraic equations with one variable, for example, $a - 30 = 40$ and $4b = 20$.

SHAPE, POSITION AND MOVEMENT

PROPERTIES OF 2D SHAPES AND 3D OBJECTS

E **MTH 0-16a** I enjoy investigating objects and shapes and can sort, describe and be creative with them.	• Recognises, describes and sorts common 2D shapes and 3D objects according to various criteria, for example, straight, round, flat and curved.
1 **MTH 1-16a** I have explored simple 3D objects and 2D shapes and can identify, name and describe their features using appropriate vocabulary.	• Names, identifies and classifies a range of simple 2D shapes and 3D objects and recognises these shapes in different orientations and sizes. • Uses mathematical language to describe the properties of a range of common 2D shapes and 3D objects including side, face, edge, vertex, base and angle. • Identifies 2D shapes within 3D objects and recognises 3D objects from 2D drawings.
MTH 1-16b I can explore and discuss how and why different shapes fit together and create a tiling pattern with them.	• Identifies examples of tiling in the environment and applies knowledge of the features of 2D shapes to create tiling patterns incorporating two different shapes.
2 **MTH 2-16a** Having explored a range of 3D objects and 2D shapes, I can use mathematical language to describe their properties, and through investigation can discuss where and why particular shapes are used in the environment. **MTH 2-16b** Through practical activities, I can show my understanding of the relationship between 3D objects and their nets. **MTH 2-16c** I can draw 2D shapes and make representations of 3D objects using an appropriate range of methods and efficient use of resources.	• Describes 3D objects and 2D shapes using specific vocabulary including regular, irregular, diagonal, radius, diameter and circumference. Applies this knowledge to demonstrate understanding of the relationship between 3D objects and their nets. • Identifies and describes 3D objects and 2D shapes within the environment and explains why their properties match their function. • Knows that the radius is half of the diameter. • Uses digital technologies and mathematical instruments to draw 2D shapes and make representations of 3D objects, understanding that not all parts of the 3D object can be seen.

ANGLE, SYMMETRY AND TRANSFORMATION

E **MTH 0-17a** In movement, games, and using technology I can use simple directions and describe positions.	• Understands and correctly uses the language of position and direction, including in front, behind, above, below, left, right, forwards and backwards, to solve simple problems in movement games.
MTH 0-19a I have had fun creating a range of symmetrical pictures and patterns using a range of media.	• Identifies, describes and creates symmetrical pictures with one line of symmetry.
1 **MTH 1-17a** I can describe, follow and record routes and journeys using signs, words and angles associated with direction and turning.	• Uses technology and other methods to describe, follow and record directions using words associated with angles, directions and turns including, full turn, half turn, quarter turn, clockwise, anticlockwise, right turn, left turn, right angle. • Knows that a right angle is 90°. • Knows and uses the compass points, North, South, East and West. • Uses informal methods to estimate, compare and describe the size of angles in relation to a right angle. • Finds right angles in the environment and in well-known 2D shapes.
MTH 1-18a I have developed an awareness of where grid reference systems are used in everyday contexts and can use them to locate and describe position.	• Identifies where and why grid references are used. • Describes, plots and uses accurate two figure grid references, demonstrating knowledge of the horizontal and vertical location.
MTH 1-19a I have explored symmetry in my own and the wider environment and can create and recognise symmetrical pictures, patterns and shapes.	• Identifies symmetry in patterns, pictures, nature and 2D shapes. • Creates symmetrical pictures and designs with more than one line of symmetry.
2 **MTH 2-17a** I have investigated angles in the environment, and can discuss, describe and classify angles using appropriate mathematical vocabulary.	• Uses mathematical language including acute, obtuse, straight and reflex to describe and classify a range of angles identified within shapes in the environment.
MTH 2-17b I can accurately measure and draw angles using appropriate equipment, applying my skills to problems in context.	• Measures and draws a range of angles to within ± 2°. • Knows that complementary angles add up to 90° and supplementary angles add up to 180° and uses this knowledge to calculate missing angles.
MTH 2-17c Through practical activities which include the use of technology, I have developed my understanding of the link between compass points and angles and can describe, follow and record directions, routes and journeys using appropriate vocabulary.	• Uses knowledge of the link between the eight compass points and angles to describe, follow and record directions.
MTH 2-17d Having investigated where, why and how scale is used and expressed, I can apply my understanding to interpret simple models, maps and plans.	• Interprets maps, models or plans with simple scales, for example, 1 cm:2 km.
MTH 2-18a I can use my knowledge of the coordinate system to plot and describe the location of a point on a grid.	• Describes, plots and records the location of a point, in the first quadrant, using coordinate notation.
MTH 2-19a I can illustrate the lines of symmetry for a range of 2D shapes and apply my understanding to create and complete symmetrical pictures and patterns.	• Identifies and illustrates line symmetry on a wide range of 2D shapes and applies this understanding to complete a range of symmetrical patterns, with and without the use of digital technologies.

INFORMATION HANDLING

DATA AND ANALYSIS

MNU 0-20a I can collect objects and ask questions to gather information, organising and displaying my findings in different ways. **MNU 0-20b** I can match objects, and sort using my own and others' criteria, sharing my ideas with others. **MNU 0-20c** I can use the signs and charts around me for information, helping me plan and make choices and decisions in my daily life.	• Asks simple questions to collect data for a specific purpose. • Collects and organises objects for a specific purpose. • Applies counting skills to ask and answer questions and makes relevant choices and decisions based on the data. • Contributes to concrete or pictorial displays where one object or drawing represents one data value, using digital technologies as appropriate. • Uses knowledge of colour, shape, size and other properties to match and sort items in a variety of different ways. • Interprets simple graphs, charts and signs and demonstrates how they support planning, choices and decision making.	E
MNU 1-20a I have explored a variety of ways in which data is presented and can ask and answer questions about the information it contains. **MNU 1-20b** I have used a range of ways to collect information and can sort it in a logical, organised and imaginative way using my own and others' criteria.	• Asks and answers questions to extract key information from a variety of data sets including charts, diagrams, bar graphs and tables. • Selects and uses the most appropriate way to gather and sort data for a given purpose, for example, a survey, questionnaire or group tallies.	1
MTH 1-21a Using technology and other methods, I can display data simply, clearly and accurately by creating tables, charts and diagrams, using simple labelling and scale.	• Uses a variety of different methods, including the use of digital technologies, to display data, for example, as block graphs, bar graphs, tables, Carroll diagrams and Venn diagrams. • Includes a suitable title, simple labelling on both axes and an appropriate scale where one unit represents more than one data value in graphs.	
MNU 2-20a Having discussed the variety of ways and range of media used to present data, I can interpret and draw conclusions from the information displayed, recognising that the presentation may be misleading. **MNU 2-20b** I have carried out investigations and surveys, devising and using a variety of methods to gather information and have worked with others to collate, organise and communicate the results in an appropriate way.	• Devises ways of collecting data in the most suitable way for the given task. • Collects, organises and displays data accurately in a variety of ways including through the use of digital technologies, for example, creating surveys, tables, bar graphs, line graphs, frequency tables, simple pie charts and spreadsheets. • Analyses, interprets and draws conclusions from a variety of data. • Draws conclusions about the reliability of data taking into account, for example, the author, the audience, the scale and sample size used.	2
MTH 2-21a I can display data in a clear way using a suitable scale, by choosing appropriately from an extended range of tables, charts, diagrams and graphs, making effective use of technology.	• Displays data appropriately making effective use of technology and chooses a suitable scale when creating graphs.	

IDEAS OF CHANCE AND UNCERTAINTY

No Experiences and Outcomes at Early Level

MNU 1-22a I can use appropriate vocabulary to describe the likelihood of events occurring, using the knowledge and experiences of myself and others to guide me.	• Uses mathematical vocabulary appropriately to describe the likelihood of events occurring in everyday situations including, probable, likely/unlikely, certain/uncertain, possible/impossible, and fair/unfair. • Interprets data gathered through everyday experiences to make reasonable predictions of the likelihood of an event occurring.	1
MNU 2-22a I can conduct simple experiments involving chance and communicate my predictions and findings using the vocabulary of probability.	• Uses the language of probability accurately to describe the likelihood of simple events occurring, for example equal chance; fifty-fifty; one in two, two in three; percentage chance; and $\frac{1}{6}$. • Plans and carries out simple experiments involving chance with repeated trials, for example, 'what is the probability of throwing a six if you throw a die fifty times?' • Uses data to predict the outcome of a simple experiment.	2

Design: © Harold Raitt / SeeHearTeach.scot (2019)   Content: © Crown copyright (2017)

RELIGIOUS & MORAL EDUCATION

PRINCIPLES & PRACTICE

WHY RME IS IMPORTANT FOR ALL CHILDREN AND YOUNG PEOPLE[1] THEY ACHIEVE THROUGH THEIR LEARNING

Scotland is a nation whose people hold a wide range of beliefs from the many branches of the Christian faith represented throughout the land to the world's other major religions and to beliefs which lie outwith religious traditions. Such diversity enriches the Scottish nation and serves as an inspiring and thought-provoking background for our children and young people to develop their own beliefs and values.

Religious and moral education enables children and young people to explore the world's major religions and views which are independent of religious belief and to consider the challenges posed by these beliefs and values. It supports them in developing and reflecting upon their values and their capacity for moral judgement. Through developing awareness and appreciation of the value of each individual in a diverse society, religious and moral education engenders responsible attitudes to other people. This awareness and appreciation will assist in counteracting prejudice and intolerance as children and young people consider issues such as sectarianism and discrimination more broadly.

> Religious and moral education is a process where children and young people engage in a search for meaning, value and purpose in life. This involves both the exploration of beliefs and values and the study of how such beliefs and values are expressed.
>
> *Building the Curriculum 1*

Children and young people must become aware that beliefs and values are fundamental to families and to the fabric of society in communities, local and global. There is an intrinsic value in learning about religion as well as learning from religion, as children and young people develop their understanding of diversity in our society and their own roles in it. The skills of reflection and critical thinking and an enhanced understanding of the beliefs and values of others are all crucial in assisting in this process.

Learning through religious and moral education enables children and young people to:

▶ recognise religion as an important expression of human experience
▶ learn about and from the beliefs, values, practices and traditions of Christianity and the world religions selected for study, other traditions, and viewpoints independent of religious belief
▶ explore and develop knowledge and understanding of religions, recognising the place of Christianity in the Scottish context

▶ investigate and understand the responses which religious and non-religious views can offer to questions about the nature and meaning of life
▶ recognise and understand religious diversity and the importance of religion in society
▶ develop respect for others and an understanding of beliefs and practices which are different from their own
▶ explore and establish values such as wisdom, justice, compassion and integrity and engage in the development of and reflection upon their own moral values
▶ develop their beliefs, attitudes, values and practices through reflection, discovery and critical evaluation
▶ develop the skills of reflection, discernment, critical thinking and deciding how to act when making moral decisions
▶ make a positive difference to the world by putting their beliefs and values into action
▶ establish a firm foundation for lifelong learning, further learning and adult life.

Religious and moral education is therefore an essential part of every child or young person's educational experience.

ORGANISATION

The experiences and outcomes allow opportunities for personalisation and choice, depth and reflection.

The experiences and outcomes are structured within three organisers to enable teachers to plan learning about and through Christianity and those other world religions which are selected for study, and to plan for the development of beliefs and values. For the major religions, the lines of development are Beliefs, Values and issues, and Practices and traditions.

The experiences and outcomes relating to the development by children and young people of their own beliefs and values do not form a separate context for planning but should be intertwined with the experiences and outcomes for Christianity and the world religions selected for study.

The fourth level outcomes have been designed to approximate to SCQF level 4.

EMPHASIS ON CHRISTIANITY

When planning for religious and moral education, schools will take account of the communities and the context in which the children and young people live and learn. Through their learning in religious and moral education all children and young people will develop an understanding of Christianity, which has shaped the history and traditions of Scotland and continues to exert an influence on national life. It is also a fundamental principle that all children and young people throughout Scotland will consider a range of faiths and views, whatever their own situation and local context. Indeed, the experiences and outcomes will lead to children and young people, as they develop, extending their learning far beyond the local context to national and international contexts.

EFFECTIVE LEARNING AND TEACHING

Learning should be coherent, progressive and meaningful, and should be planned for and taught in ways that encourage learners to recognise that the knowledge, skills and attitudes identified are inextricably linked. These aspirations can only be achieved through high quality teaching and learning and the establishment of a supportive climate for learning. All teachers have an important role in modelling and promoting an ethos of inclusion and respect for individuals.

In planning learning and teaching in religious and moral education, teachers will be able to:

▸ sensitively take account of and value the religious and cultural diversity within their own local communities, using relevant contexts which are familiar to young people
▸ actively encourage children and young people to participate in service to others
▸ develop, through knowledge and understanding and discussion and active debate, an ability to understand other people's beliefs
▸ draw upon a variety of approaches including active learning and planned, purposeful play
▸ encourage the development of enquiry and critical thinking skills
▸ create opportunities for the development of problem-solving skills
▸ build in time for personal reflection and encourage discussion in depth and debate
▸ provide opportunities for collaborative and independent learning
▸ take account of the faith background, circumstances and developmental stage of the children and young people and their capacity to engage with complex ideas
▸ recognise and build on the considerable scope for connections between themes and learning in religious and moral education and other areas of the curriculum
▸ make appropriate and imaginative use of technology
▸ build on the principles of Assessment is for Learning.

Active learning approaches, including collaborative learning, will encourage children and young people to discuss and share ideas, experiences and moral challenges in a variety of ways, as well as develop skills for life and work such as communication, working with others and problem-solving.

Teachers will ensure that children and young people from within any faith are treated with sensitivity. While some may wish to discuss their faith, others may not. Teachers should not assume that any child or young person should be automatically drawn upon as a source of information.

Viewpoints independent of religious belief can be considered within the learning and teaching approaches adopted for Christianity and world religions selected for study. The experiences and outcomes in development of beliefs and values support the development of broader understanding and permeate learning and teaching.

Above all, it is the teacher who brings the inspiration and challenge critical to achieving our aspirations for all young people.

PLANNING FOR AN APPROPRIATE RANGE OF RELIGIONS AND VIEWPOINTS INDEPENDENT OF RELIGIOUS BELIEF

In addition to study of Christianity, decisions have to be made about which world religions will be selected for study to develop depth of understanding. It is important to acknowledge local circumstances and community expectations and to involve parents in decision making. It is also important to avoid superficial coverage of too many religions and too many aspects which is potentially confusing. With this in mind it may be appropriate in many primary schools to focus on a maximum of two world religions in addition to Christianity. However, while one or more religions will be studied in depth, teachers may also want to draw upon carefully selected aspects of other religions, possibly in the context of interdisciplinary learning.

The context of study of world religions including Christianity will often lead teachers to appropriate points where viewpoints independent of religious belief, values and practices, and traditions can be considered. An illustrative example is that of the opportunity provided when exploring a religion's moral values or response to a social issue also to explore corresponding or alternative moral values which are independent of religious belief.

SUPPORTING THE DEVELOPMENT OF CHILDREN'S OWN BELIEFS AND VALUES

The processes associated with the idea of 'personal search' remain a key component of teaching and learning in religious and moral education: children and young people must learn from religious beliefs as well as learning about them. The context of study should encourage the development of a child or young person's own beliefs and values in addition to developing his or her knowledge and understanding of values, practices and traditions. This can be achieved through consideration of, reflection upon and response to the challenges presented by religious beliefs and values, and those which flow from viewpoints independent of religious belief.

A child or young person should be exploring his or her developing beliefs and values throughout the process of learning in religious and moral education. This exploration should permeate learning and teaching, and should take full account of the background, age and stage of the child or young person. Knowledge and understanding are an essential element of this personal reflection and exploration but they are not its only components. A learner may feel and express a sense of awe and wonder, may recognise patterns and order in the world, may vigorously question sources, may be reflecting on relationships and values, and may have begun to consider ultimate questions relating to meaning, value and purpose in life. The process of learning must recognise this and start from where the child or young person is.

As the child and young person learns and develops, the spiral, cyclical nature of this process is evident; accordingly, the framework of experiences and outcomes provides opportunities to visit and revisit issues as this journey continues through life. (So, for example, a sense of awe and wonder is by no means limited to any particular stage of life.) The development of a child or young person's own beliefs and values is therefore embedded in the framework, and activities relevant to and supportive of this will take place in the context of exploring religions and viewpoints which are independent of religious belief. Teachers will recognise that in this process of personal reflection not all children will adopt a religious standpoint.

BROAD FEATURES OF ASSESSMENT

Assessment in religious and moral education will focus on children and young people's knowledge and understanding of religious practices and traditions and on their skills in making informed, mature responses to issues of belief and morality.

Teachers can gather evidence of progress as part of children and young people's day-to-day learning about, and their responses to, practices and traditions and beliefs and values. The use of specific assessment tasks will also be helpful in assessing progress in knowledge, understanding and skills. From the early years through to the senior stages, children and young people will demonstrate their progress through increasingly reflective responses to the beliefs, values, practices and traditions of others, in their skills of discussion of moral issues and in their own personal response. For example, do children and young people demonstrate that they are developing more informed viewpoints and wider perspectives in their reflections on moral and ethical issues?

Assessment should identify the extent to which children and young people can reflect on the beliefs, values and traditions they have studied. Approaches to assessment will take account of the idea that there is not always a 'right answer' where issues of belief and morality are concerned. Children and young people can demonstrate their progress through:

▸ how well they respond to questions and issues
▸ the depth to which they engage with issues of belief and morality
▸ their developing abilities to think critically
▸ their awareness of how they can put their own beliefs, values and attitudes into action and show respect for those who hold different beliefs.

Assessment should also link with other areas of the curriculum, within and outside the classroom, and offer children and young people opportunities to investigate religious and cultural diversity and the impact of religion on lives and society within the local and global community.

CONTRIBUTION TO THE CURRICULUM AS A WHOLE AND CONNECTIONS WITH OTHER CURRICULUM AREAS

Values such as justice, wisdom, compassion and integrity are constantly being enacted through all aspects of the life of the school as a community. They can be further developed through exploration and discussion in religious and moral education.

Children and young people should be given opportunities to participate in service to others and to meet people who show their faith in action. They will learn from all those who offer inspiration, challenge and support.

The religious and moral education experiences and outcomes encourage links with other areas of the curriculum to provide learners with deeper, more enjoyable and active experiences. These experiences contribute much to the development of the four capacities of successful learners, confident individuals, responsible citizens and effective contributors, as described in *Building the Curriculum 1*. Religious and moral education has strong associations with learning for citizenship, enterprise, international education, creativity and sustainable development.

Practitioners are able to organise and group the experiences and outcomes in different and creative ways to bring together various elements of learning as well as linking with the school's involvement in the wider community.

Teachers will recognise the potential for valuable links between religious and moral education and all other areas of the curriculum. Aspects of health and wellbeing provide extensive opportunities for learning about moral dimensions of life including relationships. Children and young people will examine moral and ethical issues in other areas of the curriculum. Social studies and science offer opportunities to relate religious and moral education to global contexts and to raise contemporary moral and ethical issues. The expressive arts provide means, through role play and music, through creating personal artwork and through reflecting upon the artwork of others, which raise awareness and understanding of different views and beliefs and promote discussion and debate. Effective links with English and Gàidhlig will support the exploration of beliefs, values and issues through literature, poetry and other types of text.

INSIGHT AND EXPERIENCES OF SCOTLAND'S CULTURAL HERITAGE AND IDENTITY

The experiences and outcomes draw on the rich and diverse context of Scotland's cultural heritage through the use of Scottish stories, images, music and poems. As teachers make use of the experiences and outcomes they will draw on the resources of the school's community and context to inform their planning. Within practices and traditions, this can be made explicit through visits to local places of worship as well as through festivals and celebrations.

EXPERIENCES & OUTCOMES

Learning through religious and moral education[1] enables me to:

▶ recognise religion as an important expression of human experience

▶ learn about and from the beliefs, values, practices and traditions of Christianity and the world religions selected for study, other traditions and viewpoints independent of religious belief

▶ explore and develop knowledge and understanding of religions, recognising the place of Christianity in the Scottish context

▶ investigate and understand the responses which religious and non-religious views can offer to questions about the nature and meaning of life

▶ recognise and understand religious diversity and the importance of religion in society

▶ develop respect for others and an understanding of beliefs and practices which are different from my own

▶ explore and establish values such as wisdom, justice, compassion and integrity and engage in the development of and reflection upon my own moral values

▶ develop my beliefs, attitudes, values and practices through reflection, discovery and critical evaluation

▶ develop the skills of reflection, discernment, critical thinking and deciding how to act when making moral decisions

▶ make a positive difference to the world by putting my beliefs and values into action

▶ establish a firm foundation for lifelong learning, further learning and adult life.

[1]   Religious education has a statutory position in Scottish education, relating to schools but not to pre-school centres.

CHRISTIANITY (RME x-01 to x-03)

WORLD RELIGIONS SELECTED FOR STUDY (RME x-04 to x-06)

DEVELOPMENT OF BELIEFS AND VALUES (RME x-07 to x-09)

These experiences and outcomes should be addressed through the context of the experiences and outcomes for Christianity and world religions selected for study. They should not be seen as a separate area to plan for but should be intertwined with the experiences and outcomes for Christianity and the world religions selected for study. They should also enable consideration of a range of spiritual traditions and viewpoints which are independent of religious belief.

BELIEFS

E **RME 0-01a** As I explore Christian stories, images, music and poems, I am becoming familiar with some beliefs Christian people have about God and Jesus. **RME 0-04a** As I explore stories, images, music and poems, I am becoming familiar with the beliefs of the world religions I am learning about. **RME 0-07a / 1-07a / 2-07a** I am developing respect for others and my understanding of their beliefs and values.	• Shares thoughts and asks and answers questions to show and support understanding about stories, images, music and poems[1] from Christianity and at least one World Religion. • Identifies and discusses at least two aspects[2] of a religion. • Relates information and ideas about at least two beliefs to personal experiences.
1 **RME 1-01a** Through exploring Bible stories, I can describe some beliefs Christians have about God and Jesus. **RME 1-01b** By exploring some places and investigating artefacts, I am developing my knowledge of Christian beliefs and my awareness of the role of Christianity in Scottish society and the world. **RME 1-04a** Through exploring stories from world religions, I can describe some of their key beliefs. **RME 1-04b** By exploring some places and investigating artefacts, I am developing my knowledge of the beliefs of world religions and my awareness of their role in Scottish society and the world. **RME 1-01c* / RME 1-04c** I can talk about my own beliefs, or express them in other ways. **RME 0-07a / 1-07a / 2-07a** I am developing respect for others and my understanding of their beliefs and values. **RME 1-09a** I am developing an awareness that some people have beliefs and values which are independent of religion. *The following Es & Os are not listed in the Benchmarks:* **RME 1-08a / 2-08a** I am developing an increasing awareness and understanding of my own beliefs and I put them into action in positive ways.	• Describes, discusses and expresses an opinion with at least one reason on at least one belief[3] from Christianity, at least one World Religion, and at least one belief group independent of religion.[4] • Describes and discusses at least one personal belief and at least one example of how own beliefs might affect actions.
2 **RME 2-01a** Through investigating and reflecting upon biblical and other Christian stories, I can show my understanding of these stories. **RME 2-04a** Through investigating and reflecting upon stories of world religions, I can show my understanding of these stories. **RME 2-01b** Through exploring the lives and teachings of Jesus and other figures in Christianity, I am increasing my knowledge and understanding of key Christian beliefs. **RME 2-04b** Through exploring the lives and teachings of significant figures from world religions, I am increasing my knowledge and understanding of their key beliefs. **RME 2-01c** I can show understanding of Christian beliefs and explore the similarities and differences between these and my developing beliefs. **RME 2-04c** I can show understanding of the beliefs of world religions and explore the similarities and differences between these and my developing beliefs. **RME 0-07a / 1-07a / 2-07a** I am developing respect for others and my understanding of their beliefs and values. **RME 1-08a / 2-08a** I am developing an increasing awareness and understanding of my own beliefs and I put them into action in positive ways. **RME 2-09a** I am increasing my understanding of how people come to have their beliefs, and further developing my awareness that there is a diversity of belief in modern Scotland. **RME 2-09b** I am developing my understanding that people have beliefs and values based upon religious or other positions.	• Investigates, describes, explains and expresses an opinion on at least one belief[5] from Christianity, at least one World Religion, and at least one belief group independent of religion. • Discusses ways in which own beliefs can affect actions.

VALUES AND ISSUES

E **RME 0-02a* / RME 0-05a / RME 0-09a** As I play and learn, I am developing my understanding of what is fair and unfair and the importance of caring for, sharing and cooperating with others.	• Shares thoughts about what is fair, unfair, caring and sharing.
1 **RME 1-02a** Having explored biblical and other Christian stories, I can show my developing understanding of key values of Christianity and how they might be put into action in people's lives and communities. **RME 1-02b** I can describe the key features of the values of Christianity which are expressed in stories. **RME 1-05a** Having explored stories from world religions, I can show my developing understanding of key values of those faiths and how they might be put into action in people's lives and communities. **RME 1-05b** I can describe the key features of the values of world religions which are expressed in stories. *The following Es & Os are not listed in the Benchmarks:* **RME 1-09b** I can show my understanding of values such as caring, sharing, fairness, equality and love. **RME 1-09c** I am becoming aware that people's beliefs and values affect their actions.	• Describes and discusses at least one value[6] from Christianity, at least one World Religion, and at least one belief group independent of religion, illustrating how this value could be put into practice. • Describes and discusses at least one personal value and at least one example of how own values might affect actions.

RME 2-02a Through investigating and reflecting upon the lives and teachings of Jesus and key Christian figures, and drawing upon moral values as expressed in Christianity, I am beginning to understand how these have influenced Christian morality. **RME 2-05a** Through investigating and reflecting upon the lives and teachings of significant figures from world religions, and drawing upon moral values as expressed in religious scriptures and other stories, I am beginning to understand how these have influenced the morality of world religions. **RME 2-02b / 2-05b** I can share my developing views about values such as fairness and equality and love, caring, sharing and human rights. **RME 0-07a / 1-07a / 2-07a** I am developing respect for others and my understanding of their beliefs and values. **RME 2-09b** I am developing my understanding that people have beliefs and values based upon religious or other positions. **RME 2-09c** I can explain why different people think that values such as honesty, respect and compassion are important, and I show respect for others. **RME 2-09d** I am developing my understanding of how my own and other people's beliefs and values affect their actions.	• Investigates, describes, explains and expresses an opinion on at least one value from Christianity, at least one World Religion, and at least one belief group independent of religion. • Discusses ways in which own values can affect actions. • Discusses and expresses views about the importance of values such as honesty, respect and compassion. **2**

PRACTICES AND TRADITIONS

RME 0-03a I am becoming aware of the importance of celebrations, festivals and customs in Christian people's lives. **RME 0-06a** I am becoming aware of the importance of celebrations, festivals and customs in religious people's lives. **RME 0-07a / 1-07a / 2-07a** I am developing respect for others and my understanding of their beliefs and values.	• Shares thoughts and asks and answers questions to show and support understanding about at least one celebration, festival and custom in Christianity and at least one World Religion. **E**
RME 1-03a Through investigating the Christian communities in my local area, I am discovering how Christian communities demonstrate their beliefs through prayer, worship and special ceremonies. I am developing respect for the practices and traditions of others. **RME 1-03b** I am developing an awareness of the ways in which Christians celebrate different times of year and can relate these to my own life and community. **RME 1-06a** I am discovering how followers of world religions demonstrate their beliefs through prayer/meditation, worship and special ceremonies. I am developing respect for the practices and traditions of others. **RME 1-06b** I am developing an awareness of the ways in which followers of world religions celebrate different times of year and can relate these to my own life and community. **RME 0-07a / 1-07a / 2-07a** I am developing respect for others and my understanding of their beliefs and values.	• Describes and discusses the significance of at least one special ceremony, celebration and way of marking a major life event in Christianity, at least one World Religion, and at least one belief group independent of religion. **1**
RME 2-03a I am increasing my knowledge and understanding of different forms of Christian worship and artefacts and can explain their importance for Christians. **RME 2-06a** I am increasing my knowledge and understanding of different forms of worship and artefacts within world religions and can explain their importance for followers of world religions. **RME 2-03b** Through investigating the ways in which Christians mark major life events and times of year, I can explain key features of such festivals and celebrations. **RME 2-06b** Through investigating and reflecting upon the ways in which followers of world religions mark major life events and times of year, I can explain key features of such festivals and celebrations. **RME 2-03c** I can describe the practices and traditions of Christianity and have considered the way these have influenced Scottish society. **RME 2-06c** I can describe and reflect upon practices and traditions of world religions. **RME 0-07a / 1-07a / 2-07a** I am developing respect for others and my understanding of their beliefs and values. **RME 2-09d** I am developing my understanding of how my own and other people's beliefs and values affect their actions.	• Investigates, describes, explains and expresses an opinion with supporting reasons on the importance of at least two from a tradition, a practice, a ceremony, a custom, a way of marking a major life event in Christianity, at least one World Religion, and at least one belief group independent of religion. **2**

RELIGIOUS EDUCATION IN ROMAN CATHOLIC SCHOOLS

PRINCIPLES & PRACTICE

CONTEXT OF RELIGIOUS EDUCATION IN ROMAN CATHOLIC SCHOOLS

Scotland in the 21st century is an increasingly multi-cultural and diverse nation. The great majority of Scottish denominational schools are Roman Catholic, while a small number serve other faith communities. The curriculum in a denominational school will reflect its particular faith perspective. In Roman Catholic schools, it will build on the openness of Catholic schools to other young people regardless of denominations and faiths.

This framework of experiences and outcomes, the principles which underpin it and the practice that arises from it maintain continuity with established practice within Roman Catholic schools but develop that practice further in the light of *Curriculum for Excellence*. Full understanding of these principles and practice can only be achieved by reading them in conjunction with the Supplementary Guidance *This is Our Faith*, provided on the Scottish Catholic Education Service website, http://www.sces.uk.com.

It is hoped that this guidance will also be useful for the religious education of Catholic children who are attending non-denominational schools and do not have access to the provision of Catholic education.

RELIGIOUS EDUCATION

The position of religious education in denominational schools is set out in statute.[1] In Catholic schools, the Catholic Education Commission has responsibility for the faith content of the curriculum on behalf of the Bishops' Conference of Scotland. The Scottish Government is working in partnership with the Catholic Education Commission in the development of guidance for Catholic schools in keeping with the values, purposes and principles of *Curriculum for Excellence*. In Catholic schools the term 'religious education' is used in preference to 'religious and moral education'.

Religious education in Catholic schools takes place within the context of the wider Catholic faith community, in partnership with home and parish. It is an integral part of the Catholic school, which is itself a community of faith. It is designed to assist children and young people to be increasingly able to make an informed and mature response to God in faith and to nurture that faith. It offers opportunities for both evangelisation – proclaiming the Gospel message to all – and catechesis – the deepening of existing faith commitments among believers.

[1] Please note that the statutory position of religious education relates to schools and not to pre-school centres.

WHAT LEARNING IN RELIGIOUS EDUCATION IN ROMAN CATHOLIC SCHOOLS WILL ENABLE CHILDREN AND YOUNG PEOPLE TO DO

As many schools and teachers recognise, the curriculum is more than curriculum areas and subjects: it is the totality of experiences which are planned for children and young people through their education – a canvas upon which their learning experiences are formed. Learning through religious education in Roman Catholic schools is no exception, contributing to the four aspects of the curriculum from *Progress and Proposals*: the ethos and life of the school, interdisciplinary studies, curriculum areas and subjects, and opportunities for personal achievement.

Within Roman Catholic schools children and young people will be at different places in the spectrum of faith development. While most young people will be of the Catholic tradition, some will be of other denominations and faiths or have stances for living which may be independent of religious belief. Religious education should support all children and young people in their personal search for truth and meaning in life, and so it is central to their educational development. This is recognised in Church documents which offer guidance on Catholic education:

> Students will surely have different levels of faith response. The Christian vision of existence must be presented in such a way that it meets all of these levels, ranging from the most elementary evangelisation all the way to communion in the same faith.
>
> *Lay Catholics in School,*
> Sacred Congregation for Catholic Education 1982, 28

Learning through religious education enables children and young people to:

▸ develop their knowledge and deepen their understanding of the Catholic faith

▸ investigate and understand the relevance of the Catholic faith to questions about truth and the meaning of life

▸ highlight, develop and foster the values, attitudes and practices which are compatible with a positive response to the invitation to faith

▸ develop the skills of reflection, discernment, critical thinking, and deciding how to act in accordance with an informed conscience when making moral decisions

▸ nurture the prayer life of the individual and of the school community

▸ understand and appreciate significant aspects of other

Christian traditions and major world religions

▸ make a positive difference to themselves and the world by putting their beliefs and values into action.

Teachers will remain faithful to the mission of promoting an understanding of the Catholic faith and they will also teach respect for persons of different religious convictions. Religious education in the Catholic school considers the significance of faith from the perspective of the life of the person and of the faith community. It does not study religion as a phenomenon from an external perspective.

In addition to developing their understanding of the Catholic faith, children and young people will also learn respect for, and understanding of, other Christian traditions. They will also come to an appreciation of significant aspects of major world religions, recognising and respecting the sincere search for truth which takes place in other faiths. Where appropriate they will learn similarly about stances for living which are independent of religious belief.

HOW AND WHEN CHILDREN LEARN ABOUT OTHER WORLD RELIGIONS

During the pre-school period and from experiences within their local community, most children will have learned something about other world religions, for example through festivals and celebrations, and teachers will want to build on that knowledge as they gradually introduce learning about other world religions. Depending on the context of the school and its local community, other world religions would normally be taught from P3 onwards.

To provide coherence and appropriate balance in the delivery of Catholic Christianity and other world religions, Church guidance is as follows. Normally learning about aspects of Judaism and Islam would take place from P3 onwards and be further developed in S1 and S2. This will not exclude reference to the beliefs of pupils of other faith traditions represented in the school, but such references should be in response to questions or on the occasion of religious festivals, for example. This means that they are likely to be exceptional. This can widen to learning about Buddhism, Sikhism or Hinduism in the secondary stages with fourth level providing some study options in this regard.

APPROACHES TO LEARNING AND TEACHING

The process of learning in religious education in the Catholic school can be seen as a journey of faith, a quest for personal growth and response within the community of faith. To ensure that the young person is able to participate fully and actively in this journey, it is essential that they are accompanied by adults who can engage, question and explain in such a way that the young person is enabled to reflect, understand deeply and respond appropriately.

The learning approach, referred to as 'The Emmaus Approach', which can be useful at appropriate stages on the journey of faith is described overleaf.

Engaging The teacher establishes a relationship of respect and trust with learners. They recognise the importance of the learner's understanding of his or her own life experience and affirm the unique capacity of each person to reflect upon events. Activities are constructed which allow the teacher to walk with the children and young people in a supportive and discerning fashion.

Reflecting Varied, stimulating learning opportunities are presented which catch the imagination, and focus attention on a selected aspect of life. Learners are led to think in such a way that they enter their own, or another person's, life experience. They are invited to respond by identifying and declaring the thoughts and feelings which they experience.

Questioning Through questioning, the learners recognise key issues common to all people, which lie at the root of the life experience under reflection. This demands much skill and awareness on the part of the teacher and can often be best achieved through the use of open-ended questioning.

Explaining The teacher explains the meaning of aspects of Sacred Scripture and Tradition which help the learner make sense of the particular element of life experience under consideration.

Deepening The way that the teaching is unpacked contains elements which help the learner engage and understand at levels that go beyond cognitive understanding alone. Experiences such as poetry, prayer, meditation, music, drama and faith witness can open not only the mind but also the heart and soul of the learner.

Responding The teacher creates a climate of respect for the beliefs of all learners and affirms the worth of each person being able to reflect, identify and describe their personal understanding of what they believe in the context under study. Within this ethos learners are led on to reflect upon the challenge to respond to God's call which lies at the heart of the study under consideration. They are asked to describe and explain their response and how this may affect their own life and that of others.

Responding in this way, when connected to the other five elements above, presents learners within the Catholic tradition with the opportunity to deepen their existing faith commitment. Within this ethos, learners of other denominations, faiths and stances for living which may be independent of religious belief are presented with the opportunity to progress their personal search for meaning and truth.

Such dynamic experiences of learning and teaching will be achieved where teachers in their planning seek to:

- build in time for personal reflection and encourage in depth discussion of ideas, experiences and moral challenges
- help learners to recognise the significance of their experience and nurture their capacity to reflect on and evaluate it
- incorporate experiences of prayer, liturgy and reflection and other opportunities for spiritual growth, enabling children and young people to experience the life of faith
- provide opportunities for learners to experience participation in service to others and meet people who show their faith in action
- highlight the relevance of faith and learning in religious education to the lives of young people in modern society
- encourage children and young people to probe the basis of different beliefs within an ethos of inclusion and respect
- recognise and build on the considerable scope for linking with learning across the curriculum and the ethos and life of the Catholic school community
- take account of the developmental stage of children and young people and their capacity to engage with complex ideas
- help children and young people to develop critical thinking skills
- maximise opportunities for collaborative and independent learning
- draw upon a variety of creative approaches which promote active learning
- engage learners in the assessment of their own learning
- make imaginative use of resources.

BROAD FEATURES OF ASSESSMENT

Assessment in religious education in Roman Catholic schools should assist children and young people to become increasingly more able to understand and make informed, mature responses to God's invitation to relationship. Personal faith commitment is not being assessed in any shape or form. In the educational context, the assessment of children and young people's response to God's invitation to relationship demonstrates the knowledge, understanding and skills that learners have gained to support their response to learning in religious education and in the wider life of the school.

Teachers will gather evidence of progress as part of day-to-day learning and through carefully planned use of specific assessment tasks. Approaches to assessment will take account of:

- knowledge and understanding of key aspects of Catholic Christian faith, including an awareness of other Christian traditions and other world religions
- each child and young person's responses (for example through self-evaluation) which demonstrate broader and deeper understanding, through critical analysis, moral reasoning and discernment
- their awareness of ways in which they put their beliefs, values and attitudes into action.

By its nature, learning in religious education involves children and young people visiting and re-visiting topics and relating them to real-life situations as they grow and develop.

They can demonstrate progress through their abilities in analysing, evaluating and communicating their increasing understanding with coherence and confidence, and through reflecting on their own and other people's experience of life. Children and young people can also demonstrate progress in how they respond to questions and issues, in the extent to which they engage in reflection and discussion on issues of belief and morality, and through their developing abilities to think critically. Examples of progress will include increasingly thoughtful responses to questions demonstrating progressive breadth in their knowledge and depth in their perceptions.

ORGANISATION OF EXPERIENCES AND OUTCOMES

The experiences and outcomes have been organised under Strands of Faith which outline the aspects of Catholic theology underpinning Catholic religious education. By indicating associated areas of reflective focus, each strand also provides an outline of the experience from within which learning takes place. They are not discrete entities – they naturally entwine with one another. While actively exploring and responding to one strand with learners, the teacher is able to draw on some aspects of other strands.

The experiences and outcomes framework will enable teachers to create the experiences of learning outlined in the Strand of Faith, enabling the learner to reflect upon their personal response to God.

The experiences and outcomes within each strand map progression which is not always linear across levels. They do have their own distinct and intrinsic value which must be addressed in order to develop the next steps in learning. The contexts for learning include self, family, school community, local/parish community, national and international community. The role of the school, parish and diocese as source and witness in the growth of the pupil is central.

These experiences and outcomes will involve the children and the young people in active learning as they mature in faith. The outcomes envisage the children and young people on a journey of unfolding encounter with God within the context of their total experience of life. This relies on a child-centred approach where children and young people are provided with opportunities to experience such encounters, built around the key facets of Catholic faith.

Such opportunities are not only provided by teachers but by parents and families and in local parish and community settings where young people are invited to consider their beliefs and values, their actions and commitments, their traditions and practices across a range of contexts, with the support of various adults and other young people.

The nature of these learning outcomes describes, in part, some of the experiences. The active use of verbs highlights the need for children to be engaged in quality interaction with the strands.

Mystery of God

- exploring situations of wonder and mystery in life
- in the light of the Word of God as expressed in the Christian

scriptures and the teachings of the Catholic Church, considering how these situations can affect the way that we understand ourselves, our lives and the world around us.

In the Image of God

▶ reflecting on the Christian belief that all our lives have meaning and that our gifts, talents, background, experiences, family and faith can help us value the vocation which God reveals in our life.

Revealed Truth of God

▶ reflecting on the Christian belief that God who made us and invites us to fullness of life is revealed to us as Father, Son and Holy Spirit through personal relationships with Him and one another
▶ expressing our thoughts and feelings about how it affects the way that we understand the inner experiences of our spiritual life in particular conscience, will and prayer.

Son of God

▶ reflecting on the Christian belief that God is revealed in Creation in a particular way through special events and people in the unfolding history of salvation, and that this revelation was made complete when God became human in Jesus Christ, Son of God and Son of Man
▶ expressing our thoughts and feelings about this in the light of the words and actions of Jesus
▶ reflecting upon the extent to which the words and actions of Jesus can affect the attitudes, values and behaviour of ourselves and others.

Signs of God

▶ reflecting on the Catholic Christian belief that the Risen Christ is present in the Community of the Church by the power of the Holy Spirit and that its members are nourished by sharing in the life of the Trinity through the Seven Sacraments
▶ understanding that the Sacraments are encounters with Jesus who continues to guide us on our journey of Faith
▶ having considered examples of prophetic and missionary church witness we can describe our thoughts and feelings about the impact Sacraments and witness can have upon our lives and our world.

Word of God

▶ reflecting on the Catholic Christian belief that God speaks to all peoples of all times and speaks to us in a distinctive way in the Word of God, expressed in Sacred Scripture and in the Sacred Tradition of the Catholic Church
▶ having applied the Word of God to everyday situations in life, we can express our thoughts and feelings about its effects on people's lives.

Hours of God

▶ reflecting on the Christian belief that the People of God respond to God's invitation to communion through Prayer and the Sacred Liturgy of the Church
▶ expressing our thoughts and feelings about this and describing how our understanding and experience of prayer and liturgy can affect our lives and those of others.

Reign of God

▶ reflecting on the Ten Commandments and on Jesus' New Commandment
▶ responding to the call to grow in holiness in this life and forever as expressed by Jesus in the Beatitudes
▶ examining the need to respond to moral issues in the light of Catholic teaching
▶ considering how our response to Christ's proclamation to build God's kingdom of justice, love and peace can affect ourselves and others.

CONNECTIONS WITH OTHER AREAS OF THE CURRICULUM

The experiences and outcomes for religious education in the Catholic school lie at the heart of the learning experience of all who belong to a school community of faith. School managers, in planning for the effective provision of Catholic education, will take account of the school's purpose and mission, its values, identity and ethos, its partnership with home and parish.

The Catholic Education Commission has published specific advice in the *Values for Life* resource on how the Catholic school can nurture the growth of values and virtues in the lives of its students. It demonstrates how – across the life of the school – schools can teach the values of justice, wisdom, compassion and integrity, thus enabling young people to develop as successful learners, confident individuals, responsible citizens and effective contributors.

If education in faith is at the heart of the Catholic school – if Christ is at its centre – then this should be reflected in the priority it gives to religious education: in its allocation of resources, in its curriculum planning and in its programmes of professional development and formation of staff.

All Catholic schools are expected by the Bishops' Conference of Scotland to follow guidelines established by the Catholic Education Commission on the provision of adequate time for religious education within the school curriculum. These guidelines indicate a requirement for a minimum of 2.5 hours per week in primary school and 2 hours per week in all stages of secondary school.

There are, of course, meaningful links between religious education and all other areas of the curriculum which are important and complement but do not displace the need for the minimum time allocation for religious education. In particular, some aspects of health and wellbeing provide opportunities for learning about some moral dimensions of life – for example, relationships education. Other moral and ethical issues are frequently raised through topics in other curriculum areas.

Active learning approaches to learning and teaching, including collaborative learning, will encourage children and young people to discuss and share ideas, experiences and moral challenges in a variety of ways and also to develop core skills such as communication, working with others and problem-solving.

Young people in schools will also benefit from the experience of faith which they gain through acts of prayer, worship, celebration and loving service to others. They should experience participation in service to others and meet people who show their faith in action. In ways appropriate to their stage, they should have opportunities to put their own ideas for living their faith into practice. They will learn from teachers and others who offer witness and inspiration, challenge and support.

FURTHER SUPPORT FOR PRACTITIONERS

Curriculum for Excellence offers an exciting opportunity to us all to review and reinvigorate learning and teaching, which inevitably involves change and challenge. In order to assist teachers across the country in meeting this challenge, further guidance and support is being provided to support teachers in their planning and ensure the experiences and outcomes are translated into very good teaching, learning and achievement for all learners. Such explanation and exemplification is contained in the Supplementary Guidance, *This is Our Faith*, provided on the Scottish Catholic Education Service website, http://www.sces.uk.com

RELATION OF EXPERIENCES AND OUTCOMES TO EXISTING PRACTICE

The experiences and outcomes draw on the best of current practice as outlined in Curriculum for Excellence documentation and build on previous documents emanating from the Catholic community. These include:

▶ *Catechism of the Catholic Church* (1994)

▶ *Compendium to the Catechism of the Catholic Church* (2007)

▶ *General Directory for Catechesis* (1997)

▶ *Declaration on Christian Education* (1967)

▶ *Lay Catholics in Schools* (1982)

▶ *The Religious Dimension of Education in a Catholic School* (1988)

▶ *The Catholic School on the Threshold of the Third Millennium* (1998)

▶ *Educating Together in Catholic Schools* (2007)

▶ *Religious Education Syllabus for Secondary Schools* (CEC, 1992)

▶ *Effective Teaching of Religious Education: Personal Search [Roman Catholic Schools]* (Learning and Teaching Scotland, 2001)

▶ *Religious Education 5–14: Roman Catholic Schools* (Learning and Teaching Scotland, 2003)

▶ *Religious Education 5–14: Roman Catholic Schools* (SOED and CEC, 1994)

RELIGIOUS EDUCATION IN ROMAN CATHOLIC SCHOOLS

The experiences and outcomes for religious education in Roman Catholic schools are currently provisional and subject to final agreement by the Scottish Government and the Catholic Education Commission. That process is ongoing. We will notify recipients of the experiences and outcomes once it is completed. The status of the experiences and outcomes (provisional or final) can also be viewed at the website of the Scottish Catholic Education Service: http://www.sces.uk.com.

EXPERIENCES & OUTCOMES

Learning through religious education enables me to:

▶ develop my knowledge and deepen my understanding of the Catholic faith

▶ investigate and understand the relevance of the Catholic faith to questions about truth and the meaning of life

▶ highlight, develop and foster the values, attitudes and practices which are compatible with a positive response to the invitation to faith

▶ develop the skills of reflection, discernment, critical thinking, and deciding how to act in accordance with an informed conscience when making moral decisions

▶ nurture my prayer life as an individual and as part of the school community

▶ understand and appreciate significant aspects of other Christian traditions and major world religions

▶ make a positive difference to myself and the world by putting my beliefs and values into action.

[1] Please note that the statutory position of religious education relates to schools and not to pre-school centres.

CHRISTIANITY (RERC x-01 to x-03)

MYSTERY OF GOD
- exploring situations of wonder and mystery in life
- in the light of the Word of God as expressed in the Christian scriptures and the teachings of the Catholic Church, considering how these situations can affect the way that we understand ourselves, our lives and the world around us.

IN THE IMAGE OF GOD
- reflecting on the Christian belief that all our lives have meaning and dignity and that our gifts, talents, background, experiences, family and faith can help us to value the vocations which God reveals in our lives.

REVEALED TRUTH OF GOD
- reflecting on the Christian belief that God, who made us and invites us to fullness of life, is revealed to us as Father, Son and Holy Spirit through personal relationships with Him and one another
- expressing our thoughts and feelings about this and how it affects the way that we understand the inner experiences of our spiritual life, in particular conscience, will and prayer.

SON OF GOD
- reflecting on the Christian belief that God is revealed in Creation in a particular way through special events and people in the unfolding history of salvation, and that this revelation was made complete when God became human in Jesus Christ, Son of God and Son of Man
- expressing our thoughts and feelings about this in the light of the words and actions of Jesus
- reflecting upon the extent to which the words and actions of Jesus can affect the attitudes, values and behaviour of ourselves and others.

SIGNS OF GOD
- reflecting on the Catholic Christian belief that the Risen Christ is present in the Community of the Church by the power of the Holy Spirit, and that its members are nourished by sharing in the life of the Trinity through the Seven Sacraments
- understanding that the Sacraments are encounters with Jesus who continues to guide us on our journey of Faith
- having considered examples of prophetic and missionary church witness, we can describe our thoughts and feelings about the impact that Sacraments and witness can have upon our lives and our world.

WORD OF GOD
- reflecting on the Catholic Christian belief that God speaks to all peoples of all times and speaks to us in a distinctive way in the Word of God, expressed in Sacred Scripture and in the Sacred Tradition of the Catholic Church
- having applied the Word of God to everyday situations in life, we can express our thoughts and feelings about its effects on people's lives.

HOURS OF GOD
- reflecting on the Christian belief that the People of God respond to God's invitation to communion through Prayer and the Sacred Liturgy of the Church
- expressing our thoughts and feelings about this and describing how our understanding and experience of prayer and liturgy can affect our lives and those of others.

REIGN OF GOD
- reflecting on the Ten Commandments and on Jesus' New Commandment
- responding to the call to grow in holiness as expressed by Jesus in the Beatitudes through being compassionate, just and willing to contribute to the common good
- examining the need to respond to moral issues in the light of Catholic teaching
- expressing our thoughts and feelings about how the Church's invitation to build God's kingdom of justice, love and peace can affect us and others.

OTHER WORLD RELIGIONS (RERC x-25 to x-27)

Scotland in the 21st century is an increasingly multicultural and diverse nation. The curriculum in a denominational school will reflect its particular faith perspective. In Roman Catholic schools it will build on the openness of Catholic schools to other young people regardless of denominations and faiths. In addition to developing their understanding of the Catholic faith, children and young people will also come to an appreciation of significant aspects of major world religions, recognising the sincere search for truth which takes place in other faiths. During the pre-school period and from experiences within their local community, most children will have learned something about other world religions, for example through festivals and celebrations, and teachers will want to build on that knowledge as they gradually introduce learning about other world religions. Other world religions would normally be taught from P3 onwards; however, where appropriate, this can be adapted to meet the needs of a diverse school community.

These outcomes can be met through a consideration of Judaism and Islam in the primary stages (although this can be adapted, where appropriate, to include some other world religions which exist in the school context). This can widen to learning about Buddhism, Sikhism and Hinduism in the secondary stages with fourth level providing some study options in this regard.

MYSTERY OF GOD	**RERC 0-01a** I explore God's natural world and I am beginning to see the wonder and awe of this gift in the world around me.	• Talks about where they can see God's creation. Recognises and identifies signs of God's love. • Shows love for others.
IN THE IMAGE OF GOD	**RERC 0-02a** I can share my awareness of what makes me a unique child who has been given gifts from God.	• Shares what gifts they have and talks about how they are different from other people's.
REVEALED TRUTH OF GOD	**RERC 0-03a** I am aware of God's love for me and His call for me to be close to Him. **RERC 0-04a** I am becoming aware of God as Father, Son and Holy Spirit.	• Asks and answers questions about their community and gives an example of how they are part of a Catholic community.
SON OF GOD	**RERC 0-05a / 1-05a** I am familiar with the Christmas story and I know that at Christmas we celebrate the birth of Jesus the Son of God and Son of Mary. **RERC 0-07a** I am familiar with the Easter story and I understand that God raised Jesus from the dead to be with us.	• Talks about and gives an example of why Sunday is special to Catholic Christians. • Knows that prayer is us talking to God. • Prays the sign of the cross.
SIGNS OF GOD	**RERC 0-08a** I am aware of being part of a community and I have begun to explore aspects of the local Catholic community.	• Participates in school liturgies. • Shows respect for the Bible and talks about why it should be treated with respect.
WORD OF GOD	**RERC 0-11a** I am aware of some Bible stories. **RERC 0-12a / 1-12a / 2-12a** I know that the Bible is the inspired Word of God and that I should treat it with reverence.	• Talks about a story with Christian values. • Talks about the importance of Easter and Christmas for Christians.
HOURS OF GOD	**RERC 0-14a** I know that when I pray I am speaking to God. **RERC 0-15a** I am aware that Mary is the Mother of Jesus and Our Mother. **RERC 0-16a** I can share that Sunday is a special day when the Catholic Christian community meets to celebrate Mass. **RERC 0-17a** I have experienced liturgy as a community event. **RERC 0-18a** I can recognise Easter and Christmas as special times for the Christian Community.	• Recalls the Christmas story and gives a reason as to why it is important. • States that Jesus is Son of God and Son of Mary and that Mary is our Mother.
REIGN OF GOD	**RERC 0-20a** I know that God invites us to show love to others. **RERC 0-21a** I can respond to stories that reflect Christian values.	• Recalls the Easter story and gives a reason as to why it is important.

E1

MYSTERY OF GOD	**RERC 1-01a** I am discovering God's precious gift of life and reflect on how this reveals God's love for me.	• Shares thoughts and feelings that God created and loves them and how life is a gift from God.
IN THE IMAGE OF GOD	**RERC 1-02a** I know that a loving God has created me and that my uniqueness can develop according to God's plan for me.	• Expresses that it is God who asks them to love others and shares how they put into practice love of God and love of neighbour.
REVEALED TRUTH OF GOD	**RERC 1-03a** I am exploring God's relationship with others and I have reflected on how people's faith has helped them in difficult times.	• Shares thoughts and feelings about how to make good choices. Describes and discusses how forgiveness and reconciliation are important in their relationship with God and others.
	RERC 1-04a I can describe God as Father, Son and Holy Spirit and I have reflected on how God can support me in my life.	
SON OF GOD	**RERC 0-05a / 1-05a** I am familiar with the Christmas story and I know that at Christmas we celebrate the birth of Jesus the Son of God and Son of Mary.	• Participates in discussion and reflection about how God helps them and others in life and at difficult times.
	RERC 1-06a / 2-06a I have examined some political, social, historical and religious elements in first-century Palestine and gained an understanding of Jesus' life on earth.	• Discusses ways in which they know the Holy Spirit is present in people's lives.
	RERC 1-06b / 2-06b I have examined the role of Jesus as a teacher and a healer and I have reflected on how His words and actions influence my own life and the lives of others.	• Gives examples from the lives of the Saints of how the Holy Spirit strengthens faith.
	RERC 1-07a / 2-07a I have explored the events of the Passion, Death and Resurrection of Jesus and I have reflected on the Catholic meaning of eternal life.	
SIGNS OF GOD	**RERC 1-08a** I know that through the Community of the Church, people can experience God's love and care and I have reflected on how this community celebrates together.	• States the names of the Trinity. • Shares thoughts and feelings about why the Church honours Mary.
	RERC 1-09a I am exploring the Sacraments of Initiation and Reconciliation and I have reflected on how the Sacraments help to nurture faith.	
	RERC 1-10a I have examined the role of the Holy Spirit in my life and in the lives of others.	
WORD OF GOD	**RERC 1-11a** I can share some Bible stories and I can explore how God speaks to us through these stories. I have reflected on how these stories can help me to live a Christian life.	• Participates respectfully in parts of the Mass. • Says some prayers on their own and as part of a worshipping community.
	RERC 0-12a / 1-12a / 2-12a I know that the Bible is the inspired Word of God and that I should treat it with reverence.	• Uses symbols and rituals to worship God.
HOURS OF GOD	**RERC 1-14a / 2-14a / 3-14a / 4-14a** I recognise the importance of personal prayer and communal prayer in the growth of all people's relationship with God. I know a number of traditional Catholic prayers and I have developed an understanding of the meaning of these prayers. I have participated in different approaches to, and experiences of, prayer. I can describe how prayer is an important part of the liturgical and devotional life of the Church. I have reflected on how all of these are different ways of worshipping God.	• Describes and discusses how signs and symbols helps them understand more about liturgical celebrations.
	RERC 1-15a I can honour Mary as Mother of Jesus and Our Mother. I can share why we honour her.	• Engages in discussion about Bible stories and describes in their own words how God speaks through them.
	RERC 1-16a / 2-16a I know that the Mass is at the heart of Catholic community life and I am developing an understanding of how to participate fully in this celebration.	• Reflects upon and explains how these stories help them live a Christian life.
	RERC 1-17a / 2-17a I have, through liturgical experiences, reflected on an ability to respond to symbols and take part in rituals in order to worship God.	• Knows that the Bible is God's Word and shows respect for the Bible.
	RERC 1-18a / 2-18a I know some of the signs and symbols related to Lent, Easter, Pentecost, Advent and Christmastide and I can use this understanding to help me explore the themes of these celebrations.	• Actively engages with the Christmas story and discusses its importance for Christians.
	RERC 1-19a / 2-19a I know that the Holy Spirit strengthens my faith and the faith of the saints and I have reflected on how the stories of the Saints can inspire me to live a more Christian life.	• Describes some facts about life in Palestine at the time of Jesus.
REIGN OF GOD	**RERC 1-20a / 2-20a** I know that I have been called by God to grow in love, justice and peace in my relationships with others.	• Gives a personal response to Jesus as teacher and healer.
	RERC 1-21a I have explored the implications of Jesus' command to love God and love my neighbour.	• Describes and discusses the Passion, Death and Resurrection of Jesus.
	RERC 1-22a / 2-22a / 3-22a I have explored the call to forgiveness and reconciliation and have reflected on how this can restore my relationship with God and others. I can put this understanding into practice in my relationship with God and others.	• Participates in discussion and reflection about the meaning of eternal life.
	RERC 1-23a / 2-23a I know that God has given me the freedom to make choices about the way I live my life. I have reflected on how the decisions of my conscience affect my relationship with God and others.	
	RERC 1-24a / 2-24a I have considered ways in which the Catholic Christian community works together to show care for the world and for the needs of all people. I have reflected on the implications of this for my life and that of others.	
BELIEFS IN OTHER WORLD RELIGIONS	**RERC 1-25a** I am aware that the Jewish and/or Muslim communities believe in God.	• Describes and discusses basic beliefs of Jewish people / Muslims about God and family and community values.
VALUES AND ISSUES IN OTHER WORLD RELIGIONS	**RERC 1-26a** I am aware of family and community values in the Jewish and/or Muslim faiths.	• Identifies and discusses the places of worship and the role of the Holy Books of the Jewish or Muslim community.
PRACTICES AND TRADITIONS IN OTHER WORLD RELIGIONS	**RERC 1-27a** I can identify the places of worship of the Jewish and/or Muslim faith communities.	
	RERC 1-27b I know that the Jewish and/or Muslim communities have special books which are important to their beliefs.	

1

MYSTERY OF GOD	**RERC 2-01a** I examine God's precious gift of life and can reflect and act upon my God-given role. **RERC 2-01b** I explore the Biblical stories of Creation and I can reflect on how we understand these truths in our modern world.	• Participates in discussion and reflection upon the gift of life. • Explains in their own words how the Biblical Creation stories help us know more about the gift of life. • Demonstrates, through their words and actions, Church teaching on care for the world and others. • Demonstrates through words and actions how Jesus influences people's lives and values. • Uses examples from the lives of the Saints and applies these to their own life. • Acts in a loving, just and peaceful way, using their gifts and talents for the good of all; and has identified ways to develop these. • Reflects and acts upon how good choices, forgiveness and reconciliation are important in their relationship with God and others.
IN THE IMAGE OF GOD	**RERC 2-02a** I know that God wants me to develop my God-given gifts and I have reflected on how I can use them for the common good.	
REVEALED TRUTH OF GOD	**RERC 2-03a** I can examine God's relationship with myself and others. I have reflected on how the gift of faith can permeate my whole being. **RERC 2-04a** I can identify the three persons in the Holy Trinity and I have reflected on how I can honour the Holy Trinity.	
SON OF GOD	**RERC 2-05a** / 3-05a I know that Jesus is truly divine and truly human and I can acknowledge Him as our Saviour who brings the New Covenant. **RERC 1-06a** / **2-06a** I have examined some political, social, historical and religious elements in first-century Palestine and gained an understanding of Jesus' life on earth. **RERC 1-06b** / **2-06b** I have examined the role of Jesus as a teacher and a healer and I have reflected on how His words and actions influence my own life and the lives of others. **RERC 1-07a** / **2-07a** I have explored the events of the Passion, Death and Resurrection of Jesus and I have reflected on the Catholic meaning of eternal life.	
SIGNS OF GOD	**RERC 2-08a** I have explored Christian heritage and my role in the Catholic community and I have reflected on how this role can affect my life. **RERC 2-09a** Through my study of the Seven Sacraments I have developed a deeper understanding of them and I have reflected on how they strengthen my relationships with God and others. **RERC 2-09b** I can understand that the Eucharist is 'the source and summit of the Christian life'. **RERC 2-10a** I can reflect on the Holy Spirit's prophetic influence.	• Shares their knowledge of Christian heritage and the Catholic community and applies this to parts of their own life. • Explains some facts about ecumenism and discusses how it contributes to building God's Kingdom. • Identifies the three persons of the Trinity, discusses their unique characteristics and shares ways that they honour the Trinity. • Participates in discussion and reflection about the work of the Holy Spirit, sharing some examples of this. • Identifies and discusses the parts of the Bible including describing God's message in some Bible passages. • Explains the Bible is God's Word and gives their own reasons why it should be treated with reverence. Shows respect for the Bible. • Is able to discuss and give examples that show Jesus is both God and Man. • Investigates and identifies key knowledge about Palestine at the time of Jesus. • Discusses the importance of the Passion, Death and Resurrection of Jesus for an understanding of the meaning of eternal life.
WORD OF GOD	**RERC 2-11a** I have studied the structure of the Bible. I can identify the different parts of the Bible and I have explored God's message in these. **RERC 0-12a** / 1-12a / **2-12a** I know that the Bible is the inspired Word of God and that I should treat it with reverence.	
HOURS OF GOD	**RERC 1-14a** / **2-14a** / 3-14a / 4-14a I recognise the importance of personal prayer and communal prayer in the growth of all people's relationship with God. I know a number of traditional Catholic prayers and I have developed an understanding of the meaning of these prayers. I have participated in different approaches to, and experiences of, prayer. I can describe how prayer is an important part of the liturgical and devotional life of the Church. I have reflected on how all of these are different ways of worshipping God. **RERC 2-15a** I can recognise Mary's significance within the Catholic tradition and I know that celebrating her feast days and praying to God through Mary can enrich my life. **RERC 1-16a** / **2-16a** I know that the Mass is at the heart of Catholic community life and I am developing an understanding of how to participate fully in this celebration. **RERC 1-17a** / **2-17a** I have, through liturgical experiences, reflected on an ability to respond to symbols and take part in rituals in order to worship God. **RERC 1-18a** / **2-18a** I know some of the signs and symbols related to Lent, Easter, Pentecost, Advent and Christmastide and I can use this understanding to help me explore the themes of these celebrations. **RERC 1-19a** / **2-19a** I know that the Holy Spirit strengthens my faith and the faith of the saints and I have reflected on how the stories of the Saints can inspire me to live a more Christian life.	• Participates in discussions about and gives examples of how the Sacraments strengthen relationships with God and others. • Explains in their own words the importance of the Eucharist for Christian life and participates reverently in all parts of the Mass. • Says some traditional prayers and prayerfully participates in different liturgical celebrations. • Investigates and shares why signs and symbols are used at particular times of the liturgical year and uses symbols and rituals to worship God, reflecting on their purpose. • Shares ways that devotion to Mary deepens personal faith life and says in their own words why Mary is important to Catholics.
REIGN OF GOD	**RERC 1-20a** / **2-20a** I know that I have been called by God to grow in love, justice and peace in my relationships with others. **RERC 2-21a** I can recognise how my relationship with God and others can be shaped by the values of Jesus' Kingdom. **RERC 2-21b** I recognise the contribution of other Christian Churches to Jesus' Kingdom. I have explored ecumenical action and reflected upon its impact in the world. **RERC 1-22a** / **2-22a** / 3-22a I have explored the call to forgiveness and reconciliation and have reflected on how this can restore my relationship with God and others. I can put this understanding into practice in my relationship with God and others. **RERC 1-23a** / **2-23a** I know that God has given me the freedom to make choices about the way I live my life. I have reflected on how the decisions of my conscience affect my relationship with God and others. **RERC 1-24a** / **2-24a** I have considered ways in which the Catholic Christian community works together to show care for the world and for the needs of all people. I have reflected on the implications of this for my life and that of others.	
BELIEFS IN OTHER WORLD RELIGIONS	**RERC 2-25a** I have explored some beliefs of the Jewish and/or Muslim communities.	• Shares some key beliefs and guiding principles for Jewish *or* Muslim life. • Shares facts and participates in discussion about Jewish *or* Muslim customs, artefacts, places of worship and religious festivals.
VALUES AND ISSUES IN OTHER WORLD RELIGIONS	**RERC 2-26a** I can identify some of the principles by which people of the Jewish and/or Muslim faith communities live.	
PRACTICES AND TRADITIONS IN OTHER WORLD RELIGIONS	**RERC 2-27a** I can share some of the key features and rituals associated with the Jewish and/or Muslim communities' places of worship and their festivals. **RERC 2-27b** I can identify some of the customs and artefacts related to the Jewish and/or Muslim communities and their festivals.	

2

PRINCIPLES & PRACTICE

Science is an important part of our heritage and we use its applications every day in our lives at work, at leisure and in the home. Science and the application of science are central to our economic future and to our health and wellbeing as individuals and as a society. Scotland has a long tradition of scientific discovery, of innovation in the application of scientific discovery, and of the application of science in the protection and enhancement of the natural and built environment. Children and young people are fascinated by new discoveries and technologies and become increasingly aware of, and passionate about, the impact of science on their own health and wellbeing, the health of society and the health of the environment.

Through learning in the sciences, children and young people develop their interest in, and understanding of, the living, material and physical world. They engage in a wide range of collaborative investigative tasks, which allows them to develop important skills to become creative, inventive and enterprising adults in a world where the skills and knowledge of the sciences are needed across all sectors of the economy.

MAIN PURPOSES OF LEARNING

Children and young people participating in the experiences and outcomes in the sciences will:

▶ develop a curiosity and understanding of their environment and their place in the living, material and physical world

▶ demonstrate a secure knowledge and understanding of the big ideas and concepts of the sciences

▶ develop skills for learning, life and work

▶ develop skills of scientific inquiry and investigation using practical techniques

▶ develop skills in the accurate use of scientific language, formulae and equations

▶ recognise the role of creativity and inventiveness in the development of the sciences

▶ apply safety measures and take necessary actions to control risk and hazards

▶ recognise the impact the sciences make on their lives, the lives of others, the environment and on society

▶ develop an understanding of the Earth's resources and the need for responsible use of them

▶ express opinions and make decisions on social, moral, ethical, economic and environmental issues based upon sound understanding

▶ develop as scientifically literate citizens with a lifelong interest in the sciences

▶ establish the foundation for more advanced learning and, for some, future careers in the sciences and the technologies.

FRAMEWORK STRUCTURE

The sciences curriculum area within *Curriculum for Excellence* has to meet some significant challenges. While every child and young person needs to develop a secure understanding of important scientific concepts, their experience of the sciences in school must develop a lifelong interest in science and its applications.

Content has been updated and account has been taken of research evidence on learning in science and of international comparisons. As a result, there is a strong emphasis on the development of understanding and on critical evaluation, and expectations in some areas have been raised.

The key concepts have been clearly identified using five organisers:

▶ **Planet Earth**
▶ **Forces, electricity and waves**
▶ **Biological systems**
▶ **Materials**
▶ **Topical science.**

Further explanation of the rationale for each organiser is provided within the framework. Through these organisers, the framework provides a range of different contexts for learning which draw on important aspects of everyday life and work.

The experiences and outcomes tap into children's and young people's natural curiosity and their desire to create and work in practical ways. They can act as a motivation for progressively developing skills, knowledge, understanding and attitudes, and so maximise achievement.

The level of achievement at the fourth level has been designed to approximate to that associated with SCQF level 4. As in other curriculum areas, the fourth level experiences and outcomes provide possibilities for choice: it is not intended that any individual young person's programme of learning would include all of the fourth level outcomes.

Schools and teachers will plan to offer different combinations of the experiences and outcomes to provide programmes that meet the needs of children and young people and provide a sound basis for more advanced study within the discrete sciences.

USEFUL APPROACHES TO LEARNING AND TEACHING

Although the content of the curriculum is important, the high aspirations of the sciences curriculum within *Curriculum for Excellence* will only be achieved through high quality learning and teaching. The sciences experiences and outcomes are designed to stimulate the interest and motivation of children and young people and to support staff in planning challenging, engaging and enjoyable learning and teaching activities. They allow flexibility and choice for both teachers and learners to meet individual learning needs.

Effective learning and teaching approaches extend experiential learning from the early years into primary school and beyond. As children and young people progress in their learning of the sciences, teachers can take advantage of opportunities for study in the local, natural and built environments, as an opportunity to deepen their knowledge and understanding of the big ideas of the sciences. Teaching and learning approaches should promote thinking as well as provide opportunities to consolidate and apply learning.

In the sciences, effective learning and teaching depends upon the skilful use of varied approaches, including:

▶ active learning and planned, purposeful play

▶ development of problem-solving skills and analytical thinking skills

▶ development of scientific practical investigation and inquiry

▶ use of relevant contexts, familiar to young people's experiences

▶ appropriate and effective use of technology, real materials and living things

▶ building on the principles of Assessment is for Learning

▶ collaborative learning and independent thinking

▶ emphasis on children explaining their understanding of concepts, informed discussion and communication.

Through involvement in a wide range of open-ended experiences, challenges and investigations, including those related to the applications of science in areas such as engineering, medicine and forensics, children and young people develop skills of critical thinking and appreciate the key role of the scientific process both in generating new knowledge and in applying this to addressing the needs of society.

SKILLS DEVELOPED IN THE SCIENCES

The experiences and outcomes in science provide opportunities for children and young people to develop and practise a range of inquiry and investigative skills, scientific analytical thinking skills, and develop attitudes and attributes of a scientifically literate citizen; they also support the development of a range of skills for life and skills for work, including literacy, numeracy and skills in information and communications technology (ICT).

These skills are embedded in the contexts detailed in the experiences and outcomes. The progressive development of these skills throughout the levels is supported through the increasing complexity of the scientific contexts and concepts being developed and through revisiting and reinforcing the skills. The experiences and outcomes support the development of the attributes and capabilities of the four capacities of Curriculum for Excellence by encouraging teachers to consider the purposes of learning and to plan for active learning.

The skills detailed below draw on research from other countries and on the signposts to the four capacities detailed in the HMIE 2008 publication Science – A portrait of current practice in Scottish schools.

INQUIRY AND INVESTIGATIVE SKILLS

Through experimenting and carrying out practical scientific investigations and other research to solve problems and challenges, children and young people:

▶ ask questions or hypothesise

▶ plan and design procedures and experiments

▶ select appropriate samples, equipment and other resources

▶ carry out experiments

▶ use practical analytical techniques

▶ observe, collect, measure and record evidence, taking account of safety and controlling risk and hazards

▶ present, analyse and interpret data to draw conclusions

▶ review and evaluate results to identify limitations and improvements

▶ present and report on findings.

The main approaches to science inquiry are:

▶ observing and exploring – careful observation of how something behaves, looking for changes over time and exploring 'what happens if...?' and 'how could I...?' questions

▶ classifying – through identifying key characteristics

▶ fair testing – through identifying all possible variables and then changing only one while controlling all others

▶ finding an association – linking two variables to determine relationships.

SCIENTIFIC ANALYTICAL THINKING SKILLS

Children and young people develop a range of analytical thinking skills in order to make sense of scientific evidence and concepts. This involves them:

▶ being open to new ideas and linking and applying learning

▶ thinking creatively and critically

▶ developing skills of reasoning to provide explanations and evaluations supported by evidence or justifications

▶ making predictions, generalisations and deductions

▶ drawing conclusions based on reliable scientific evidence.

PLANNING FOR PROGRESSION IN THE SKILLS OF SCIENTIFIC INVESTIGATIONS, INQUIRY AND ANALYTICAL THINKING

Throughout the framework, these investigation and cognitive skills are signalled within the experiences and outcomes across all levels. The skills become more complex as learners' conceptual understanding develops within increasingly complex science contexts.

Teachers can plan to focus on the development of specific skills through investigations, inquiries or challenges, with occasional opportunities for more detailed and comprehensive activities, recognising that any one investigation does not always require children and young people to develop the full range of skills.

A broad indication of expectations for the development of these skills at second level and at third/fourth level may be helpful.

Second level

Children take part in a range of scientific investigations and inquiries which develop their understanding of the underlying scientific concepts appropriate for second level. They develop a growing awareness of themselves and the world around them through observation, collecting specimens and carrying out experiments. They develop their ability to formulate questions or predictions based on observations or information that can be answered through experimentation, inquiry and research. As they answer these questions, they show an increasing awareness of the factors that could be changed and can plan a 'fair test' that involves keeping all the factors the same except one.

While conducting experiments, children are able to safely use simple tools, equipment, apparatus and procedures. They make observations, collect information and make measurements accurately using relevant devices and standard units and ICT where appropriate. They can select, with assistance, appropriate methods to record their findings.

Learners at this level use simple charts and diagrams to present, analyse and interpret their findings, identifying simple relationships, making links to their original questions or predictions and drawing conclusions consistent with findings. They can present their findings in writing, orally or visually using a variety of media.

Third and fourth level

Young people take part in a range of scientific investigations and inquiries which develop their understanding of the underlying scientific concepts appropriate for third and fourth levels. They will take a more quantitative and formalised approach to investigations and inquiries. As learners plan and design their investigations, they identify a number of key questions, formulating hypotheses and predictions based on observation or their knowledge. They control and vary an increased number of more complex variables.

Learners become more evaluative and increasingly take the initiative in decision making about samples, measurements, equipment and procedures to use. They demonstrate increased precision in their use of terminology, units and scales. They apply safety measures and take the necessary action to control risk and hazards. They collect and analyse increasingly complex data and information including using data loggers and software analysis tools.

Young people establish links between their findings and the original question, hypothesis or prediction. They establish relationships between variables and use a relationship, equation or formulae to find a qualitative or quantitative solution. They evaluate a range of aspects of their investigation or inquiry including the relevance and reliability of the evidence.

Young people provide explanations of their findings based on evidence in terms of cause and effect and by applying their understanding of the underlying scientific concepts. They begin to consider alternative explanations and apply or extend conclusions to new situations or identify further studies. They communicate effectively in a range of ways including orally and through scientific report writing.

DEVELOPING THE SKILLS AND ATTRIBUTES OF SCIENTIFICALLY LITERATE CITIZENS

Children and young people develop as scientifically literate citizens with a lifelong interest in science by:

- developing scientific values and respect for living things and the environment
- assessing risk and benefit of science applications
- making informed personal decisions and choices
- expressing opinions and showing respect for others' views
- developing informed social, moral and ethical views of scientific, economic and environmental issues
- developing self-awareness through reflecting on the impact, significance and cultural importance of science and its applications to society
- demonstrating honesty in collecting and presenting scientific information/data and showing respect for evidence
- being able to read and understand essential points from sources of information including media reports
- discussing and debating scientific ideas and issues
- reflecting critically on information included or omitted from sources/reports including consideration of limitations of data.

The experiences and outcomes clearly indicate opportunities for developing these skills and attributes.

BROAD FEATURES OF ASSESSMENT

Assessment in the sciences will focus on children and young people's knowledge and understanding of key scientific concepts in the living, material and physical world, inquiry and investigative skills, scientific analytical and thinking skills, scientific literacy and general attributes. Teachers can gather evidence of progress as part of day-to-day learning, and specific assessment tasks will also be important in assessing progress at key points of learning.

From the early years through to the senior stages, children and young people will demonstrate progress through their skills in planning and carrying out practical investigations, inquiries and challenges, working individually and collaboratively, and describing and explaining their understanding of scientific ideas and concepts. They will also demonstrate evidence of progress through their abilities and skills in reasoning, presenting and evaluating their findings through debate and discussion, expressing informed opinions and making decisions on social, moral, ethical, economic and environmental issues.

Approaches to assessment should identify the extent to which children and young people can apply these skills in their learning and their daily lives and in preparing for the world of work. For example:

▸ How well do they contribute to investigations and experiments?

▸ Are they developing the capacity to engage with and complete tasks and assignments?

▸ To what extent do they recognise the impact the sciences make on their lives, on the lives of others, on the environment and on society?

Progression in knowledge and understanding can be demonstrated, for example, through children and young people:

▸ providing more detailed descriptions and explanations of increasingly complex scientific contexts and concepts

▸ using a wider range of scientific language, formulae and equations

▸ presenting, analysing and interpreting more complex evidence to draw conclusions and make sense of scientific ideas.

They will demonstrate their progress through investigations, inquiries and challenges, and through how well they apply scientific skills in increasingly complex learning situations. For example, investigations and inquiries will become more evaluative, deal with an increasing range and complexity of variables, and involve collecting and analysing increasingly complex information.

Through developing these skills, children and young people will demonstrate growing confidence and enjoyment of the sciences. Assessment should also link with other areas of the curriculum, within and outside the classroom, to allow children and young people to demonstrate their increasing awareness of the impact of scientific developments on their own health and wellbeing, society and the environment.

CONNECTIONS WITHIN AND BEYOND THE SCIENCES

The sciences experiences and outcomes encourage links between the sciences and with other curriculum areas in order to foster deeper, more enjoyable and active learning. Experiences and outcomes relating to Earth science are located in both the social studies and the sciences frameworks and therefore offer an excellent vehicle for interdisciplinary working. Links exist between, and across, the sciences and other areas of the curriculum: for example, engineering offers possible links among the sciences, mathematics and the technologies. Such practice provides children and young people with opportunities to recognise the connectivity which exists across curriculum areas as a means of understanding the world around them.

All science teachers will look for opportunities both to develop and reinforce science knowledge and skills within their teaching activities and to work with their colleagues in other areas to plan interdisciplinary studies and a coherent approach to the development of literacy and numeracy skills, aspects of health and wellbeing and ICT.

Through self-evaluation, schools and departments will plan for an appropriate balance of learning and teaching approaches, progression in skills, and effective use of interdisciplinary work to deepen and extend learning.

EXPERIENCES & OUTCOMES

The sciences framework provides a range of different contexts for learning which draw on important aspects of everyday life and work. Learning in the sciences will enable me to:

▸ develop curiosity and understanding of the environment and my place in the living, material and physical world

▸ demonstrate a secure knowledge and understanding of the big ideas and concepts of the sciences

▸ develop skills for learning, life and work

▸ develop the skills of scientific inquiry and investigation using practical techniques

▸ develop skills in the accurate use of scientific language, formulae and equations

▸ apply safety measures and take necessary actions to control risk and hazards

▸ recognise the impact the sciences make on my life, the lives of others, the environment and on society

▸ recognise the role of creativity and inventiveness in the development of the sciences

▸ develop an understanding of the Earth's resources and the need for responsible use of them

▸ express opinions and make decisions on social, moral, ethical, economic and environmental issues based upon sound understanding

▸ develop as a scientifically-literate citizen with a lifelong interest in the sciences

▸ establish the foundation for more advanced learning and future careers in the sciences and the technologies.make a positive difference to myself and the world by putting my beliefs and values into action.

SCIENTIFIC SKILLS

The tables below have been included as a helpful guide to the scientific skills to be developed within the sciences at each level.

▼ SKILLS AT EARLY LEVEL

INQUIRY AND INVESTIGATIVE SKILLS	**Plans and designs scientific investigations and enquiries** ▸ Explores and observes through play. ▸ Asks questions arising from play activities. ▸ Makes simple predictions of what might happen. ▸ Makes suggestions about what to do to answer the selected question. **Carries out practical activities within a variety of learning environments** ▸ Discusses obvious risks and takes appropriate steps to protect themselves and others. ▸ Uses their senses to acquire information. ▸ Measures using simple equipment and non-standard units. **Analyses, interprets and evaluates scientific findings** ▸ Presents and sorts data/information, for example, using displays, photographs, simple charts and drawings. ▸ Provides oral descriptions of what was done and what happened. ▸ Recognises similarities, patterns and differences in the findings and links these to the original question. ▸ Discusses, with support, how the experiment might be improved. ▸ Relates findings to everyday experiences. ▸ Identifies and discusses new knowledge and understanding. **Presents scientific findings** ▸ Communicates findings to others verbally and through drawings, photographs, displays and simple charts. ▸ Responds to questions about their investigation.
SCIENTIFIC ANALYTICAL THINKING SKILLS	▸ Demonstrates natural curiosity and shows development of basic skills of analysis in simple and familiar contexts, for example, through asking questions, experimenting and making predictions. ▸ Demonstrates creative thinking by offering suggestions and solutions to everyday problems. ▸ Demonstrates reasoning skills by explaining choices and decisions.
SKILLS AND ATTRIBUTES OF SCIENTIFICALLY LITERATE CITIZENS	▸ Talks about science, showing developing understanding of risks and benefits, and listens to the views of others. ▸ Demonstrates awareness of the importance of respecting living things and the environment and of managing the Earth's resources responsibly. ▸ Demonstrates a developing understanding of science in the world around them. ▸ Explores the ways in which people use science and science skills as part of their job.

▼ SKILLS AT FIRST LEVEL

INQUIRY AND INVESTIGATIVE SKILLS	**Plans and designs scientific investigations and enquiries** ▸ Collaborates with others to identify questions to find out more about a specific scientific concept, idea or issue. ▸ Makes predictions about the scientific investigation/enquiry being planned. ▸ Contributes to the design of procedures for carrying out scientific investigations. **Carries out practical activities in a variety of learning environments** ▸ Identifies risks and hazards and ensures safe use of all tools, equipment and procedures. ▸ Collaborates to undertake investigations. ▸ Observes and collects information and makes measurements using appropriate equipment and units. **Analyses, interprets and evaluates scientific findings** ▸ Records and presents data/information using a range of methods including tables, charts and diagrams, using labelling and scales. ▸ Organises data and information and identifies significant patterns and relationships. ▸ Interprets findings and discusses links to the original question. ▸ Reports on limitations of their investigation and possible improvements. ▸ Relates findings to their wider experiences of the world around them. ▸ Identifies and discusses additional knowledge or understanding gained. **Presents scientific findings** ▸ Presents data/information using a range of methods including tables, charts and diagrams, using labels and scales. ▸ Reports in writing, orally or visually using a variety of media. ▸ Structures a presentation or report, with support, to present findings in a coherent and logical way.
SCIENTIFIC ANALYTICAL THINKING SKILLS	▸ Applies learning in the sciences. ▸ Provides creative solutions to scientific issues and problems. ▸ Contributes to the design processes and uses components to make models. ▸ Demonstrates reasoning skills and draws on understanding of science concepts to make and test predictions. ▸ Provides explanations which are supported by evidence.
SKILLS AND ATTRIBUTES OF SCIENTIFICALLY LITERATE CITIZENS	▸ Expresses informed views of scientific issues, both orally and in writing, and respects the views of others. ▸ Makes connections between science and their own health and wellbeing. ▸ Demonstrates awareness of their own impact on the world. ▸ Demonstrates awareness of how people use science in their everyday lives and in a variety of jobs and careers. ▸ Discusses science topics in real-life contexts including those appearing in the media.

	▼ SKILLS AT SECOND LEVEL
INQUIRY AND INVESTIGATIVE SKILLS	**Plans and designs scientific investigations and enquiries** ▶ Formulates questions and predictions (hypotheses), with assistance, based on observations and information. ▶ Identifies the independent, dependent and controlled variables, with assistance. ▶ Anticipates some risks and hazards. **Carries out practical activities in a variety of learning environments** ▶ Applies appropriate safety measures. ▶ Contributes to carrying out all the procedures. ▶ Makes observations and collects information and measurements using appropriate devices and units. ▶ Manages identified controlled variables to ensure validity of results. **Analyses, interprets and evaluates scientific findings** ▶ Selects appropriate methods to record data/information. ▶ Identifies relationships between the independent and dependent variables. ▶ Makes links to original questions or predictions. ▶ Relates findings to the wider world. ▶ Draws basic conclusions consistent with findings. ▶ Identifies and discusses additional knowledge and understanding gained. ▶ Recognises anomalous results and suggests possible sources of error. ▶ Evaluates the investigation and suggests one way of improving it if it was to be repeated. **Presents scientific findings** ▶ Presents data/information by choosing from an extended range of tables, charts, diagrams, graphs, including bar graphs and line graphs. ▶ Reports collaboratively and individually using a range of methods. ▶ Collates, organises and summarises findings, with assistance, using headings or questions to provide structure for presentations. ▶ Uses appropriate scientific vocabulary and acknowledges sources, with assistance.
SCIENTIFIC ANALYTICAL THINKING SKILLS	▶ Applies scientific analytical thinking skills, with assistance, working with less familiar (or familiar but more complex) contexts. ▶ Applies understanding, and a combination of more than one science concept, to solve problems and provide solutions. ▶ Demonstrates further development of creative thinking including through the engineering processes of design, construction, testing and modification.
SKILLS AND ATTRIBUTES OF SCIENTIFICALLY LITERATE CITIZENS	*At Second Level, it is anticipated that learners will be able to demonstrate the skills below with assistance:* ▶ Presents a reasoned argument based on evidence, demonstrating understanding of underlying scientific concepts, and engages with the views of others. ▶ Demonstrates understanding of the relevance of science to their future lives and the role of science in an increasing range of careers and occupations. ▶ Demonstrates increased awareness of creativity and inventiveness in science, the use of technologies in the development of sciences and the impact of science on society. ▶ Expresses informed views about scientific and environmental issues based on evidence.

2

PLANET EARTH

BIODIVERSITY AND INTERDEPENDENCE

Learners explore the rich and changing diversity of living things and develop their understanding of how organisms are interrelated at local and global levels. By exploring interactions and energy flow between plants and animals (including humans) learners develop their understanding of how species depend on one another and on the environment for survival. Learners investigate the factors affecting plant growth and develop their understanding of the positive and negative impact of the human population on the environment.

E		
	SCN 0-01a I have observed living things in the environment over time and am becoming aware of how they depend on each other.	• Explores and sorts objects as living, non-living or once living. • Describes characteristics of livings things and how they depend on each other, for example, animals which depend on plants for food.
	SCN 0-03a I have helped to grow plants and can name their basic parts. I can talk about how they grow and what I need to do to look after them.	• Explores, observes and discusses basic needs of plants and what they need to grow including water, heat, sunlight and soil. • Demonstrates understanding of how plants grow from seeds.

1		
	SCN 1-01a I can distinguish between living and non living things. I can sort living things into groups and explain my decisions.	• Explains the difference between living and non-living things, taking into consideration movement, reproduction, sensitivity, growth, excretion and feeding. • Creates criteria for sorting living things and justifies decisions. • Sorts living things into plant, animal and other groups using a variety of features.
	SCN 1-02a I can explore examples of food chains and show an appreciation of how animals and plants depend on each other for food.	• Demonstrates awareness of how energy from the sun can be taken in by plants to provide the major source of food for all living things. • Interprets and constructs a simple food chain, using vocabulary such as 'producer', 'consumer', 'predator' and 'prey'.
	SCN 1-03a I can help to design experiments to find out what plants need in order to grow and develop. I can observe and record my findings and from what I have learned I can grow healthy plants in school.	• Observes, collects and measures the outcomes from growing plants in different conditions, for example, by varying levels of light, water, air, soil/nutrients and heat. • Structures a presentation or report, with support, to present findings on how plants grow.

2		
	SCN 2-01a I can identify and classify examples of living things, past and present, to help me appreciate their diversity. I can relate physical and behavioural characteristics to their survival or extinction.	• Classifies living things into plants (flowering and non-flowering), animals (vertebrates and invertebrates) and other groups through knowledge of their characteristics. • Begins to construct and use simple branched keys which can be used to identify particular plants or animals. • Identifies characteristics of living things and their environment which have contributed to the survival or extinction of a species. • Describes how some plants and animals have adapted to their environment, for example, for drought or by using flight.
	SCN 2-02a I can use my knowledge of the interactions and energy flow between plants and animals in ecosystems, food chains and webs. I have contributed to the design or conservation of a wildlife area.	• Describes how energy flows between plants and animals in more complex food chains and webs and ecosystems, using vocabulary such as 'producers', 'consumers' and 'herbivore'.
	SCN 2-02b Through carrying out practical activities and investigations, I can show how plants have benefited society.	• Relates findings from practical investigations to describe how plants have benefited society, for example, in medicine, dyes, fuels, construction, prevention of soil erosion and by influencing the balance of gases in the air.
	SCN 2-03a I have collaborated in the design of an investigation into the effects of fertilisers on the growth of plants. I can express an informed view of the risks and benefits of their use.	• Collaborates with others to present a reasoned argument, based on evidence, of the risks and benefits of using fertilisers, demonstrating understanding of the underlying scientific concepts.

ENERGY SOURCES AND SUSTAINABILITY

Learners explore types, sources and uses of energy and develop their understanding of how energy is transferred and conserved. They consider the relevance of these concepts to everyday life. They explore the nature and sustainability of energy sources and discuss benefits and assess possible risks to form an informed view of responsible energy use.

E		
	SCN 0-04a I have experienced, used and described a wide range of toys and common appliances. I can say 'what makes it go' and say what they do when they work.	• Ask questions and describes what can 'make things go', for example, batteries, wind-up toys and sunlight. • Talks about toys and common appliances and what they do when they work, for example, produce heat, light, movement or sound.

1		
	SCN 1-04a I am aware of different types of energy around me and can show their importance to everyday life and my survival.	• Identifies and talks about types of energy that we get from different energy sources, for example, light, sound, heat and electrical. • Uses knowledge of different energy sources, for example, sun, food, fuel, wind and waves, to discuss the importance of different types of energy for everyday life and survival.

SCN 2-04a By considering examples where energy is conserved, I can identify the energy source, how it is transferred and ways of reducing wasted energy.	• Demonstrates understanding of the law of conservation of energy (energy can be converted from one form to another but cannot be created or destroyed). • Identifies the common types of energy (kinetic, potential, electrical, chemical, light, sound and heat) used in energy transfers and transformations that occur in everyday appliances. • Explains that when energy transfers and transformations take place, energy is converted into 'useful' and 'wasted' energy, for example a mechanical braking system transforms kinetic energy into heat energy which is dissipated to the atmosphere as 'waste' heat.	2
SCN 2-04b Through exploring non-renewable energy sources, I can describe how they are used in Scotland today and express an informed view on the implications for their future use.	• Researches non-renewable sources of energy, such as fossil fuels and nuclear, and discusses how these are used in Scotland. • Draws on increasing knowledge and understanding to suggest ways in which they can reduce their own energy use and live more sustainably.	
TCH 2-06a[1] I can analyse how lifestyles can impact on the environment and Earth's resources and can make suggestions about how to live in a more sustainable way. TCH 2-07a[1] I can make suggestions as to how individuals and organisations may use technologies to support sustainability and reduce the impact on our environment.	• [Explains how and why it is important to conserve energy.] • [Discusses the advantages and disadvantages of how technologies impact on the environment for example, renewable energy technologies.]	

PROCESSES OF THE PLANET

Learners explore the changing states of matter and the physical and chemical processes which influence Earth's atmosphere and oceans. They learn about climate change as a natural process in time as well as the result of human activity. Through connections with collaborative studies of landscape, weather and climate in social studies they build up an integrated picture of the dynamic nature of Earth.

SCN 0-05a / 1-05a By investigating how water can change from one form to another, I can relate my findings to everyday experiences.	**Early Level:** • Investigates the different properties of water and shares their findings with others. • Talks about water in nature and how it influences their everyday lives. • Identifies three main states of water (ice, water and steam) and uses scientific vocabulary such as 'melting', 'freezing' and 'boiling' to describe changes of state. **1st Level:** • Uses more complex vocabulary to describe changes of states of water, for example, 'condensation' and 'evaporation'. • Contributes to the design of an experiment to determine the temperature at which water boils, freezes and melts, ensuring appropriate use of units. • Knows that pure water boils at 100°, melts at 0° and freezes at 0°.	E 1
SCN 2-05a I can apply my knowledge of how water changes state to help me understand the processes involved in the water cycle in nature over time.	• Discusses the necessity of water for life, for example, for the growth of crops, for drinking and in river formation/flow. • Demonstrates understanding of the processes involved in the water cycle.	2

SPACE

Learners develop their understanding of the Earth's position within the universe while developing a sense of time and scale. They develop their understanding of how our knowledge of the universe has changed over time and explore ideas of future space exploration and the likelihood of life beyond planet Earth.

SCN 0-06a I have experienced the wonder of looking at the vastness of the sky, and can recognise the sun, moon and stars and link them to daily patterns of life.	• Describes how the rotation of the Earth in relation to the sun gives us day and night. • Talks about how the pattern of night and day changes over the course of a year.	E
SCN 1-06a By safely observing and recording the sun and moon at various times, I can describe their patterns of movement and changes over time. I can relate these to the length of a day, a month and a year.	• Describes how the Earth spins around its axis in 24 hours resulting in day and night. • Observes and records the different patterns of movement of the moon and explains why the moon appears to have different shapes and positions in the sky at different times in a lunar month. • Demonstrates understanding of how the Earth takes one year to completely orbit the sun. • Demonstrates understanding of how the tilt of the Earth on its axis as it circles the sun causes the pattern of the seasons and changes to the number of daylight hours over the course of a year.	1
SCN 2-06a By observing and researching features of our solar system, I can use simple models to communicate my understanding of size, scale, time and relative motion within it.	• Reports collaboratively on the key features of the planets including size, distance from the sun, length of day, length of year, temperature, materials from which they are predominantly made and the number of moons. • Uses simple models to communicate understanding of size, scale, time and relative motion within our Solar System, including how solar & lunar eclipses occur.	2

---

[1] [When the Es & Os for Technologies were updated in November 2016, the Science Es & Os were not updated, and still contain the following deprecated entry: "TCH 2-02b I can investigate the use and development of renewable and sustainable energy to gain an awareness of their growing importance in Scotland or beyond." *Benchmarks* makes no reference to Technologies at this point.]

FORCES, ELECTRICITY AND WAVES

FORCES

Learners first develop an understanding of how forces can change the shape or motion of an object, considering both forces in contact with objects and those which act over a distance. They investigate the effects of friction on motion and explore ways of improving efficiency in moving objects and systems. Study of speed and acceleration of an object leads to an understanding of the relationship between its motion and the forces acting on it. This is linked to transport safety. Learners develop their understanding of the concept of buoyancy force and density.

E	**SCN 0-07a** Through everyday experiences and play with a variety of toys and other objects, I can recognise simple types of forces and describe their effects.	• Explores and sorts toys and objects into groups according to whether they need to be pushed or pulled. • Measures, using simple equipment, how the movement of an object is affected by the size of the force or the weight of the object. • Demonstrates, through play, how a force can make an object stay still, start to move, speed up, slow down and change shape.
1	**SCN 1-07a** By investigating forces on toys and other objects, I can predict the effect on the shape or motion of objects.	• Predicts and then investigates how a force can make an object change speed, direction or shape, and uses vocabulary such as pushing, pulling, stretching, squashing and twisting to describe forces. • Investigates balanced forces and explains that if a push and pull are equal in strength and opposite in direction then there is no change in movement.
	SCN 1-08a By exploring the forces exerted by magnets on other magnets and magnetic materials, I can contribute to the design of a game.	• Reports in writing, visually, orally how magnets exert a non-contact force on each other and attract certain materials. • Demonstrates through practical activities that like poles repel and opposite poles attract. • Gives at least two examples for how magnets are used in everyday life.
2	**SCN 2-07a** By investigating how friction, including air resistance, affects motion, I can suggest ways to improve efficiency in moving objects.	• Describes friction as a force which opposes the motion of moving objects, for example, two solid surfaces rubbing against one another or a solid surface moving through air or water. • Finds an association between air resistance (drag), the speed of the object being investigated and the surface area exposed to the air, making links to original predictions. • Demonstrates understanding of how friction and air resistance can both be useful, for example, in braking systems, and also a problem, for example, causing moving parts to wear. • Describes efficient movement as that which requires the least possible energy and suggests ways to improve efficiency in moving objects, for example, by streamlining.
	SCN 2-08a I have collaborated in investigations to compare magnetic, electrostatic and gravitational forces and have explored their practical applications.	• Measures gravitational force with a force meter or newton meter and records results using appropriate units (newtons). • Explains how some objects may become electrically charged by rubbing two surfaces together and how the charges produce an electrostatic force. • Investigates and demonstrates understanding that magnetic and electrostatic forces can both repel and attract. • Describes practical applications of magnetic, electrostatic and gravitational forces, for example, magnetised needle in a compass.
	SCN 2-08b By investigating floating and sinking of objects in water, I can apply my understanding of buoyancy to solve a practical challenge.	• Explores the factors which affect floating, for example, the object's shape and the density of the material that the object is made of, and collates, organises and summarises findings with assistance.

ELECTRICITY

The learner's knowledge about electricity begins with knowing how to use it safely and this aspect is reinforced throughout their learning. They develop their understanding of electricity as a means of transferring energy by investigating circuits and building chemical cells. Learners develop their understanding of series and parallel circuits and of electrical and electronic components and apply their knowledge to the process of designing, constructing, testing and modifying.

E	**SCN 0-09a** I know how to stay safe when using electricity. I have helped to make a display to show the importance of electricity in our daily lives.	• Groups objects into those which get electricity either from mains electrical sockets or alternative sources, such as batteries and solar cells. • Talks about the importance of electricity in their daily lives. • Identifies the risks that can be caused by electricity and recognises how to stay safe.
1	**SCN 1-09a** I can describe an electrical circuit as a continuous loop of conducting materials. I can combine simple components in a series circuit to make a game or model.	• Builds simple circuits containing bulbs, switches, bells and batteries.
2	**SCN 2-09a** I have used a range of electrical components to help to make a variety of circuits for differing purposes. I can represent my circuit using symbols and describe the transfer of energy around the circuit.	• Designs and builds a variety of electrical circuits for differing purposes, using an increasing range of components. • Draws circuit diagrams using appropriate symbols to denote a bulb, switch, motor, bell, buzzer, wires, cell and a battery. • Describes how components in a circuit transfer energy into different forms.
	SCN 2-10a To begin to understand how batteries work, I can help to build simple chemical cells using readily-available materials which can be used to make an appliance work.	• Applies knowledge and understanding to build simple batteries (chemical cells) and demonstrates understanding that a battery (cell) is a portable energy source which has a store of chemical energy. • Explains the process of energy transformation from battery (cell) to electrical components.

VIBRATIONS AND WAVES

Learners explore the nature of sound, light and radiations in the electromagnetic spectrum. They use musical instruments to explore the relationship between vibrations and sounds produced. They develop their understanding of the properties of light and other forms of electromagnetic radiations. They explore how different waves relate to the environment and how we make use of them in health, medicine and communications.

SCN 0-11a Through play, I have explored a variety of ways of making sounds.	• Predicts, then investigates, ways to make sounds louder and quieter. • Identifies different sources of sound.	E
SCN 1-11a By collaborating in experiments on different ways of producing sound from vibrations, I can demonstrate how to change the pitch of the sound.	• Demonstrates how sounds can be made higher or lower pitch by altering tightness, length, width or thickness or other physical characteristics of the sound source. • Explains that sound is caused by a vibration in a material.	1
SCN 2-11a Through research on how animals communicate, I can explain how sound vibrations are carried by waves through air, water and other media. **SCN 2-11b** By exploring reflections, the formation of shadows and the mixing of coloured lights, I can use my knowledge of the properties of light to show how it can be used in a creative way.	• Discusses and demonstrates through experiments how sound travels differently through air, water and solids. • Explains how hearing is limited by a range of factors, for example, age, position, and flexibility (direction) of ears. • Demonstrates and records, through practical investigations, that light travels in straight lines, can be reflected by highly-polished surfaces and that curved faces can distort the image. • Predicts and investigates how the position, shape and size of a shadow depend on the position of the object in relation to the light source. • Demonstrates that white light/sunlight can be dispersed to show the colours of the visible spectrum and identifies the colours and order of the rainbow as red, orange, yellow, green, blue, indigo and violet. • Explains that we see objects because they give out or reflect light rays that enter our eyes. • Draws on findings from practical investigations to describe the effect that coloured filters have on white light and how they can be used to make other colours. • Explains how we can recognise the colour of an object due the reflection and absorption of particular parts of the visible spectrum.	2

Design: © Harold Raitt / SeeHearTeach.scot (2019)   Content: © Crown copyright (2017)

BIOLOGICAL SYSTEMS

BODY SYSTEMS AND CELLS

Learners develop their knowledge and understanding of the structure and function of organs of the body, including the senses. They learn about cells as the basic units of life, and their organisation to form familiar body systems. Through observation, research and practical investigation learners explore the risk and impact of microorganisms in relation to health, and then in industrial processes. They experience the use of technology in monitoring health and improving the quality of life and develop informed views on the moral and ethical implications of controversial biological procedures.

E	
SCN 0-12a I can identify my senses and use them to explore the world around me.	• Identifies specific parts of the body related to each of the senses. • Uses their senses to describe the world around them, giving examples of things they see, hear, smell, taste and feel.
HWB 0-47b[1] / 1-47b I am aware of my growing body and I am learning the correct names for its different parts and how they work.	• [Describes how bodies change as they grow. Identifies body parts using correct names, for example, penis, testicles, vulva and nipples.]

1	
SCN 1-12a[1] By researching, I can describe the position and function of the skeleton and major organs of the human body and discuss what I need to do to keep them healthy.	• Uses components to make simple models of a skeleton which identify the skull, spine, ribcage and some bones of the arms and leg and which show how the skeleton gives us support and protects our organs. • Describes the position and function of major organs including the brain, heart, lungs, stomach and bladder. • Describes how skin, as an organ, provides a barrier to infection and helps to control our temperature. • Structures a presentation or report, with support, on how to have a healthy lifestyle, for example, through a balanced diet, regular exercise, sufficient sleep and by avoiding substance misuse.
SCN 1-12b[1] I have explored my senses and can discuss their reliability and limitations in responding to the environment.	• Uses their senses to detect information and explains how they help to keep people safe. • Investigates the reliability and limitations of the senses, for example, using taste tests, limits of sound, optical illusions and blind-fold games.
SCN 1-13a I know the symptoms of some common diseases caused by germs. I can explain how they are spread and discuss how some methods of preventing and treating disease benefit society.	• Describes the symptoms of some common diseases including colds, mumps, measles, chicken pox and flu. • Provides explanations, supported by evidence, of how some diseases spread and discusses ways in which some diseases can be prevented through good hygiene and vaccination.

2	

SCN 2-12a[1] By investigating some body systems and potential problems which they may develop, I can make informed decisions to help me to maintain my health and wellbeing.	*The expectation is that at least two of the following body systems will be studied at Second Level.*
	• **Respiratory system**
	  – Describes the function of the respiratory system (lungs, windpipe and bronchi), for example, in gas exchange.
	  – Discusses the main preventable causes of bronchitis, lung cancer and asthma, for example, smoking.
	• **Circulatory system**
	  – Describes the function of the circulatory system (heart and blood vessels), for example, transport of food, oxygen and waste materials.
	  – Discusses the main preventable causes of heart disease or stroke, for example, obesity, lack of exercise, smoking and high (saturated) fat diet.
	• **Digestive system**
	  – Describes the function of the digestive system (mouth, oesophagus, stomach, liver, small intestine, large intestine, rectum and anus), for example, breakdown of food and absorption of nutrients, minerals and water.
	  – Discusses the main preventable causes of liver disease, for example, alcohol and drug misuse.
	• **Reproductive system**
	  – Describes the function of the reproductive system (penis, testes, sperm tube/duct, ovaries, egg tube/duct, uterus and vagina), for example, to make a baby.
	  – Discusses some preventable causes of fertility problems, for example, alcohol misuse, anorexia and obesity.
	• **Skeletal system**
	  – Describes the function of the skeleton (skull, spine, ribcage some bones of the arm and leg), for example, to provide support, protection and enable movement.
	  – Discusses some common problems of bones (for example, arthritis, osteoporosis and breaks) and how their incidence can be reduced (for example, through calcium in the diet and weight-bearing exercise).

SCN 2-12b[1] I have explored the structure and function of sensory organs to develop my understanding of body actions in response to outside conditions.	• Describes how senses work individually or together to keep people safe from harm. • Demonstrates understanding of how, if one sense is impaired, it can have an effect on the other senses, either positively or negatively. • Describes how light enters the eye through the pupil and how the pupil changes size in dark/light conditions.
SCN 2-13a I have contributed to investigations into the role of microorganisms in producing and breaking down some materials.	• Demonstrates understanding of how microorganisms, including bacteria, viruses and fungi, can multiply rapidly. • Investigates and explains the action of some microorganisms used in food production, for example, yeast in bread and bacteria in yoghurt. • Describes how some micro-organisms break down food causing it to be inedible or harmful if digested, and how others exist in the gut to break down food to aid digestion. • Investigates, observes and records how microscopic organisms are necessary for the process of decomposition (the breaking down of dead material – decay).

INHERITANCE

Starting with observations of similarities and differences between individuals, learners develop their understanding of how organisms develop and pass on genetic information to the next generation. They begin to develop their knowledge of genetics and of the role of DNA and examine moral and ethical questions which arise from technological developments.

HWB 0-47a / 1-47a I recognise that we have similarities and differences but are all unique.	• [Identifies body differences and similarities.]	E
SCN 1-14a By comparing generations of families of humans, plants and animals, I can begin to understand how characteristics are inherited.	• Uses their own experiences to illustrate how inherited characteristics are passed from one generation to the next. • Knows that genetic information determines characteristics such as colour of eyes and shape of petals. • Demonstrates understanding of the variations within family groups.	1
SCN 2-14a By investigating the lifecycles of plants and animals, I can recognise the different stages of their development.	**Plants** • Describes how pollination occurs when the male cell (pollen) lands on the stigma. • Describes how fertilisation (sexual reproduction) occurs when the genetic information in the male cell fuses (joins) with the genetic information in the female cell. • Describes how the fertilised ovule develops into a seed and how the ovary ripens to form a fruit. • Investigates and explains how a seed germinates into a plant using water, oxygen, a food store and warmth. **Animals** • Identifies and compares the two distinct groups of animals – vertebrates and invertebrates. • Researches the lifecycles of the five main types of vertebrates including fish (spawn), birds (eggs which are rigid but fragile), amphibians (spawn and metamorphosis), reptiles (leathery shelled eggs) and mammal (live young), and communicates findings using a range of media. • Compares the lifecycles of some invertebrates, for example, ladybird and spider.	2
SCN 2-14b By exploring the characteristics offspring inherit when living things reproduce, I can distinguish between inherited and non-inherited characteristics.	• Knows that genetics is the study of inherited characteristics and that inherited characteristics are carried on genes and can sometime skip a generation. • Explores and categorises characteristics into inherited (eye and hair colour, height and right/left handedness) and non-inherited (native language spoken and favourite colour). • Describes how every living thing has its own DNA fingerprint.	

[1]   [A close link exists between **SCN 12** and Health & Wellbeing at all levels, not just at the level of **SCN 0-12** (although this is the only link drawn out explicitly in the Es & Os).

The links include:
• **SCN 12a** → **HWB 47/48** and **HWB 15**
• 'Respiratory system', 'Digestive system' and 'Reproductive system' in **SCN 2-12a** → **HWB 2-38a**
• 'Circulatory system' and 'Skeletal system' in **SCN 2-12a** → **HWB 2-32a** (and related Es & Os at Third Level).

In common with most inter-disciplinary links made in the Es & Os, these links are not shown at all in *Benchmarks*.]

MATERIALS

PROPERTIES AND USES OF SUBSTANCES

By exploring the properties of different substances and how they can be changed, learners gradually develop their understanding of the connection between structure and properties. They explore the development of new substances which have useful properties, and begin to relate physical and chemical properties to models of atomic structure. Learners begin to use symbols and chemical formulae as a way of communicating information about elements and compounds.

E	**SCN 0-15a** Through creative play, I explore different materials and can share my reasoning for selecting materials for different purposes.	• Explores and sorts materials into different groups depending on their properties, for example, whether they are strong, smooth, rough and if they float or sink. • Justifies the selection of appropriate materials for different uses based on their physical properties.
1	**SCN 1-15a** Through exploring properties and sources of materials, I can choose appropriate materials to solve practical challenges.	• Classifies materials into natural and human-made (synthetic). • Identifies properties of different materials, for example, rigidity, flexibility, rough, smooth and waterproof, and their uses linked to their properties.
	SCN 1-16a I can make and test predictions about solids dissolving in water and can relate my findings to the world around me.	• Links new knowledge of dissolving to real-life examples of things that dissolve and things that don't dissolve. • Predicts, investigates and records how solubility is affected by heat and stirring.
2	**SCN 2-15a** By contributing to investigations into familiar changes in substances to produce other substances, I can describe how their characteristics have changed.	• Investigates and explains physical changes to the properties of materials which are fully and partially reversible, for example, salt dissolving in water, chocolate melting and water freezing. • Uses scientific vocabulary such as 'melting', 'freezing', 'evaporating' and 'condensing' to describe changes of state. • Investigates and records chemical changes to the properties of materials which are irreversible, for example, cooking, rusting and striking a match. • Observes and identifies some of the signs of a chemical reaction, for example, production of bubbles, colour/texture change and heat given out/taken in. • Explores and describes the characteristics of solids, liquids and gases, for example, solids retain the same volume and shape, liquids keep the same volume but the shape changes to fit the container and that gases change shape and volume to fill the container.
	SCN 2-16a I have participated in practical activities to separate simple mixtures of substances and can relate my findings to my everyday experience.	• Draws on findings from practical investigations to explain how a mixture of solids of different sizes can be separated using a sieve or magnet, for example, sand and peas or salt and iron filings. • Selects the most appropriate practical technique for separating insoluble solids, for example, filtering or sieving. • Explains why a dissolved solid cannot be separated from the solvent by filtering but can be separated by evaporation. • Uses scientific vocabulary such as 'soluble', 'insoluble', 'dissolve' and 'solution' in context. • Relates findings of practical investigations about dissolving to everyday experiences, for example, recycling, salt production and water purification.
	SCN 2-16b By investigating common conditions that increase the amount of substance that will dissolve or the speed of dissolving, I can relate my findings to the world around me.	• Finds an association between the quantity of substance that dissolves and a range of conditions – temperature, time, particle size, stirring and quantity of solvent. • Investigates how a range of factors such as particle size and heat can affect the rate of dissolving. • Relates learning about the quantity and rate of dissolving to everyday examples such as dissolving sugar in tea or salt in water (granules or big crystals, hot or cold liquid, stirred or not stirred).

EARTH'S MATERIALS

Learners develop their knowledge and understanding of substances that make up the Earth's surface. Properties, uses and methods of extraction of such materials are explored. Opportunities exist to discuss the importance of carbon compounds derived from crude oil to our lives.

No Experiences and Outcomes at Early Level

1	**TCH 1-06a**[2] I can take appropriate action to ensure conservation of materials and resources, considering the impact of my actions on the environment.	• [Identifies ways in which energy can be saved.] • [Understands how and where we waste materials and resources.]
2	**SCN 2-17a** Having explored the substances that make up Earth's surface, I can compare some of their characteristics and uses.	• Analyses and compares samples of rocks, soil and minerals and reports their characteristics and uses, using a range of media.

[2] [When the Es & Os for Technologies were updated in November 2016, the Science Es & Os were not updated, and still contain the following deprecated entry: "**TCH 1-02a** Throughout all my learning, I take appropriate action to ensure conservation of materials and resources, considering the impact of my actions on the environment." *Benchmarks* makes no reference to Technologies at this point.]

CHEMICAL CHANGES

Learners gradually develop an understanding of chemical changes. They consider processes which take place in the environment and in the laboratory, and develop their understanding of the environmental impact of some changes. They develop their understanding of energy changes in chemical reactions and some of the factors affecting the rates of reactions. Learners develop the use of chemical names, formulae and equations as a way of conveying information about chemical changes.

No Experiences and Outcomes at Early or First Level

SCN 2-18a I have investigated different water samples from the environment and explored methods that can be used to clean and conserve water and I am aware of the properties and uses of water.	• Uses knowledge of the water cycle to explain how the quantity of water on the Earth has remained approximately the same. • Investigates and discusses the methods used to purify water, for example, sedimentation, filtration, evaporation, desalination and the addition of chemicals such as chlorine. • Researches methods used to conserve water within the home, school and globally and communicates findings to others. • Discusses the many uses of water, for example, to support all living things, in preservation (ice) and to generate electricity.	**2**
SCN 2-19a I have collaborated in activities which safely demonstrate simple chemical reactions using everyday chemicals. I can show an appreciation of a chemical reaction as being a change in which different materials are made.	• Collaborates with others to safely demonstrate simple chemical reactions, for example, effervescence. • Investigates examples of everyday chemical reactions, such as burning and corrosion, and names some of the new substances which are produced. • Uses prior knowledge to identify when a chemical reaction has occurred to produce a new substance.	

TOPICAL SCIENCE

TOPICAL SCIENCE

By considering current issues of science, learners increasingly develop their understanding of scientific concepts and their capacity to form informed social, moral and ethical views. They reflect upon and critically evaluate media portrayal of scientific findings.

SCN 0-20a I can talk about science stories to develop my understanding of science and the world around me.	• Talks about the science they encounter in their everyday experiences. • Explores, through role-play, how science and science skills are used in a variety of jobs.	**E**
SCN 1-20a I have contributed to discussions of current scientific news items to help develop my awareness of science.	• Discusses and expresses opinions about science topics in real-life contexts, including those featured in the media. • Discusses how people use science in their everyday lives. • Describes a variety of jobs and careers which require scientific knowledge and skills.	**1**
SCN 2-20a Through research and discussion I have an appreciation of the contribution that individuals are making to scientific discovery and invention and the impact this has made on society.	• Researches historic and contemporary scientists (ensuring gender balance) and their scientific discoveries and reports collaboratively to others using a range of methods. • Describes the impact of scientific discovery, creativity and invention on society past and present, for example, in design, medicine and agriculture. • Demonstrates understanding of how science impacts on every aspect of our lives. • Relates the development of scientific skills in the classroom to an increasingly wide variety of science, technology, engineering and mathematics (STEM) careers.	**2**
SCN 2-20b I can report and comment on current scientific news items to develop my knowledge and understanding of topical science.	• Explores items of current scientific interest within the school, local community, nationally or in the global media and collates, organises and summarises findings, with assistance. • Shares opinions about a variety of topical scientific issues considering, for example, moral, ethical, societal, cultural, economic and environmental aspects.	

SOCIAL STUDIES

PRINCIPLES & PRACTICE

WHAT WILL LEARNING IN SOCIAL STUDIES ENABLE CHILDREN AND YOUNG PEOPLE TO DO?

Through social studies, children and young people develop their understanding of the world by learning about other people and their values, in different times, places and circumstances; they also develop their understanding of their environment and of how it has been shaped. As they mature, children and young people's experiences will be broadened using Scottish, British, European and wider contexts for learning, while maintaining a focus on the historical, social, geographic, economic and political changes that have shaped Scotland. Children and young people learn about human achievements and about how to make sense of changes in society, of conflicts and of environmental issues. With greater understanding comes the opportunity and ability to influence events by exercising informed and responsible citizenship.

Children and young people as they participate in experiences and outcomes in social studies will:

▶ develop their understanding of the history, heritage and culture of Scotland, and an appreciation of their local and national heritage within the world
▶ broaden their understanding of the world by learning about human activities and achievements in the past and present
▶ develop their understanding of their own values, beliefs and cultures and those of others
▶ develop an understanding of the principles of democracy and citizenship through experience of critical and independent thinking
▶ explore and evaluate different types of sources and evidence
▶ learn how to locate, explore and link periods, people and events in time and place
▶ learn how to locate, explore and link features and places locally and further afield
▶ engage in activities which encourage enterprising attitudes
▶ develop an understanding of concepts that encourage enterprise and influence business
▶ establish firm foundations for lifelong learning and for further specialised study and careers.

ORGANISATION OF THE EXPERIENCES AND OUTCOMES

The social studies experiences and outcomes have been structured under the three main organisers:

▶ people, past events and societies
▶ people, place and environment
▶ people in society, economy and business.

These organisers recognise the special contribution made by each of the social subjects, whilst enabling them to reflect local contexts. Teachers will use this framework to provide children and young people with opportunities for effective interdisciplinary working by making connections across and between subject boundaries. Teachers should not feel constrained by the organisers and should explore the opportunities to plan within and across curriculum areas as outlined below to enhance learning. The organisers will assist with the collaborative planning of coherent programmes of learning within and between establishments.

The fourth level provides a range of experiences and outcomes within which there can be choice and scope for depth, challenge, enjoyment and personalisation. Schools and their partners will consider how they can offer and plan different combinations of the experiences and outcomes to provide a sound basis for more advanced study. The level of achievement at the fourth level has been designed to approximate to that associated with SCQF level 4.

APPROACHES TO LEARNING AND TEACHING

Although the content of the curriculum is important, our aspirations can only be achieved through high quality learning and teaching. The social studies experiences and outcomes will support staff in planning challenging, engaging and enjoyable learning and teaching activities which will stimulate the interest and motivation of children and young people. They allow flexibility and choice for both teachers and learners which can sustain interest and enthusiasm.

In social studies, effective learning and teaching will draw upon a variety of approaches including:

▶ active learning which provides opportunities to observe, explore, experiment and play
▶ use of relevant contexts and experiences familiar to children and young people
▶ appropriate and effective use of technology
▶ building on the principles of Assessment is for Learning
▶ both collaborative and independent learning
▶ discussion and informed debate
▶ interdisciplinary learning experiences
▶ learning outdoors, field trips, visits and input by external contributors.

SKILLS DEVELOPMENT

The development of skills is an essential aspect of learning in social studies and the experiences and outcomes provide frequent opportunities for applying these skills in new and more complex contexts. Terms such as 'investigating', 'exploring', 'discussing' and 'presenting' are used throughout the experiences and outcomes from early to fourth level, recognising that at all stages learners are capable of exercising these skills at a level appropriate to their development. The framework ensures that social studies provide an important context for the development of literacy and numeracy skills.

Children and young people as they learn within the social studies will develop a range of skills including:

▶ observing, describing and recording

▶ comparing and contrasting to draw valid conclusions

▶ exploring and evaluating different types of sources and evidence

▶ development of curiosity and problem-solving skills and capacity to take initiatives

▶ interacting with others and developing an awareness of self and others

▶ planning and reviewing investigation strategies

▶ developing the capacity for critical thinking through accessing, analysing and using information from a wide variety of sources

▶ discussion and informed debate

▶ developing reasoned and justified points of view

▶ developing and using maps in a variety of contexts

▶ developing and applying skills in interpreting and displaying graphical representation of information

▶ developing an awareness of sequence and chronology

▶ presentation skills – oral, written, multimedia.

Teachers will support children and young people as they progressively develop these skills by applying them in new and more complex contexts. Skills are to be regarded as a continuum and should not be 'capped' at any particular level. The professional judgement of teachers is essential in ensuring that individual learners are faced with the appropriate level of challenge in developing skills.

BROAD FEATURES OF ASSESSMENT

Assessment in social studies will focus on children and young people's knowledge, understanding and skills in their studies of people, past events, society, place, environment, economy and business.

Teachers can gather evidence as part of day-to-day learning, as children and young people describe and record, explore and analyse sources, interpret and display information, talk and debate with peers and adults, undertake investigations and present their thinking orally, in writing or in a multimedia format. Specific assessment tasks will be valuable in assessing progress. From the early years through to the senior stages, children and young people can demonstrate their progress through their skills in using differing sources of evidence, in assessing its validity and reliability, and in applying these in everyday life and work. This will include assessment of how well children and young people can use their knowledge and understanding to interpret evidence and present an informed view, progressing to being able to sustain a line of argument. Learners can also demonstrate evidence of progress through their abilities in applying their knowledge and skills in increasingly demanding and/or unfamiliar contexts, such as environmental issues, citizenship, and their awareness of the world and Scotland's place in it.

Approaches to assessment should identify the extent to which children and young people can apply these skills in their learning and their daily lives and in preparing for the world of work. For example:

▶ Do they show awareness of the importance of participating in decision-making processes?

▶ How well are they prepared to contribute to discussions on local, national and global issues?

Children and young people can demonstrate progression in knowledge, understanding and skills by how well they deal with increasingly demanding and challenging concepts within a wide range of economic, geographical, historical, political and social contexts. Progress can be seen in their:

▶ growing abilities to understand the complexity of such issues with increasing maturity and empathy

▶ increasingly sophisticated views

▶ skills in supporting these by reference to carefully-considered evidence and sources

▶ abilities to draw together their learning to demonstrate the depth of their understanding, for example of Scotland's history.

Assessment should also link with other areas of the curriculum, within and outside the classroom, offering children and young people opportunities to develop awareness of social issues such as sustainability and enterprise through field trips, visits to local and national heritage sites, and meetings with members of the community.

CONNECTIONS WITH OTHER AREAS OF THE CURRICULUM

Social studies experiences and outcomes encourage links with other areas of learning to provide learners with a deeper, more enjoyable and active experience.

The promotion of active citizenship is a central feature of learning in social studies as children and young people develop skills and knowledge to enable and encourage participation. Within social studies, practitioners will plan opportunities for children and young people to become involved in their local community and the wider world to support them in considering and developing their roles as active and informed citizens.

All staff teaching social studies will identify opportunities to develop and reinforce social studies knowledge and skills both, within their own teaching activities and through working with their colleagues to plan interdisciplinary studies and a coherent approach to the development of literacy, numeracy, citizenship, creativity, enterprise and sustainability.

Teachers have opportunities to combine statements of experiences and outcomes in various ways. They can group them around important concepts in social studies; they can organise statements to provide a basis for a subject-based approach; they can group experiences and outcomes around common learning contexts in social studies.

Through self-evaluation, schools, departments and teachers will plan a balance of learning and teaching approaches, learning that develops all the attributes and capabilities of the four capacities, a coherent approach to important themes such as citizenship and enterprise, progression in skills and understanding, and effective use of interdisciplinary work to deepen and extend learning.

EXPERIENCES & OUTCOMES

Learning in the social studies will enable me to:

▶ develop my understanding of the history, heritage and culture of Scotland, and an appreciation of my local and national heritage within the world

▶ broaden my understanding of the world by learning about human activities and achievements in the past and present

▶ develop my understanding of my own values, beliefs and cultures and those of others

▶ develop my understanding of the principles of democracy and citizenship through experience of critical and independent thinking

▶ explore and evaluate different types of sources and evidence

▶ learn how to locate, explore and link periods, people and events in time and place

▶ learn how to locate, explore and link features and places locally and further afield

▶ engage in activities which encourage enterprising attitudes

▶ develop an understanding of concepts that stimulate enterprise and influence business

▶ establish firm foundations for lifelong learning and for further specialised study and careers.

PEOPLE, PAST EVENTS AND SOCIETIES

SOC 0-01a I am aware that different types of evidence can help me to find out about the past.	• Identifies at least two different types of evidence which can provide information about the past, for example, pictures, family stories, artefacts.	**E**
SOC 0-02a I can make a personal link to the past by exploring items or images connected with important individuals or special events in my life.	• Recalls past events from their own life or that of their family, for example learning to ride a bike, a special party.	
SOC 0-04a I have explored how people lived in the past and have used imaginative play to show how their lives were different from my own and the people around me.	• Recognises that people in the past lived differently. • Uses knowledge of the past to demonstrate a difference between their life today and life in the past. For example, diet, lifestyle, clothing.	
SOC 1-01a I understand that evidence varies in the extent to which it can be trusted and can use this in learning about the past.	• Identifies the difference between a more and less trustworthy source.	**1**
SOC 1-02a By exploring places, investigating artefacts and locating them in time, I have developed an awareness of the ways we remember and preserve Scotland's history.	• Draws a short timeline and can locate two or more events on the line in the correct order.	
SOC 1-03a I can use evidence to recreate the story of a place or individual of local historical interest.	• Uses information learned from sources to relate the story of a local place or individual of historic interest though media such as drawings models or writing.	
SOC 1-04a I can compare aspects of people's daily lives in the past with my own by using historical evidence or the experience of recreating an historical setting.	• Draws comparisons between modern life and life from a time in the past.	
SOC 1-06a Having selected a significant individual from the past, I can contribute to a discussion on the influence of their actions, then and since.	• Names a figure from the past and comments on their role in events.	
SOC 2-01a I can use primary and secondary sources selectively to research events in the past.	• Uses both primary and secondary sources of evidence in an investigation about the past.	**2**
SOC 2-02a I can interpret historical evidence from a range of periods to help to build a picture of Scotland's heritage and my sense of chronology.	• Places an event appropriately within a historical timeline.	
SOC 2-03a I can investigate a Scottish historical theme to discover how past events or the actions of individuals or groups have shaped Scottish society.	• Describes at least two ways in which past events or the actions of individuals or groups have shaped Scottish society.	
SOC 2-04a I can compare and contrast a society in the past with my own and contribute to a discussion of the similarities and differences.	• Describes and discusses at least three similarities and differences between their own life and life in a past society.	
SOC 2-06a I can discuss why people and events from a particular time in the past were important, placing them within a historical sequence.	• Contributes two or more points to the discussion (in any form) as to why people and events from the past were important. • Places those people and events on a timeline.	

PEOPLE, PLACE AND ENVIRONMENT

E

SOC 0-07a I explore and discover the interesting features of my local environment to develop an awareness of the world around me. **SOC 0-08a** I explore and appreciate the wonder of nature within different environments and have played a part in caring for the environment. HWB 0-35a I explore and discover where foods come from as I choose, prepare and taste different foods.	• Identifies simple features of the local environment, for example, hill, river, road, railway. • Identifies different methods of taking journeys. • Expresses thoughts about which ways of travelling impact the environment both positively and negatively. • Talks about something they have done to care for the environment.
SOC 0-09a I have experimented with imaginative ways such as modelling and drawing, to represent the world around me, the journeys I make and the different ways I can travel.	• Draws or produces simple models of aspects of the local area, for example roads or buildings. • Draws a simple map, or shares a relevant experience of the route of a straightforward journey, and the method of transport which was used.
SOC 0-12a While learning outdoors in differing weathers, I have described and recorded the weather, its effects and how it makes me feel and can relate my recordings to the seasons.	• Names and talks about at least two different kinds of weather. • Draws pictures to record the weather for three days. • Describes how weather affects the activities they can undertake. • Talks about how they feel about different kinds of weather. • Describes which weather is likely to be related to which season.

1

SOC 1-07a I can describe and recreate the characteristics of my local environment by exploring the features of the landscape.	• Draws or makes a model of features in their local landscape, for example, hill, river, building.
SOC 1-08a I can consider ways of looking after my school or community and can encourage others to care for their environment.	• Identifies a way in which the school looks after its environment.
SOC 1-09a Having explored the variety of foods produced in Scotland, I can discuss the importance of different types of agriculture in the production of these foods.	• Identifies at least two forms of agriculture in Scotland and foods associated with these, for example, arable, dairy or pastoral.
SOC 1-11a By exploring my community and the groups within it, I can identify and consider different types of housing and how they meet needs.	• Identifies at least two different types of housing and the kinds of households who may inhabit them.
SOC 1-12a By using a range of instruments, I can measure and record the weather and can discuss how weather affects my life. **SOC 1-12b** By exploring climate zones around the world, I can compare and describe how climate affects living things.	• Uses instruments to measure and record at least two different weather elements, for example, temperature, rainfall, wind direction. • Contributes to a discussion giving reasoned opinions on how the weather affects life. • Draws two conclusions about how living things adapt to the climate in any chosen area.
SOC 1-13a Having explored the landscape of my local area, I can describe the various ways in which land has been used.	• Describes at least three different ways in which land is used in the local area, for example shops, houses, farming.
SOC 1-13b By exploring a natural environment different from my own, I can discover how the physical features influence the variety of living things.	• Draws at least two conclusions as to the effects the landscape has had on how people can use it, for example desert, rainforest.
SOC 1-14a Through activities in my local area, I have developed my mental map and sense of place. I can create and use maps of the area.	• Produces a basic map for a familiar journey.

2

SOC 2-07a I can describe the major characteristic features of Scotland's landscape and explain how these were formed.	• Identifies at least three features of Scotland's landscape and can provide a basic explanation of how these are formed.
SOC 2-07b I can describe the physical processes of a natural disaster and discuss its impact on people and the landscape.	• Describes the causes of a natural disaster such as a volcano, earthquake or extreme weather event. • Describes the impact of the natural disaster giving at least three examples for people and one for the landscape. Impact can be positive or negative.
SOC 2-08a I can discuss the environmental impact of human activity and suggest ways in which we can live in a more environmentally-responsible way.	• Identifies at least three impacts of human activity on the environment. • Suggests at least three ways in which people can live in a more environmentally responsible way.
SOC 2-08b I can consider the advantages and disadvantages of a proposed land use development and discuss the impact this may have on the community.	• Describes at least two advantages and two disadvantages of a land use development proposal. • Explores at least two impacts on the community either verbally or in writing.
SOC 2-09a Having explored the ways journeys can be made, I can consider the advantages and disadvantages of different forms of transport, discussing their impact on the environment.	• Identifies at least four ways in which journeys can be made. • Describes at least one advantage and disadvantage for each form of transport. • Shares knowledge about the impact of the various types of transport on the environment either verbally or in writing.
SOC 2-10a Having explored my local area, I can present information on different places to live, work and relax and interesting places to visit.	• Presents information in any preferred form on the local area including local area names, two major employers/types of employment, for example, call centres, local attractions, leisure facilities.
SOC 2-12a By comparing my local area with a contrasting area outwith Britain, I can investigate the main features of weather and climate, discussing the impact on living things.	• Compares and contrasts the differing effects of the weather on the people and society of Britain and a contrasting area, providing at least three similarities and/or differences.
SOC 2-13a I can explain how the physical environment influences the ways in which people use land by comparing my local area with a contrasting area.	• Provides explanation as to why their local physical environment influences the way in which people use land in comparison to a contrasting areas.
SOC 2-14a To extend my mental map and sense of place, I can interpret information from different types of maps and am beginning to locate key features within Scotland, UK, Europe or the wider world.	• Extracts information from more than one kind of map. • Locates continent names, country names, capital cities, rivers and railways on maps of Scotland, the UK, Europe and areas further afield.

PEOPLE IN SOCIETY, ECONOMY AND BUSINESS

SOC 0-15a I am aware that different types of evidence can help me to find out about the world around me.	• Identifies at least two sources of evidence which provide information about the world, for example, newspapers and television.	**E**
SOC 0-16a By exploring my local community, I have discovered the different roles people play and how they can help.	• Identifies at least two people who provide help in the community. • Talks about ways that each of those people help.	
SOC 0-17a I make decisions and take responsibility in my everyday experiences and play, showing consideration for others.	• Takes on appropriate roles during imaginative play.	
SOC 0-18a Within my everyday experiences and play, I make choices about where I work, how I work and who I work with.		
SOC 0-20a In real-life settings and imaginary play, I explore how local shops and services provide us with what we need in our daily lives.	• Identifies at least two different types of shops or services families might use, for example, supermarket or health centre.	
SOC 1-15a I understand that evidence varies in the extent to which it can be trusted and can use this in learning about current issues in society.	• Identifies a reliable and an unreliable source of evidence.	**1**
SOC 1-16a I can contribute to a discussion of the difference between my needs and wants and those of others around me.	• Identifies needs and wants using examples from their own experience.	
SOC 1-17a By exploring the ways in which we use and need rules, I can consider the meaning of rights and responsibilities and discuss those relevant to me.	• Presents an informed opinion on rights and responsibilities using their own experience.	
SOC 1-18a I have participated in decision making and have considered the different options available in order to make decisions.	• Makes informed decisions on an issue having listened to others.	
SOC 1-20a I have developed an understanding of the importance of local organisations in providing for the needs of my local community.	• Names two local organisations who provide for needs in the local community and describe what they do.	
SOC 1-21a I can work out the amount of money I need to buy items, understanding that I may not always be able to afford the items I want.	• Demonstrates relevant numeracy skills to do a simple budget.	
SOC 1-22a I have experienced the different jobs involved in running a business enterprise and understand the role each one plays in its success.	• Describes at least two different types of jobs and give a reason why each contributes to the success of the business or enterprise.	
SOC 2-15a I can use evidence selectively to research current social, political or economic issues.	• Selects appropriate evidence and uses it to research a social, political or economic issue.	**2**
SOC 2-16a I can explain how the needs of a group in my local community are supported.	• Provides a basic explanation as to how the needs of a particular group within the local community can be supported, using relevant examples.	
SOC 2-16b I can gather and use information about forms of discrimination against people in societies and consider the impact this has on people's lives.	• Uses evidence to form a valid opinion of the impact of discrimination or prejudice on people's lives, for example, racism or the effect of immigration.	
SOC 2-16c I can discuss issues of the diversity of cultures, values and customs in our society.	• Discusses in any form at least three issues related to cultures, values and customs in our society, for example, the role of family, traditions and gender stereotyping.	
SOC 2-17a I can describe the main features of a democracy and discuss the rights and responsibilities of citizens in Scotland.	• Describes the main features of a democracy. • Identifies links between rights and responsibilities.	
SOC 2-18a I can investigate the features of an election and the work of representatives at a local, national or European level to begin to develop my understanding of how democracy works.	• Presents information (in any preferred form) about the features of local, national or European elections and discusses the work of the appropriate representative.	
SOC 2-19a By comparing the lifestyle and culture of citizens in another country with those of Scotland, I can discuss the similarities and differences.	• Compares and contrasts the lifestyle and culture of the citizens of Scotland as compared to the citizens of another country. • Describes the basic needs of human beings. • Draws valid conclusions as to why some countries can meet these needs better than others.	
SOC 2-20a Through exploring ethical trading, I can understand how people's basic needs are the same around the world, discussing why some societies are more able to meet these needs than others.	• Describes and pros and cons of using Fairtrade products and community service providers such as credit unions.	
SOC 2-21a I can identify essential goods and services, discuss the different ways to pay for them, considering the benefits and risks of each method.	• Identifies which goods and services would be essential in society. • Describes the main ways of paying for goods and services acknowledging that there may be advantages and disadvantages of each method.	
SOC 2-22a By experiencing the setting up and running of a business, I can collaborate in making choices relating to the different roles and responsibilities and have evaluated its success.	• Identifies the main business functions such as production, sales, marketing, and administration. • Takes a role in setting up or running a small enterprise. • Evaluates the success of the enterprise. • Identifies profit and non-profitmaking organisations/enterprises including those who services are free at the point of delivery, for example health and education.	

TECHNOLOGIES

PRINCIPLES & PRACTICE

WHAT DOES LEARNING IN THE TECHNOLOGIES ENABLE CHILDREN AND YOUNG PEOPLE TO DO?

Technology – the application of knowledge and skills to extend human capabilities and to help satisfy human needs and wants – has had profound effects on society.

Scotland has a strong tradition of excellence and innovation in technological research. This is especially true in areas such as engineering, electronics, optoelectronics, biomedical research, genomics and cell engineering. Scotland's people need to be skilled in technologies and to be aware of the impact of technologies on society and the environment, now and in the future. Learning in the technologies provides a strong foundation for the development of skills and knowledge which are, and will continue to be, essential in maintaining Scotland's economic prosperity.

Within *Curriculum for Excellence*, the technologies curriculum area relates particularly to contexts that provide scope for developing technological skills, knowledge, understanding and attributes through creative, practical and work-related activities. For this reason, the framework provides experiences and outcomes which can be applied in business, computing science, food, textiles, craft, design, engineering, graphics and applied technologies. These experiences and outcomes offer a rich context for the development of all of the four capacities and for developing the life skills that are recognised as being important for success in the world of work. They also offer an excellent platform for a range of technology-related careers.

The technologies framework offers challenging activities which involve research, problem-solving, exploration of new and unfamiliar concepts, skills and materials, and the rewarding learning which often results from creating products which have real applications. It provides progression in cognitive skills. Children and young people will develop their creativity and entrepreneurial skills and be encouraged to become innovative and critical designers of the future. These attributes are essential if, in the future, our children and young people are to play a major part in the global economy and embrace technological developments in the 21st century.

MAIN PURPOSES OF LEARNING

Learning in the technologies enables children and young people to be informed, skilled, thoughtful, adaptable and enterprising citizens, and to:

▶ develop understanding of the role and impact of technologies in changing and influencing societies

▶ contribute to building a better world by taking responsible ethical actions to improve their lives, the lives of others and the environment

▶ gain the skills and confidence to embrace and use technologies now and in the future, at home, at work and in the wider community

▶ become informed consumers and producers who have an appreciation of the merits and impacts of products and services

▶ be capable of making reasoned choices relating to the environment, to sustainable development and to ethical, economic and cultural issues

▶ broaden their understanding of the role that information and communications technology (ICT) has in Scotland and in the global community

▶ broaden their understanding of the applications and concepts behind technological thinking, including the nature of engineering and the links between the technologies and the sciences

▶ experience work-related learning, establish firm foundations for lifelong learning and, for some, for specialised study and a diverse range of careers.

ORGANISATION OF THE EXPERIENCES AND OUTCOMES

The technologies framework has been organised to offer opportunities for personalisation and choice using diverse contexts for learning.

The technologies framework has six organisers, namely:

▶ **technological developments in society**
▶ **ICT to enhance learning**
▶ **business**
▶ **computing science**
▶ **food and textiles**
▶ **craft, design, engineering and graphics.**

The final four organisers are contexts for developing technological skills and knowledge.

These organisers recognise the special contribution made by each context for learning, whilst enabling teachers to plan opportunities to reflect individual and local needs. The important purposes of the technologies depend upon effective interdisciplinary working through connections across and between subject boundaries. It is important that teachers do not feel constrained by the organisers but view them as opportunities for children and young people to experience the differing contexts for learning.

In secondary schools, teachers of business education, computing, home economics and technical education will recognise how they can make their specialist contributions within the framework. Schools and teachers will plan different combinations of the experiences and outcomes to provide programmes that meet young people's needs and provide a sound basis for more advanced study within an area of specialism. As in other curriculum areas, the fourth level experiences and outcomes provide possibilities for choice: it is not intended that any individual young person's programme of learning would include all of the fourth level outcomes.

Teachers in their planning will use the framework to ensure that children and young people develop their understanding of important themes such as the impact of technology, informed attitudes to technology, sustainability, and social, economic and ethical issues. These will underpin and continually reinforce learning within the technologies.

The framework contains some statements which span two levels. These provide space for teachers to plan for progression over an extended period of time, enabling children and young people to explore contexts in increasing depth and develop their creativity through independent learning.

The framework allows opportunity for personalisation and choice, depth and relevance. The level of achievement at the fourth level has been designed to approximate to that associated with SCQF level 4. The technologies framework offers children and young people opportunities to develop a set of skills that can be utilised in Skills for Work programmes.

SKILLS WHICH ARE DEVELOPED

The technologies provide frequent opportunities for active learning in creative and work-related contexts. Learning in the technologies thus provides opportunities to continually develop, use and extend skills that are essential components for life, work and learning, now and in the future, including planning and organisational skills. Learning in the technologies therefore makes a strong contribution to achieving the aim clearly articulated in *Skills for Scotland: a Lifelong Learning Strategy* of '... ensuring that *Curriculum for Excellence* provides vocational learning and the employability skills needed for the world of work and is the foundation for skills development throughout life'.

Well-designed practical activities in the technologies offer children and young people opportunities to develop:

▸ curiosity and problem-solving skills, a capacity to work with others and take initiative
▸ planning and organisational skills in a range of contexts
▸ creativity and innovation, for example though ICT and computer aided design and manufacturing approaches
▸ skills in using tools, equipment, software and materials
▸ skills in collaborating, leading and interacting with others
▸ critical thinking through exploration and discovery within a range of learning contexts
▸ discussion and debate
▸ searching and retrieving information to inform thinking within diverse learning contexts
▸ making connections between specialist skills developed within learning and skills for work
▸ evaluating products, systems and services
▸ presentation skills.

USEFUL APPROACHES TO LEARNING AND TEACHING

The experiences and outcomes are intended to tap into children's and young people's natural inventiveness and their desire to create and work in practical ways. They act as a motivation for progressively developing skills, knowledge, understanding and attitudes, and so maximise achievement. Effective learning and teaching will draw upon a wide variety of approaches to enrich the experience of children and young people, particularly through collaborative and independent learning.

The experiences and outcomes are well suited for learning beyond school: in colleges, in the voluntary sector and in partnership with businesses, where children and young people may experience learning activities that are relevant to employment or future vocational learning.

Proficiency in ICT is an ideal vehicle for shared learning between and amongst children, young people and teachers. Many teachers may need to build their own knowledge and confidence, often learning with and from children and young people, in this area of continually evolving developments.

THE MEANING OF ICT

ICT refers to forms of technology that are used to transmit, store, create, display, share or exchange information by electronic means. This broad definition of ICT currently includes such technologies as media, telecommunications, and computer hardware and software; it also includes equipment and services associated with these technologies, such as videoconferencing, email and blogs.

HOW ICT CAN ENHANCE LEARNING AND TEACHING

In the words of the HMIE publication Improving *Scottish Education: ICT in Learning and Teaching* (2007),

'... staff in pre-school centres and in primary schools recognised that learners developed awareness of the world in which they live more effectively when this included engagement with the world through ICT.'

Being skilled in using ICT is essential if children and young people are to be effective contributors able to communicate and interact on a global scale. Across the curriculum, skills in ICT will be developed in the context of the learning and teaching as appropriate to the child or young person's maturity. All teachers, in all sectors, in all departments and in all settings, have opportunities to apply, reinforce and extend ICT skills within and across curriculum areas to equip children and young people with the learning and employability skills required for the 21st century.

Several curriculum areas including the technologies provide opportunities for children and young people to consider security aspects associated with ICT, for example keeping personal data secure, and the important consequences of these for individuals. It is important for children and young people to recognise security risks when handling information across the curriculum, and act accordingly.

THE DIFFERENCE BETWEEN COMPUTING AND ICT

ICT, as defined here, brings together different forms of technologies and applies them to communication and learning, whereas computing, as an area of specialised study, provides deeper theoretical and practical understanding of how hardware and software can be developed and applied in a range of contexts. This area of specialist study has particular relevance in preparing children and young people for the challenges of rapidly changing digital technologies. It will enable learners to prepare for more advanced specialised study and careers within computing science.

BROAD FEATURES OF ASSESSMENT

Assessment in the technologies will focus on practical, problem-solving and collaborative activities which enable children and young people to show that they know, understand and can use technological skills and concepts across all the contexts for learning in the technologies.

Teachers can gather evidence as part of children and young people's day-to-day learning, and specific assessment tasks will also contribute to assessing progress. From the early years through to the senior stages, children and young people can demonstrate progress in their skills in making models and preparing food, in planning and carrying out practical investigations and solving problems, in discussing and debating ideas with peers and adults, and in recording and presenting their thinking in different ways, including using ICT.

Approaches to assessment should identify the extent to which children and young people can apply these skills and use them creatively in their learning and their daily lives and in preparing for the world of work. For example:

▶ How well do they contribute ideas and suggestions and develop team working skills?
▶ How well do they collaborate and independently participate in learning activities which lead to products with real uses?

Children and young people can show progress by responding enthusiastically to more demanding and challenging concepts in technologies, showing increasing depth of understanding in their explanations, and applying knowledge and skills in more demanding or unfamiliar contexts. They can also demonstrate progress through their increasing independence and confidence when carrying out tasks and their increasing resilience in facing challenges. Progress includes increasingly well-structured explanations and well-argued opinions and conclusions, including developing informed views on environmental, ethical and economic issues. Assessment should also link with other areas of the curriculum, both within and outside the classroom, and in the context of the world of work.

MAKING CONNECTIONS WITHIN AND BEYOND THE TECHNOLOGIES

Technologies are connected strongly with all other areas of the curriculum, through extending and applying the specialist knowledge and understanding developed in the sciences, through the creative use of technology in the expressive arts, through interdisciplinary learning, for example linking mathematics, science and technologies in an engineering context, and through the use of technologies to enhance learning.

In order to foster deeper, more enjoyable and active learning, the technologies experiences and outcomes enable clear links to be made with all other curriculum areas. For example, design, creative thinking and aesthetics are central to both the technologies and the expressive arts and can provide a platform for planning exciting interdisciplinary working as well as presenting rich contexts for reinforcing the four capacities. Such connections mutually enhance the application and interpretation of designing, offering learners opportunities to become independent in designing solutions to meet real-life needs and challenges, and adept at solving problems of increasing scale and complexity. They extend the creative process, building on the interests of children and young people to provide enjoyable learning opportunities and enhance self-esteem, for example the relationship and interaction of engineering with technologies and with science. In a wider context, the experiences and outcomes have the capacity to link with fundamental concepts, including those of engineering, mathematics and science.

Through planning and self-evaluation, establishments and departments will need to ensure an appropriate balance of learning and teaching approaches, progression in skills, and effective use of interdisciplinary work to deepen and extend learning and reinforce themes.

In planning, it is important to recognise that experiences and outcomes should not be considered as requiring particular amounts of time. Many are very open, allowing the opportunity for exploration and depth.

[The Principles & Practice document for Technologies available at education.gov.scot still contains a heading 'What is the significance of the italicised experiences and outcomes in ICT?'. This relates to the original Es & Os for Technologies, and is no longer applicable.]

EXPERIENCES & OUTCOMES NOVEMBER 2016[1]

The technologies framework provides a range of different contexts for learning, including the themes across learning; learning for sustainability, global citizenship, enterprise, that draw on important aspects of everyday life and work.

The framework develops knowledge, skills, attributes and capabilities around 13 key concepts/significant aspects of learning in the technologies.

▶ Awareness of technological developments (Past, Present and Future), including how they work.
▶ Impact, contribution, and relationship of technologies on business, the economy, politics, and the environment.
▶ Using digital products and services in a variety of contexts to achieve a purposeful outcome
▶ Searching, processing and managing information responsibly
▶ Cyber resilience and internet safety
▶ Understanding the world through computational thinking
▶ Understanding and analysing computing technology
▶ Designing, building and testing computing solutions
▶ Food and textile technologies
▶ Designing & constructing models/products
▶ Exploring uses of materials
▶ Representing ideas, concepts and products through a variety of graphic media
▶ Application of Engineering

Within each of the key concepts/significant aspects of learning learners will develop and demonstrate:

▶ knowledge and understanding of the key concepts in the technologies
▶ curiosity, exploration and problem solving skills

▶ planning and organisational skills in a range of contexts
▶ creativity and innovation
▶ skills in using tools, equipment, software, graphic media and materials
▶ skills in collaborating, leading and interacting with others
▶ critical thinking through exploration and discovery within a range of learning contexts
▶ discussion and debate
▶ searching and retrieving information to inform thinking within diverse learning contexts
▶ making connections between specialist skills developed within learning and skills for work
▶ evaluating products, systems and services
▶ presentation and communication skills.
▶ awareness of sustainability

The framework includes creative, practical and work-related experiences and outcomes which develop skills for business, digital literacy, computing science, food, textiles, craft, design, engineering, graphics and applied technologies. Learning, teaching and assessment in the technologies should span a range of the 13 key significant aspects of learning, for example when planning business education in S1 to S3 it should cover Digital Literacy significant aspects of learning and Technological Developments in Society and Business significant aspects of learning (as well as Social subject significant aspects of learning).

As with literacy, numeracy and health and wellbeing, digital literacy should be placed at the heart of all learning, not only the technologies area of the curriculum. Digital literacy outcomes could be met in any/all curriculum areas and so all practitioners can contribute to and reinforce them.

[1] [The original Es & Os for Technologies from 2009 can be found as an appendix to *Curriculum for Excellence: Complete Edition* (see back cover).]

DIGITAL LITERACY

USING DIGITAL PRODUCTS AND SERVICES IN A VARIETY OF CONTEXTS TO ACHIEVE A PURPOSEFUL OUTCOME

E	TCH 0-01a I can explore digital technologies and use what I learn to solve problems and share[1] ideas and thoughts.	• Recognises different types of digital technology. • Identifies the key components of different types of digital technology. • Logs on to a preferred device with a given password. • Identifies icons for different applications. • Opens and close a pre-saved file. • Identifies and consistently use the close icon. • Uses digital technologies in a responsible way and with appropriate care.
1	TCH 1-01a I can explore and experiment with digital technologies and can use what I learn to support and enhance my learning in different contexts.	• Communicate and collaborate with others using digital technology for example, email, Glow or other platforms. • Opens and saves a file to and from a specific location. • Identifies the key components of frequently used digital technology and whether it is a piece of hardware or software. • Uses digital technology to collect, capture, combine and share text, sound, video and images.
2	TCH 2-01a I can extend and enhance my knowledge of digital technologies to collect, analyse ideas, relevant information and organise these in an appropriate way.	• Identifies and saves in a range of standard file formats • Saves files using an organised filing system. • Stores, shares and collaborates using an online cloud based service for example, Glow or other platforms. • Identifies the key features of input, output and storage devices. • Selects and use applications and software to capture, create and modify text, images, sound and video. • Selects the most appropriate digital software to perform a task.

SEARCHING, PROCESSING AND MANAGING INFORMATION RESPONSIBLY

E	TCH 0-02a I can use digital technologies to explore how to search and find information.	• Identifies and uses images and key words when searching for specific information. • Demonstrates an understanding of how information can be found on websites as text, audio, images and video. • Demonstrates an understanding of how they should not use materials owned by others without permission.
1	TCH 1-02a Using digital technologies responsibly I can access, retrieve and use information to support, enrich or extend learning in different contexts.	• Demonstrates an understanding of the concept of ownership of material and ideas. • Demonstrates an understanding of the different functions of a browser and search engine. • Recognises what should and shouldn t be searched for on the Internet.
2	TCH 2-02a I can use digital technologies to search, access and retrieve information and am aware that not all of this information will be credible.	• Uses search engines to search the internet for specific or relevant information for example, using quotation marks to narrow the results. • Access websites and use navigation skills to retrieve information for a specific task. • Demonstrates an understanding of usage rights and can apply these within a search for example creative commons.

CYBER RESILIENCE AND INTERNET SAFETY

E	TCH 0-03a I can explore, play and communicate using digital technologies safely and securely.	• Demonstrates an understanding of appropriate behaviour and language in the digital environment. • Demonstrates an understanding of the importance of passwords and passcodes for example access to school building.
1	TCH 1-03a I can extend my knowledge of how to use digital technology to communicate with others and I am aware of ways to keep safe and secure.	• Demonstrates understanding of my rights and responsibilities as a digital citizen. • Demonstrates understanding of the potential dangers online and who to go to for advice and who to report a concern to. • Demonstrates an understanding for the need for strong passwords. • Explains the need to get a person's permission before taking a picture or video of them.
2	TCH 2-03a I can explore online communities demonstrating an understanding of responsible digital behaviour and I'm aware of how to keep myself safe and secure.	• Demonstrates an understanding of the content they should include in an online profile. • Discusses the importance of being a responsible digital citizen, giving examples of appropriate online behaviours and actions. • Identifies appropriate ways to report concerns. • Uses strong passwords. • Has an understanding of the law as it relates to inappropriate or illegal online behaviours, for example, the sharing of inappropriate images.

[1] [In *Benchmarks*, the word 'share' is italicised.]
[2] [Wordings of the Benchmarks differ slightly from those attached to the identical Es & Os in 'Health & Wellbeing: Food Health' on pages 36-37.]
[3] [*Es & Os* and *Benchmarks* use the word 'their' here. This has been changed to 'my', in keeping with the first person nature of the Es & Os.]

FOOD AND TEXTILE TECHNOLOGY[2]

TCH 0-04a I enjoy exploring and working with foods in different contexts.	• Demonstrates simple food preparation techniques, for example, peeling, slicing, mixing, spreading.	E
TCH 0-04b I enjoy experimenting with a range of textiles.	• Demonstrates simple techniques with textiles, for example, threading cards, selecting materials, gluing.	
TCH 0-04c I can share my[3] thoughts with others to help further develop ideas and solve problems.	• Explores and identifies at least two ideas by using given resources to solve the problem. • Selects an appropriate solution.	
TCH 1-04a I can use a range of simple food preparation techniques when working with food.	• Demonstrates a range of practical skills when preparing foods for example washing, using a peeler, juicing, grating, cutting, simple knife skills (claw grip/bridge hold).	1
TCH 1-04b I can use a range of tools and equipment when working with textiles.	• Uses a range of equipment when working with textiles, for example, scissors, rulers/tape measures, bodkin and wool.	
TCH 1-04c I am developing and using problem solving strategies to meet challenges with a food or textile focus.	• Investigates a simple problem/challenge which includes given criteria. • Explores and identifies a range of ideas to solve the challenge/problem.	
TCH 1-04d I can adapt and improve ideas and can express my own thinking in different ways.	• Selects and uses resources to make the solution/solve the problem. • Assesses solution against original criteria.	
TCH 2-04a I am developing dexterity, creativity and confidence when preparing and cooking food.	• Demonstrates an increasing range of practical skills and cooking techniques for example accurate weighing and measuring, kneading, chopping, baking, grilling.	2
TCH 2-04b I am developing dexterity, creativity and confidence when working with textiles.	• Demonstrates manual dexterity, for example, cutting more intricate shapes, manipulating fabrics and embellishments to create designs on fabric, using a needle and thread, attaching designs onto fabric.	
TCH 2-04c I can extend and explore problem solving strategies to meet increasingly difficult challenges with a food or textile focus.	• Investigates a challenge/problem. • Identifies and demonstrates ways to solve the challenge/problem. • Identifies and selects appropriate resources to solve the challenge/problem. • Plans and makes the solution.	
TCH 2-04d I can discuss, debate and improve my ideas with increasing confidence and clear explanations.	• Assesses solution against own criteria. • Identifies at least one possible improvement.	

TECHNOLOGICAL DEVELOPMENTS IN SOCIETY AND BUSINESS

AWARENESS OF TECHNOLOGICAL DEVELOPMENTS (PAST, PRESENT AND FUTURE), INCLUDING HOW THEY WORK

TCH 0-05a I enjoy playing with and exploring technologies to discover what they can do and how they can help us.	• Discusses times when they have used different technologies.	E
TCH 1-05a I can explore the latest technologies and consider the ways in which they have developed.	• Identifies changes to technologies for example, televisions and mobile phones.	1
TCH 2-05a I can investigate how product design and development have been influenced by changing lifestyles.	• Gives examples of how our changing lifestyles have impacted on product design.	2

IMPACT, CONTRIBUTION, AND RELATIONSHIP OF TECHNOLOGIES ON BUSINESS, THE ECONOMY, POLITICS, AND THE ENVIRONMENT

TCH 0-06a To help care for the environment, I reduce, re-use and recycle the resources I use.	• Understands what can be reduced, re-used and recycled.	E
TCH 0-07a I understand how local shops and services use technologies to provide us with what we need and want in our daily lives.	• Gives examples of how people (for example police, fire, healthcare) who help us use technologies in their everyday work.	
TCH 1-06a I can take appropriate action to ensure conservation of materials and resources, considering the impact of my actions on the environment.	• Identifies ways in which energy can be saved. • Understands how and where we waste materials and resources.	1
TCH 1-07a I understand how technologies help provide for our needs and wants, and how they can affect the environment in which we live.	• Demonstrates an understanding of how technologies, by meeting our needs and wants, affect the environment in which we live.	
TCH 2-06a I can analyse how lifestyles can impact on the environment and Earth's resources and can make suggestions about how to live in a more sustainable way.	• Explains how and why it is important to conserve energy.	2
TCH 2-07a I can make suggestions as to how individuals and organisations may use technologies to support sustainability and reduce the impact on our environment.	• Discusses the advantages and disadvantages of how technologies impact on the environment for example, renewable energy technologies.	

CRAFT, DESIGN, ENGINEERING AND GRAPHICS

DESIGN AND CONSTRUCT MODELS/PRODUCT

E	TCH 0-09a I explore ways to design and construct models.	• Builds models using different materials eg. junk modelling, wooden blocks. • Uses tools and materials (paper, card, wood, plastic) to create models.
1	TCH 1-09a I can design and construct models and explain my solutions.	• Creates and justifies a solution to a given design challenge considering who is it for, where and how will it be used. • Uses appropriate tools and joining methods to construct a model.
2	TCH 2-09a I can extend and enhance my design skills to solve problems and can construct models.	• Uses tools and equipment in order to carry out a task safely. • Uses a range of methods to join and strengthen materials. • Estimates and then measures accurately using appropriate units and tools. • Creates a range of ideas and chooses a suitable solution. • Evaluates solutions and explains why they are or are not suitable.

EXPLORING USES OF MATERIALS

E	TCH 0-10a I explore everyday materials in the creation of pictures/models/concepts.	• Describes materials by touch for example sticky, squidgy, soft, fluffy, hard, rough, wet, heavy, light • Uses a range of materials when creating a pictures/models/concepts[1]. • Identifies when a material is suitable or not for specific function or task[1].
1	TCH 1-10a I can recognise a variety of materials and suggest an appropriate material for a specific use.	• Identifies different materials. • States the properties of materials (hard, soft …) • Recognises different materials and why they have been selected for a task. • Selects materials to use in a specific task.
2	TCH 2-10a I can recognise basic properties and uses for a variety of materials and can discuss which ones are most suitable for a given task.	• Recognises characteristics of groups of materials such as wood, plastic and metal. • Selects suitable materials to use in a task. • Discusses the uses of materials.

REPRESENTING IDEAS, CONCEPTS AND PRODUCTS THROUGH A VARIETY OF GRAPHIC MEDIA

E	TCH 0-11a I explore and discover different ways of representing ideas in imaginative ways.	• Uses a range of materials (natural and man-made) and resources to create pictures. • Shares ideas with others. • Recognise 2D shapes and how they can be used to visually represent ideas/concepts.
1	TCH 1-11a I can explore and experiment with sketching, manually or digitally, to represent ideas in different learning contexts.	• Recognises 2D and 3D shapes and how they can be used to visually represent ideas/concepts. • Creates manual and/or digital sketches to represent ideas.
2	TCH 2-11a I can use a range of graphic techniques, manually and digitally, to communicate ideas, concepts or products, experimenting with the use of shape, colour and texture to enhance my work.	• Sketches geometric shapes to create objects. • Produces sketches to communicate ideas that include pattern and texture. • Draws geometric shapes accurately. • Sketches 2D and 3D drawings of objects. • Describes primary and secondary colours and the moods/feeling associated with each. • Demonstrates planning for a targeted audience when creating a of graphic display.

APPLICATION OF ENGINEERING

E	TCH 0-12a I explore a variety of products covering a range of engineering disciplines.	• Recognises engineering in the world around them for example bridges, construction, electronics, computers.
1	TCH 1-12a I explore and discover engineering disciplines and can create solutions.	• Recognises and identifies different engineering disciplines. • Builds a solution to a specific task, which has moving parts.
2	TCH 2-12a I can extend my knowledge and understanding of engineering disciplines to create solution.	• Understands the difference between different engineering disciplines. • Understands different energy types. • Builds/simulates solutions to engineering problems.

[1] [This Benchmark as printed ends with "eg …". It appears that the authors intended to furnish us with a list of examples, but neglected to do so.]

COMPUTING SCIENCE

UNDERSTANDING THE WORLD THROUGH COMPUTATIONAL THINKING

TCH 0-13a I can explore computational thinking processes involved in a variety of everyday tasks and can identify patterns in objects or information.	• Identifies and sequences the main steps in an everyday task to create instructions/an algorithm, for example, washing hands. • Classifies objects and groups them into simple categories for examples, groups toy bricks according to colour. • Identifies patterns, similarities and differences in objects or information such as colour, size and temperature and simple relationships between them.	E
TCH 1-13a I can explore and comment on processes in the world around me making use of core computational thinking concepts and can organise information in a logical way.	• Follows sequences of instructions/algorithms from everyday situations for example, recipes or directions, including those with selection and repetition. • Identifies steps in a process and describes precisely the effect of each step. • Makes decisions based on logical thinking including IF, AND, OR and NOT for example, collecting balls in the gym hall but NOT basketballs, line up if you are left-handed OR have green eyes. • Collects, groups and orders information in a logical, organised way using my own and others' criteria (**MNU 1-20a / 1-20b**).	1
TCH 2-13a I understand the operation of a process and its outcome. I can structure related items of information.	• Compares activities consisting of a single sequence of steps with those consisting of multiple parallel steps, for example, making tomato sauce and cooking pasta to be served at the same time. • Identifies algorithms/instructions that include repeated groups of instructions a fixed number of times and/or loops until a condition is met. • Identifies when a process is not predictable because it has a random element for example, a board game which uses dice. • Structures related items of information for example, a family tree (**MNU 2-20b**). • Uses a recognised set of instructions/an algorithm to sort real worlds objects for examples, books in a library or trading cards.	2

UNDERSTANDING AND ANALYSING COMPUTING TECHNOLOGY

TCH 0-14a I understand that sequences of instructions are used to control computing technology. **TCH 0-14b** I can experiment with and identify uses of a range of computing technology in the world around me.	• Demonstrates an understanding of how symbols can represent process and information. • Predicts what a device or person will do when presented with a sequence of instructions for example, arrows drawn on paper. • Identifies computing devices in the world (including those hidden in appliances and objects such as automatic doors).	E
TCH 1-14a I understand the instructions of a visual programming language and can predict the outcome of a program written using the language. **TCH 1-14b** I understand how computers process information.	• Demonstrates an understanding of the meaning of individual instructions when using a visual programming language (including sequences, fixed repetition and selection). • Explains and predicts what a program in a visual programming language will do when it runs for example, what audio, visual or movement effect will result. • Demonstrates an understanding that computers take information as input, process and store that information and output the results.	1
TCH 2-14a I can explain core programming language concepts in appropriate technical language. **TCH 2-14b** I understand how information is stored and how key components of computing technology connect and interact through networks.	• Explains the meaning of individual instructions (including variables and conditional repetition) in a visual programming language • Predicts what a complete program in a visual programming language will do when it runs, including how the properties of objects for example, position, direction and appearance change as the program runs through each instruction. • Explains and predicts how parallel activities interact. • Demonstrates an understanding that all computer data is represented in binary for example, numbers, text, black and white graphics. • Describes the purpose of the processor, memory and storage and the relationship between them. • Demonstrates an understanding of how networks are connected and used to communicate and share information, for example the internet.	2

DESIGNING, BUILDING AND TESTING COMPUTING SOLUTIONS

TCH 0-15a I can develop a sequence of instructions and run them using programmable devices or equivalent.	• Designs a simple sequence of instructions/algorithm for programmable device to carry out a task for example, directional instructions: forwards/backwards. • Identifies and corrects errors in a set of instructions.	E
TCH 1-15a I can demonstrate a range of basic problem solving skills by building simple programs to carry out a given task, using an appropriate language.	• Simplifies problems by breaking them down into smaller more manageable parts. • Constructs a sequence of instructions to solve a task, explaining the expected output from each step and how each to contributes towards solving the task. • Creates programs to carry out activities (using selection and fixed repetition) in an visual programming language. • Identifies when a program does not do what was intended and can correct errors/bugs. • Evaluates solutions/programs and suggests improvements.	1
TCH 2-15a I can create, develop and evaluate computing solutions in response to a design challenge.	• Creates programs in a visual programming language including variables and conditional repetition. • Identifies patterns in problem solving and reuses aspects of previous solutions appropriately for example, reuse code for a timer, score counter or controlling arrow keys. • Identifies any mismatches between the task description and the programmed solution, and indicates how to fix them.	2

FREQUENTLY ASKED QUESTIONS

1	Does a learner have to achieve all Benchmarks to achieve a level?	In order to achieve a CfE level, it is not necessary for learners to demonstrate mastery of every individual aspect of learning in the Benchmarks for that level. However, it is important that there are no major gaps in children's and young people's learning when looking across the major organisers in each curriculum area.
2	What is the timeframe for implementation of the Benchmarks across all curriculum areas? What are the expectations of HMI?	In ELC settings and primary schools, the introduction of Benchmarks for 'other curriculum areas' needs to be proportionate and manageable. Teachers and other practitioners should be given time to engage in professional discussion to become familiar with the Benchmarks for 'other curriculum areas', and start to use them in line with their school improvement plans. Secondary school departments are expected to be engaging with the Benchmarks for their area of the curriculum. Secondary teachers need to be clear about what CfE level young people have attained in order to inform decisions about National Qualifications in the senior phase. They are expected to be using the Benchmarks for their subject areas to ensure better understanding of standards, and in particular to ensure suitably challenging learning from S1 to S3 which prepares young people for N5 in S4.
3	Why are all Es & Os not included in the Benchmarks documents?	For Expressive Arts and RME only, some Es & Os are not included in the Benchmarks documents. This is because these specific Es & Os focus mainly on experiences and do not make reference to outcomes that can be assessed. See below for the Es and Os in question. ▶ **Expressive Arts:** EXA 0-01a / EXA 1-01a / EXA 2-01a / EXA 3-01a / EXA 3-01b / EXA 4-01a. ▶ **RME:** 1-08a to 4-08a.
4	Why have the 'significant aspects of learning' (SALs) been removed?	Benchmarks draw together and streamline a wide range of previous assessment guidance (including significant aspects of learning, progression frameworks and annotated exemplars) into one key resource to support teachers' and other practitioners' professional judgement of children's and young people's progress across all curriculum areas. We know that many schools found the SALs useful in developing progression frameworks to support detailed planning for learning, teaching and assessment. Although the SALs have been superseded, many schools still have the physical education (PE) SALs posters on display, and teachers continue to find them very helpful.
5	There have been big QAMSO events to support understanding of the Benchmarks in literacy and numeracy. Will there be the same for other areas of the curriculum?	There are currently no plans to have QAMSO events for 'other curriculum areas' as there have been for literacy and numeracy. Education Scotland has been working with a number of local authorities and subject networks to support practitioners in using the Benchmarks for 'other curriculum areas' and will continue to offer similar support for local authorities, and through the new Regional Improvement Collaboratives.
6	Are the QAMSOs able to help me with moderation and Benchmarks in my curriculum area?	The moderation cycle works in exactly the same way in other curriculum areas as it does in literacy and numeracy, and Benchmarks are part of the cycle. Depending on local circumstances, QAMSOs may be able to help practitioners with moderation in all curriculum areas. Numeracy QAMSOs include science and design and technology teachers. If a practitioner needs help to understand the standards described in the Benchmarks, this should be done as part of school or local authority moderation arrangements.
7	As a secondary teacher, how can I get help to support me to use Benchmarks in an area I teach that is not my specialism?	It is the responsibility of schools and local authorities to ensure that staff are appropriately supported in delivering and assessing any curricular area they teach. Practitioners should seek support from their school leadership team to support them in engaging with relevant professional learning to ensure that learners receive their entitlement to high-quality learning and robust assessment processes.
8	What sort of documents should I use at moderation meetings?	Moderation is an ongoing process. It is not the same as cross-marking or verification. Effective moderation is where teachers work together to plan learning, teaching and assessment, to review evidence of learners' progress and achievement, and to plan next steps in learning. For effective moderation to take place, staff are likely to refer to: ▶ Experiences and Outcomes ▶ Planning folders ▶ Observations of day to day learning within the classroom ▶ Observation and feedback from learning activities that take place in other environments, for example, outdoors ▶ Coursework, including tests ▶ Learning conversations ▶ Planned periodic holistic assessment ▶ Practical investigations ▶ Projects ▶ Jotter work Further guidance can be found at the following links: ▶ National Improvement Hub: https://education.gov.scot/improvement/learning -resources/The%20Moderation%20 Cycle ▶ Moderation Hub on Glow: https://glowscotland.sharepoint.com/sites/PLC/moderationhub/SitePages/Home.aspx
9	How will the Benchmarks help me ensure that learners make appropriate choices and are presented at an appropriate level for National Qualifications in the senior phase?	Schools need to make judgments about the most appropriate senior phase pathway for each learner. These decisions must be informed by effective tracking and monitoring of learners' progress through the Broad General Education (BGE). A clear understanding of the curriculum level achieved, or that a learner is working at, in each subject area at the end of BGE is a critical piece of information to inform this decision and to ensure a smooth progression in learning for all learners as they move into the senior phase. Decisions should also be informed by discussions with parents and learners about the range of pathways open to young people. Effective use of the Benchmarks should support all of these steps.

10	Are we expected to report nationally on CfE levels for curriculum areas other than literacy and numeracy?	Current arrangements for reporting on all areas of the curriculum by schools at local level should be maintained. All schools are expected to report on curriculum level achievement for literacy and numeracy, and data will be collected and collated for reporting at national level. For the purposes of national reporting, schools are not currently expected to report on CfE levels for any other areas of the curriculum. For ELC settings and primary schools, this will not necessarily mean using Benchmarks as yet for all areas to inform reporting at local level. ELC settings and primary schools are expected to be using the Benchmarks for literacy and numeracy currently, to become familiar with the Benchmarks for 'other curriculum areas', and start to use them in line with their school improvement plans.
11	I am a single member of department, teaching up to 200 pupils a week. What approach should I take to assessing and monitoring progress for each pupil?	It is important to keep workload manageable in any context. However, practitioners still need to ensure that learners are making progress and that progress can be meaningfully reported on. If practitioners feel that that they need support to use the Benchmarks and monitor progress, they should seek advice at school and/or local authority level. Cluster and subject networking can be considered to allow practitioners to discuss learners' progress with other colleagues working across the BGE.
12	Will Education Scotland be publishing examples of holistic assessments for different subject areas, showing how literacy and numeracy Benchmarks can be assessed in subject areas?	Education Scotland will not be producing examples of holistic assessments. Having national banks of holistic assessments does not reflect the distinct nature of learning needs at local level.
13	What are my responsibilities with regard to assessing literacy and numeracy if I teach subjects other than mathematics or English in secondary school?	Teachers of all curriculum areas and subjects have a responsibility to understand literacy and numeracy standards in order to plan activities at the appropriate level, and thus help learners develop their skills in literacy and numeracy across the curriculum. All teachers should know the levels of literacy and numeracy of each of their pupils, so that they do not provide work that has literacy or numeracy content that is either too easy or too difficult for the pupil. Teachers of areas other than mathematics and English need to understand literacy and numeracy standards so they can give appropriate feedback to their pupils on how to improve.
14	Some secondary teachers of subjects other than English and mathematics are being asked by headteachers to report on their pupils' levels in literacy and numeracy? Should this be happening?	Education Scotland would not expect secondary teachers of subjects other than English and mathematics to be asked to report on their pupils' achievement of a literacy or numeracy level. It is very unlikely that teachers of these subjects would have sufficient evidence to make that judgement. However, work produced across a range of curriculum areas can contribute to the range of evidence required to indicate achievement of a literary or numeracy level, and in particular can provide evidence of application of literacy and numeracy skills.
15	Why are there no Benchmarks for 'Health and Wellbeing (HWB): Responsibility of All', similar to Literacy and Numeracy Benchmarks?	The Experiences and Outcomes that sit within HWB Responsibility of All span across all four levels to recognise the nature of development and learning in HWB. For many learners progression in HWB is neither linear nor coherent. Life circumstances can change so quickly with a subsequent impact on mental, emotional, social and physical wellbeing that it does not make sense to assign levels in this aspect of HWB. However, the Experiences and Outcomes should be regularly revisited through a wide range of relevant and realistic learning experiences to ensure that every child and young person is progressing in his or her development and learning. Children and young people should self-report on their progress using the wellbeing indicators. This then should open up a conversation with a key adult who knows the child really well.

A number of the frequently-asked questions correspond directly or indirectly to the key messages about 'what to do' and 'what to avoid', contained in the table in the introduction to every Benchmarks document [page 3 of this book]. The key messages table is included below and the corresponding frequently-asked questions are indicated.

WHAT TO DO	WHAT NOT TO DO
✓ Use literacy and numeracy Benchmarks to help monitor progress towards achievement of a level, and to support overall professional judgement of when a learner has achieved a level.	✗ Avoid undue focus on individual Benchmarks which may result in over-assessing or recording of learners' progress.
✓ Become familiar with other curriculum area Benchmarks over time. *(The answer to frequently-asked question 2 relates to this key message)*	✗ Avoid the requirement to spend time collating excessive evidence to assess learners' acwhievement.
✓ Use Benchmarks to help assess whether learners are making suitable progress towards the national standards expected and use the evidence to plan their next, challenging steps in learning.	✗ There is no need to provide curriculum level judgements in all curriculum areas – stick to literacy and numeracy. *(The answer to frequently-asked question 2 & 10 relate to this key message)*
✓ Discuss Benchmarks within and across schools to achieve a shared understanding of the national standards expected across curriculum areas.	✗ Do not create excessive or elaborate approaches to monitoring and tracking. *(The answer to frequently-asked question 11 relates to this key message)*
	✗ Do not assess Benchmarks individually. Plan periodic, holistic assessment of children's and young people's learning. *(The answer to frequently-asked question 12 relates to this key message)*
	✗ Do not tick off individual Benchmarks.

Printed in Germany
by Amazon Distribution
GmbH, Leipzig